A HISTORY
OF
CROATIA

A HISTORY
OF
CROATIA

STEPHEN GAZI

BARNES
&NOBLE
BOOKS
NEW YORK

TABLE OF CONTENTS

PREFACE

I wrote "A History of Croatia" with the intention to tell my children and their children's children the history of the land and people of their ancestors. It could only be done with the most scrupulous respect to the historically documented facts.

The result is this book, which is a general survey of the history of Croatia and its people. While it is based on the texts of leading Croatian historians, Tadija Smiciklas, *Povijest Hrvatska*, Vjekoslav Klaic, *Povijest Hrvata*, Ferdo Sisic, *Pregled povijesti hrvatskoga naroda*, Rudolf Horvat, *Povijest Hrvatske*, Lovre Katic, *Pregled povijesti Hrvata*, Josip Horvat, *Politicka povijest Hrvatske*, Ante Dabinovic, *Hrvatska drzavna i pravna povijest*, the more recent contributions of Mihovil Barada, Jaroslav Sidak, Stjepan Sakac, Dominik Mandic and Nada Klaic are also taken into account.

The book could be essentially divided into two parts. The first ten chapters contain a general narrative dealing with the Croatian past up to the nineteenth century, following the pattern established by the above listed textbooks. The second part could be considered an analysis of the modern Croatia's history. For the benefit of those who are not familiar with Croatian history some of the most crucial documents are extensively quoted. An additional chapter covering the Literature and Arts is also included.

The included historical maps, especially covering the Middle Ages, cannot be interpreted in the spirit of modern nationalism which is prone to imitate our contemporary "real-estate" concept of historical geography.

A Chronological Outline is included.

INTRODUCTION

The emergence of the Croats from their prehistorical past took place during the sixth and seventh centuries and was directly linked to the great migration of peoples. In association with the Avars, and other related Slavic tribes, they followed in the footsteps of the Goths and Huns, invading in their own turn the different territories of the Roman Empire. Although initially they participated in the destruction of the classical Roman civilization in Pannonia and Dalmatia, ultimately they settled in these two provinces and fell heir to the surviving remnants of Roman culture. During the same period they made their debut on the European historical scene, sometimes appearing independently, while at other times appearing in association with their surrounding and frequently more powerful neighbors. Thus, a study of the history of the Croats makes a simultaneous study of Byzantium, the Republic of Venice, Hungary, Serbia, and, above all, the Habsburg and Ottoman Empires mandatory.

* * *

After enjoying two and one-half centuries of independent national existence, in the early Middle-Ages Croatia entered into something of a commonwealth with Hungary. Nevertheless, by the fifteenth century a considerable portion of her territory had fallen into the hands of the Ottoman Empire and Venice. Yet, despite these difficulties, the Croats progressively weaved their own distinctive thread into the historical events of Europe.

* * *

Modern Croatian historiography dates back to the period of the National Reawakening, which was characterized by romantic nationalism. This period saw Croatia rise in a bitter struggle for national survival against the more powerful and aggressive nationalisms of the Magyars, Italians, Germans, and even the Serbs. The danger to which the Croats were exposed prompted Croatian historians to overstress their Slavic past to the detriment of a more objective assessment of their country's history, including the many contributions and influences of non-Slavic elements. Herderian philosophy, nascent Pan-Slavism, and its local offshoot, Yugoslavism, were the motivating factors in the merger of the study of the Croatian past with the history of the whole Slavic race.

This fateful assimilation can still be felt today despite attempts to re-evaluate historical happenings and their causes and consequences. Today, new interpretations based on dogmatic historical materialism make up the official historiography of contemporary Yugoslavia (of which Croatia forms a part) and add one more bias to historical hermeneutics.

Thus, any further contributions to the understanding of Croatian history must renew the old difficulties which biased interpretations have so neatly side-stepped, and, in the face of these, attempt to arrive at a more realistic characterization of Croatia's past. In doing so, as should always be the case in the study of historical events, the scholar must be wary of the many intrigues, as well as the interplaying and sometimes side-tracking influences, which tend to confuse the central issues. Moreover, if the scholar wishes to develop and relate a comprehensive view of history, his task is made even more difficult by the lack of authentic documents and the need to sort out and evaluate an abundance of contradictory and inadequate material. In fact, in certain instances, due to a general lack of valid sources, the historian has to fall back on ancient chronicles which more often than not express the views of prejudiced individuals.

Therefore, in general, in order to shed sufficient light on historical events and their consequences, as well as to establish their various causes, the historian is compelled to examine and re-examine all of the given data of a particular age.

* * *

The sources of Croatian history are scarce and incomplete. Many factors have contributed to this state of affairs. During her early independence, from the ninth to the twelfth centuries, Croatia was repeatedly exposed to Norman, Venetian, Byzantine and Hungarian invasions which brought plunder and devastation to the land. Furthermore, the Crusaders, on their way to Constantinople during the First Crusade, plunged the country into additional misery (1097). In 1202 the knights of the Fourth Crusade set out, in the name of the mighty Republic of Venice, to conquer Zadar, the most important city of medieval Croatia, and ultimately razed it. This fact is of crucial importance to the historian because Zadar had at one time been the See of the Imperial Province of Dalmatia and thereby the repository for many official documents.

The Tartar invasion (1242) followed the Fourth Crusade. Then came a long period of crusading onslaughts directed against the Bosnian and Croatian Patarens. The Ottoman wars occurred in the subsequent centuries (1415-1790) and added a heavy toll to the already sorely tried country. Indeed, the devastation inflicted by these invaders became so notorious that it was immortalized in this popular saying: "Wherever Turkish hoofs step down, the grass does not grow anymore."

It therefore seems reasonable to assume, in the face of this evidence of centuries of tribulation, that many valuable documents and sources have been lost. Thus, there is little left for the historian to do but pick up the pieces and make the best of them.

Yet, to further complicate matters and to add to the historian's grief, other great international repositories of historical documents, such as Papal Rome and Imperial Constantinople, underwent great upheavals and were plunged into chaos at precisely the time Croatia passed through the most critical period of her history; viz., her demise as an independent kingdom. In fact, during the eleventh and twelfth centuries, the Church and Empire passed through some of the darkest crises of their history and could not be expected to have had time for the preservation of documents pertaining to Croatia.

Those documents dealing with Croatia that are extant despite all of these difficulties, are oftentimes confusing in their terminology. Conflicting names are given to Croatia herself, as well as to many of her sections. Byzantine documents refer to the country as Croatia; but Roman, i.e. Church, documents persist in the use of Illyricum for church matters and Slavonia for affairs with political implications. Venice, which had a permanently dominant involvement in Croatian affairs, used the term Slavonia in reference to the country, but called the people of the country *Schiavoni*. The majority of Western European sources show a preference for the name Slavonia.

* * *

A systematic compilation of historical documents concerning the past of Croatia has only recently been initiated, which is to say, in the latter part of the nineteenth century. The most important published collections are: Franjo Racki (ed.), *Documenta historiae croaticae periodum antiquam illustrantia* (Zagreb: JAZU, 1877); Tadija Smiciklas, Marko Kostrencic, Emilije Laszowsky (ed.), *Codex diplomaticus regni Croatiae, Dalmatiae et Slavoniae* (Zagreb: JAZU, 1904-), 15 vls.; Ivan Tkalcic, Emilije Laszowsky, Ljudevit Dobronic (eds.), *Monumenta historica Lib. reg. civitatis Zagrabiae* (Zagreb, 1899-), 18 vls.; Emilije Laszowsky (ed.), *Monumenta historica nobilis comunitatis Turopolje* (Zagreb, 1904-1908), 4 vls.; Ivan Kukuljevic (ed.), *Jura regni Croatiae, Dalmatiae et Slavoniae* (Zagreb, 1861-1862), 3 vls.; Sime Ljubic (ed.), *Listiane o odnosajima izmedju Juznoga Slavenstva i mletacke republike* (Zagreb: JAZU, 1868-1891), 9 vls.; Agustin Theiner (ed.), *Vetera monumenta historica Hungariam sacram illustrantia* (Rome, 1859-1860), 2 vls.; Agustin Theiner (ed.), *Vetera monumenta Slavorum meridionalum historiam illustrantia* (Rome-Zagreb, 1863-1875), 2 vls.; Euzebije

Fermedzin (ed.), *Acta Bosniae potissimum ecclesiastica* (Zagreb: JAZU, 1892); Josip Glecic (ed.), *Diplomarium relationum reipublicae Ragusinae cum regno Hungariae* (Budapest: Hungarian Academy of Science, 1887); Ferdo Sisic (ed.), *Acta Comitialia regni Croatiae, Dalmatiae et Slavoniae* (Zagreb: JAZU, 1912-1918), 5 vls.; Emilije Laszowsky (ed.), *Monumenta Habsburgica regni Croatiae, Dalmatiae et Slavoniae* (Zagreb: JAZU, 1914-1917), 3 vls.; Radoslav Lopasic (ed.), *Spomenice hrvatske Krajine* (Zagreb: JAZU, 1884-1889), 3 vls.; Karlo Horvat (ed.), *Monumenta Historiam Uscocchorum illustrantia* (Zagreb: JAZU, 1910-1913), 2 vls.; Franjo Racki (ed.), *Isprave o uroti bana Petra Zrinskoga i kneza Frana Frankopana* (Zagreb: JAZU, 1873); Valtazar Bogisic (ed.), *Acta conjurationem Petri a Zrinio et Francisci de Frankopan illustrantia* (Zagreb: JAZU, 1888); Franjo Racki (ed.), *Gradja za Povijest Trvatske seljacke bune* (Zagreb: JAZU, 1876).

Among the most important chronicles dealing with Croatian history should be mentioned: Constantinus Porfirogenetus, *Opera*, vol. III — *De administrando imperio* (Recognovit Bekkerus: Bonn, 1840); Vladimir Mosin (ed.), *Ljetopis popa Dukljanina* (Zagreb: JAZU, 1949); Franjo Racki (ed.), Thomas archidiaconus *Historia Salonitana* (Zagreb: JAZU, 1849); Vinko Foretic (ed.), *Korculanski kodeks 12. stoljeca* (Zagreb: JAZU — *Starine* XLVI, 1956); Andreas Dandolo, *Cronicum Venetum — Scriptores rerum Italicorum*, vl. XII (Milano, 1728); Ivan Thuroczy, *Chronica Hungarorum* (Brno, 1488); Stjepan Ivsic (ed.), Franjo Crnko, *Podsjedanje i osvojenje Sigeta* (Zagreb: JAZU, 1918), Antun Vramec, *Kronika* (Ljubljana, 1578); Nikola Istanffy, *Historiarum de rebus Hungaricis libri XXXIV* (Köln, 1622).

* * *

The first written history of Croatia, *Memoria regum and banorum regnorum Dalmatiae, Croatiae et Slavoniae* (Vienna, 1652), we owe to Juraj Ratkay. He was followed by several others: Ivan Lucius, *De regno Dalmatiae et Croatiae libri sex* (Amsterdam, 1666); Adam Kerscelich, *Historiarum cathedralis ecclesiae Zagrabiensis partis primae tomus I* (Zagreb, 1770); —, *De regnis Dalmatiae, Croatiae, Sclavoniae notitiae praeliminares* (Zagreb, 1770); Josip Mikoczy, *Otiorum Croatiae liber unus* (Budapest, 1806).

With the foundation of the Yugoslav Academy of Arts and Sciences in Zagreb (1867), there began a systematic study of the Croatian past, with collected documents appearing in regularly published collections: *Monumenta spectantia historiam Slavorum meridionalum* (46 vls. to the present); *Monumenta historico — juridica Slavorum meridionalum* (12 vls. to the present); *Starine* (50 vls. to the present); *Rad* (59 vls. to the present); *Codex diplomaticus* (14 vls. to the present).

In more recent times a series of general histories of Croatia have been written on the basis of historical documents and critical historical research. Among the most noteworthy are: Tadija Smiciklas, *Povijest Hrvatska* (Zagreb: Matica Hrvatska, 1879-1882), 2 vls.; Vjekoslav Klaic, *Povijest Hrvata* (Zagreb, 1899-1911), 5 vls.; Ferdo Sisic, *Pregled povijesti hrvatskoga naroda* (Zagreb: Matica Hrvatska, 1914); —. *Hrvatska povijest od najstarijih dana* (Zagreb: Matica Hrvatska, 1925-1944), 2 vls.; Lovre Katic, *Pregled povijesti Hrvata* (Zagreb: Matica Hrvatska, 1938); Rudolf Horvat, *Povijest Hrvatske* (Zagreb: Dionicka Tiskara, 1904); Josip Horvat, *Politicka Povijest Hrvatske* (Zagreb: Binoza, 1936-1938), 2 vls.; Ante Dabinovic, *Hrvatska drzavna i pravna povijest* (Zagreb: Matica Hrvatska, 1940).

A separate history of Croatia in the English language does not exist, except for the attempts of two men: Francis Preveden, *A History of the Croatian People* (New York: Philosophical Library, 1955-1964), 2vls.; and Stanko Guldescu, *History of Medieval Croatia* (The Hague: Mouton & Co., 1964). In many works, Croatia's past has, as a rule, been treated superficially as a part of general work dealing with the Slavs or South Slavs; or it has been treated in an even more sweeping fashion in connection with a history of the Habsburg Empire or Southeastern Europe.

Beyond these two attempts, some specific aspects of Croatian history, particularly of the immediate past, have been treated in English as topics for research and doctoral dissertations by contemporary American and English scholars. But considering that the works just enumerated are the extent of Croatia's showing in the historiography of the English-speaking world, it does not need to be said that she is poorly represented, nor is it anything but a disheartening consolation to learn that her history is just as poorly represented in other languages.

CHAPTER I

THE LAND

Geographic situation — Topographic characteristics — Prehistory — Ancient population: Illyrians and Celts — Greek colonization — Roman conquest — Roman provinces — Barbarians: Goths, Huns, Avars and Slavs.

The Croats settled in their present country, the ancient Roman provinces of Dalmatia and Pannonia, during the great migration of peoples in the sixth and seventh centuries. Situated in the northwestern part of the Balkan Peninsula and the southwestern section of the Danubian plain, Croatia lies between the Adriatic Sea to the south, and the rivers Drava and Danube to the north; as well as between the rivers Rasa, Kupa and Sutla to the west and the river Drina to the east. This territory basically includes the Socialist Republics of Croatia and Bosnia — Hercegovina in contemporary Yugoslavia.

Croatia can be divided into three distinct topographical areas. The Mediterranean area is the narrow coastal belt which extends along the shores of the Adriatic Sea and which includes a multitude of islands. This section is separated from the northern plains by mountain chains which cover a major part of the land. These mountains constitute a formidable communication barrier between the south and the north. The northern area is a rich plain interrupted by moderately low mountains and hills. It lies between the rivers Drava and Danube to the north and the northern slopes of the Croatian and Bosnian mountains to the south.

These three distinct geographic areas are correspondingly different in their climates and economics. Moreover, due to topographical differences and pressures, they have developed close connections with Southern, Eastern and Central Europe respectively, which have put each of them under the influence of a different culture. Communication between northern Croatia and the Adriatic shores has always posed a serious problem, and, in the course of history, has often been completely interrupted. Thus it is clear that geographic factors have decisively influenced the cultural, political, social and economic development of the Croatian people.

The beginning of human life in the Croatian lands can be traced to the early Stone Age (Paleolithic). Some of the oldest remnants of this age in Europe have been found at Krapina in northwestern Croatia. Several human skeletons of different ages, primitive stone weapons, utensils and tools, and numerous bones of diluvial animals have been discovered there. Relics of an even greater amount and value from the younger Stone Age (Neolithic), and the Copper and Bronze Ages, have been found throughout the country. The most important of these finds has been at Butmir, near Sarajevo in Bosnia.

The first inhabitants of Croatia, the Illyrians, were situated on the land during the Iron Age. This age can be traced back to as early as the tenth century B.C.

* * *

Divided into several tribes, the Illyrians spread from the Po Valley in Italy — including present-day Austria and Western Hungary — to the confines of Greece. The most important Illyrian tribes on Croatian territory were the Liburnians, Delmates and Ardiaces. These tribes occupied the coastal regions and the adjacent mountains.

The Celts, or the Gauls, crossed the Alps and appeared on

the scene in the fourth century B.C. They defeated the Romans in 391 B.C., and under the leadership of Brennes, conquered and plundered Rome. Ultimately they settled on the Danubian plains and the region between the Drava and Sava rivers. On the land between these two rivers, their most important tribes, the Yapudes and Yasses, formed a strong state. The capital city of this state was Segesta (Sisak).

*　*　*

During the same period the Ionian Greeks penetrated into the Adriatic region and established several colonies. The Greek Adriatic island colonies included Issa (Vis), Pharos (Hvar), Brattia (Brac), Korkyra (Korcula) and Meleda (Mljet). Their colonies on the mainland were Tragurium (Trogir), Epitetum (Stobrec, near Split), Narona (Vid, near Metkovic), Epidaurum (Cavtat) and Risonia (Risan). With the establishment of these Greek settlements, the country entered her historical period.

Due to Greek colonization — which brought with it thriving settlements and increased navigation and trade — the Illyrians began attacking the colonies and practicing piracy on the open sea. When the Roman Republic became more and more involved in Greek affairs, the colonies that were being attacked placed themselves under her protection. Under the leadership of Agron, King of Ardean, the Illyrians reacted by forming, among several tribes, a military and naval alliance directed against both Greeks and Romans. Eventually, due to Agron's death, which weakened the alliance, the Romans were able to establish a short and precarious peace. But the Republic soon vacated the Adriatic region when it became involved in the first Punic War with Carthage. Thereupon, Queen Teuta, Agron's widow, who was supported by Demetrius of Pharos, renewed the old Illyrian alliance. By this action she broke the terms of the peace settlement and reopened hostilities.

Roman attempts to negotiate Teuta into compliance with the established order failed. Thus the Republic equipped and dispatched an army which invaded the eastern shore of the

Adriatic. This army consisted of two hundred ships, twenty thousand infantry and two thousand cavalry. After two years of war (229-227 B.C.), Consul Gnaeus Flavius Gentimanlius forced Teuta to sign a peace treaty that terminated both the piracy on the sea and the attacks on the Greek colonies. When he returned to Rome, Flavius celebrated his victory over the Illyrians and received the surname "Illyricus".

As soon as the Romans left the Adriatic shores they found themselves involved in the third Punic War, as well as a new military adventure in Asia Minor. The Illyrians, together with the Celts, took this opportunity to form a new, strong, military alliance and through it began a general harrassment of the Romans. They succeeded in imposing permanent warfare on the Romans until the time of Emperor Caesar Octavius Augustus, who, in his turn, was able to force peace and order upon them for a time. This did not last long, however, and the Emperor sent his foster son, Tiberius, to resolve the situation. Tiberius had to use a great number of men to subdue the Illyrians and the Celts, but in the end he established a definite and lasting peace (10 A.D.). According to the Roman historian Seutonius Tranquilius, next to Carthage, Illyricum burdened the Romans with their longest and most bitter wars.

With the final submission of the Illyric and Celtic tribes, there began a systematic Romanization of the conquered territory. The Romans introduced their political, social, economic, legal and military system. Ultimately, they were instrumental in bringing in Christianity. In the course of Romanization, the original population lost its primitive characteristics and was gradually transformed into a Roman population. In fact, some of its most prominent sons were later called upon to play crucial roles in the history of the Roman Empire.

The Romans organized the country, commonly known as Illyricum, into two separate provinces. The first, Pannonia, was situated in the north, covering the northern Croatian plains, as well as Slovenia of today and what is now the western part of Hungary. This province was subsequently divided into Pannonia Superior, with the capital at Emona (Ljubljana), and Pannonia Inferior, with the capital at Sirmium (Mitrovica). Dalmatia, on the other hand, was situated along the Adriatic coast, as well as in the mountain area, and had her capital at Salona (Solin). Both of these provinces, viz. Pannonia and Dalmatia, were assigned to the western part of the Roman Empire when the Emperor Diocletian established the eastern-western division. This division was ultimately confirmed by Emperor Theodosius the Great when he divided the Empire between his sons in 395 A.D.

Roman rule proved to be beneficial to both provinces because general progress occurred in a short period of time. The Romans built a number of military roads, with suitable fortresses at the crossroads. These fortresses eventually developed into flourishing towns, and transformed the country into a center for the thriving Roman civilization. Salona soon became one of the most beautiful cities of the Empire, while the smaller towns rapidly developed into the prospering coastal communities of Albona (Labin), Aenona (Nine), Iadera (Zadar), Tragurium (Trogir), Mericcurum (Makarska), Epidaurum (Cavtat), and the interior communities of Metulum (Ogulin), Stridon — the birthplace of St. Jerome (near Bihac) and Delminium (Duvno). It is, however, a reasonable guess that Roman civilization did not establish deep roots in the interior of the country.

In the province of Pannonia, besides that of the capital city of Sirmium, a certain preeminence was achieved by Siscia (the Celtic Segesta, Sisak), Aqua Viva (Varazdin), Aqua Iassae (Varazdinske Toplice), Andotonia (Scitarjevo, near Zagreb), Aquae Belissae (Daruvar), Marsonia (Brod), Cibaliae (Vinkovci), Murciae (Osijek), and Taurunum (Zemun).

The Pannonian and Dalmatian towns were organized along the traditional Roman pattern. The principal cities, Sirmium and Salona, were distinguished by their size, the beauty of their public buildings and the political and cultural position they held in the life of the Empire.

When Christianity spread throughout the Empire, the first Christian communities could be found in both provinces. Moreover, the repeated persecution of these Christians resulted in martyrdom for many of them. Subsequent to the official recognition of Christianity, the Church itself was organized in both provinces. Two archbishoprics, Salona and Sirmium, and several bishoprics, one for each town of any importance, were founded. Religious life developed as a matter of course, and eventually Dalmatia brought forward one of her sons (St. Jerome) to become one of the Fathers of the Church.

The population consisted of a mixture of several different kinds of peoples. Initially there were the Illyrians and Celts. Then there were added the Greeks and Romans who lived primarily in the Dalmatian towns and on islands, but who could be found in all of the principal settlements as well. There were barbarians who were brought in as slaves by the conquering Roman armies. As an example, Diocletian brought in a considerable number of Sarmatians who were obviously Slavs.

Within a certain period of time, the superior Roman civilization Romanized the indigenous population. Gradually it accepted the fruits of the Roman culture, as well as the use of the Latin language. In fact, its heirs, at the time of the Croatian immigration and the formation of the Croatian political state, called themselves Latins for short.

The social organization followed, in a general way, the Roman pattern, which consisted of free citizens, viz. both patricians and plebeians, and slaves. Frequently the slaves became freemen and they, or their descendants, were able to rise to the highest positions of the Empire. The sons of the Illyrian peasants, or slaves, were able to robe themselves in imperial purple during the times of crisis which faced the Roman world. Lucius Domitius Aurelianus (227-275) initiated a period of Illyrian emperors of which the most impressive were Marcus Aurelius Probus (267-282) and Gaius Aurelius Valerious Iovius Diocletianus (284-305).

Diocletianus, the son of an Illyrian peasant-slave, used his outstanding military career to elevate himself to the imperial throne. Following his resignation, he retired to his native land where he built a beautiful palace for himself near the capital city, Salona. The present-day city of Split was built on the grounds of this palace and preserves within it many remnants and monuments of the glory of the imperial past.

Roman administration excelled in building fortresses, towns, public buildings, baths, theaters, circuses, aqueducts, and, above all, incomparable military roads. Pannonia and Dalmatia were strategically situated between Italy and the Danube line of defense and were permanently exposed to barbarian invasions; thus they were well garrisoned. Legions, other than watching the barbarians, were used to promote agriculture, especially vine culture, which was introduced into these provinces by the Romans. For three centuries both provinces enjoyed a flourishing economy because the Romans opened mines excavating iron ore, copper, silver and zinc, and because the Romans promoted salt production from the Adriatic Sea.

Because of the enormous extent of the Empire and thereby the ultimate depletion of the native population, or because of the obliteration of the population's military characteristics, the Roman emperors enlisted the services of different barbaric peoples and eventually settled them on imperial territory. This happened in the cases of Pannonia and Dalmatia. The Emperor Diocletian, after waging a successful war against the Goths and their Sarmatian allies, brought a considerable number of the latter to Dalmatia. Jacob Burckhardt suggests that the Sarmatians were in reality Slavs. Thus, on this hypothesis, Diocletian would be responsible for bringing the first Slavs to Dalmatia.

During the bitter contests and bloody struggles for power that regularly occurred between the different emperors and their rivals, Pannonia became the arena where the destiny of the Empire was decided. At the Battle of Murciae in 258 the contest between Gallienus and Ingenius was settled; a settlement was determined between Constantine and Licinius at Cibaliae

7

in 314; and Theodosius and Maximianus resolved their quarrel at Sisciae in 388.

Internal strife and a general weakening of the Empire prevented the Empire from turning back the Hunic invasion of Western Europe. The beginning of the great migration of peoples (375) followed in the wake of this invasion.

Under Hunic pressure, the Goths, whose kingdoms were destroyed by the Huns, crossed the Danube, destroying Murciae and plundering the whole of Pannonia (395). Pannonia, as well as Dalmatia, were alloted to the Western Empire as a result of Theodosius' division. However, the Western Empire could not even protect itself or the city of Rome let alone be of any help to those outpost provinces that were subject to these first barbarian thrusts. Invasions followed in regular succession until Attila finally opened wide the imperial frontiers. The end of the Empire itself was at hand.

The Empire breathed its last breath when the Gothic leader, Odoaker, simply dismissed the boy-emperor, Romulus Augustulus, and proclaimed himself the king of the Goths (476). He established his power over Pannonia and Dalmatia as well. His rule, however, was short. With Byzantine support, the Ostrogothic leader, Theodoric, defeated Odoaker and established his own kingdom within the same territory. But this new kingdom also proved ephemeral. The Roman population had endured the Gothic rule when it was exposed to the uninhibited flow of barbaric invasions from across the Danube. Upon the first favorable occasion, however, it turned to the Eastern Empire for protection.

Pannonia and Dalmatia came once more under imperial authority when Emperor Justinian (527-567) was able to establish partial unification of the Empire. But Justinian's efforts were short-lived. After his death, imperial authority was once again hedged in, and a permanent settlement of Avars was permitted on the Danubian plains. This settlement indicated that the Roman defensive system along the Danube was permanently broken. The Avars and their subjects, as well as their Slavic allies, began to initiate regular intrusions upon Roman territory. Among the intruding forces could be found the ancestors of the Croats.

CHAPTER II

THE ORIGINS

Ancient Slavs — Theories of Croatian origin — Original homeland — Gothic influence — Hunnish sway — Old Slavonic society — Religion — Frankish impact — First Slavic immigration to Pannonia and Dalmatia — Avars — Emperor Heraclius — White Croatia — Croatian settlement of Dalmatia — Christian contacts — Bulgarians — Establishment of political units.

The Croats belong to the southern Slavic linguistic group which also includes the Slovenes, the Serbs, the Bulgarians and the Macedonians.

The origins of the Croatian nation, like those of any other people, are lost in the darkness of a prehistory which permits the development of only a few more or less acceptable theories about the primeval beginnings, the original land and the name. The most important of these theories can be briefly outlined.

According to Constantine Porfirogenetus, the Croats are, quite simply, "the people with many lands." The Slovak philologist Jan Safaryk, thinks the name Croat derives from that of the Carpathian Mountain chain (*Karpati - Horvati*). The Russian historian, Braun, thinks that the Germanic Bastrians named the Carpathians *Harvalda* and thereby named the inhabitants *Harvati, Horvati, Hrvati, Chrobaten* (Croats). The Russian historians, Pogodin and Miler, discovered some old Iranian inscriptions on the Don River (Tanais) in which a name similar to that of Croat (*Horuatus*) can be found. This discovery sup-

11

ports the theory that the name is derived from the Iranian language and means "true friends," or "who has true friends," or, in a word, "ally."

Around these principal theories there developed a few more. The most important of these are Gumplowicz's theory of the Gothic origins of the Croats, and Sakac's theory of their Irano-Sarmatian origins.

* * *

The Croats finally appeared on the European historical scene at the time of the Avar invasion of the Roman Empire in the sixth century. Ancient Greek, Roman and Arab historians such as Herodotus, Claudius Ptolomeus, Plinius the Older and Tacitus had already mentioned the Slavs in a vague way, while some had identified them as Sarmatians. The first positive facts about the ancient Slavs are given by the German historian Jordanes. He identifies the Slavs under such denominations as Sarmatians, Slavs and Antes. In later German sources they are known as Wenden, Venedi and Winden. But, generally speaking, all of these sources are extremely vague and uncertain.

With some veracity, one could say that the first known land of the Slavs was situated in the territory between the Carpathian Mountains and the Vistula, Desna, Dnieper, Western Drina and Don Rivers. The Dnieper River divided the tribes into two separate groups: the Slavs to the west and the Antes to the east. The Croats belonged to the eastern group (Antes), but gradually shifted toward the west. The neighbors of the Slavs were: the Balts, who settled to the north; the Finns or Tschudi, who settled to the northeast; the Scythians, who occupied the land to the southeast; the Germans, who inhabited the territory to the west; and the Celtic Tracians, who lived to the south.

The Iranian Scythians were the first to gain ascendancy over the Slavic tribes on the Don River. They subjected them to their rule and imposed their political and military organizations on them.

But the influence exercised by the Germanic Bastrians, and

especially by the Goths, on the political, social and military development of the different Slavic tribes was far more important. The Ostrogoths conquered the Slavic territory and ruled the Slavic tribes during the third and fourth centuries. The Gothic domination ended with the Hunnish invasion of Europe. By 375, these Uralo-Altaic nomads destroyed the Ostrogothic Kingdom and imposed their rule upon both the Goths and the Slavs. Henceforth, until the termination of Hunnish power, the Goths and the Slavs participated in the Hunnish invasions of the territory of the Roman Empire. During these invasions, the Slavic tribes started their migrations to the west and south.

*   *   *

According to old historical descriptions, the ancient Slavs were men of high stature, blue eyes, blond or reddish hair and long beards. They had monogamist marital customs, and a social structure based on family life. Several interrelated families formed a family-tribe, from which developed the institution of the home-cooperative (*kucna zadruga*), which was headed by an elderman (*starjesina*). Tribal brotherhoods (*pleme* or *bratstvo*) were formed from several home-cooperatives and were ruled by an appointed tribal chief (*celnik*). The clan (*pleme*), which was composed of several tribal brotherhoods, was the highest social organization that the ancient Slavs achieved. Within the context of the clan, the tribal system of justice — just as with other peoples on the same level of development — took the form of the pre-institutional bloody *vendetta*.

Eventually the clans joined into clannish comitats, i.e., counties (*plemenska zupa*) headed by a count (*zupan*). The *zupan* was the supreme political chief, judge and commander of the army. He probably represented the most influential clan within the comitat, and ruled from the central town of the territory.

Agriculture was the principal occupation of the ancient Slavs. The land was held in common ownership by means of a co-operative institution that has been preserved, under changed circumstances, even til recent times. Cattle-breeding, maintaining apiaries, hunting and fishing were some of the other tribal activities.

The religion of the ancient Slavs took the form of naturalistic polytheism. Their deities were symbols for natural phenomena; e.g., *Dazhbog* was the god of the sun and *Perun* was the god of thunder. The experience of the mystery of death produced a few beliefs that prevail today in death-related customs. Dragons, fairies, witches and vampires were feared and worshipped. The memory of these primitive beliefs is retained in a rich variety of popular sagas, customs and poetry.

Religious ceremonies were held in natural settings like groves, meadows and hills, and involved the sacrifice of domestic animals and products from the land. These sacrifices were followed by common prayers, songs, dances and plays. The dead were buried under high artificial hills (*mogila*) upon which the death play (*strava*) was enacted in honor of the departed. Many of the customs that originated in these early religious settings found their way into Christian ceremonies. For example, on principal Christian feast days traditional visits (*koleda*), star worship (*zvijezda*) and ritual dances (*kolo*) occur.

The different Slavic peoples appeared when the primitive tribal units developed into larger political entities. This transformation occurred in its most definite form under the influence of the Avars, and especially under that of the Franks. The new territorial and political units that developed out of the unification of the different tribes were composed along the lines of Frankish duchies and counties. Usually they were ruled by a duke (*knez*). (The name *knez* is of unknown origin, but could easily have been derived from the old German name *Kuning.*) He was assisted by tribal chieftains who met together at assemblies which became known among Croats as *sabor*.

* * *

According to some historians, a few Slavic settlements could be found in Pannonia and Dalmatia as early as the second century A.D. Following his successful campaign, near the end

14

of the third century, Diocletian brought in some Sarmatian slaves. But, whatever the case, Slavic settlements had definitely been established in both provinces dating from 536. These permanent settlements were built by the Avars.

The Avars were nomads of Asiatic-Turanian origin who initially appeared in Europe as Emperor Justinian's allies (558). Subsequently they followed a prototypical pattern: These barbaric allies of the Empire changed sides and became its enemy. In 568 they crossed the Danube, invaded the Balkans and pushed the German Langobards out of the Pannonian plain. Between the Danube and Tisa Rivers they established a strong military state under the leadership of Hagan Bajan. Some Slavic tribes were already living in this area, and the Avars brought in more. These additional tribes were both subjects and allies.

From this strategic vantage point, the Avars and their allies gazed upon the rich and fabulous Roman civilization. They were lured again and again across its borders, until their plundering invasions became a regularity. After repeated invasions, the Avars conquered and destroyed Sirmium, the capital city of Pannonia (597). With this conquest the entire province passed into their hands.

Pannonia served as a foothold for a series of devastating attacks on Dalmatia. In 614 Salona was conquered and destroyed, and from this conquest followed the total subjugation of Dalmatia herself, i.e., a similar fate awaited other Dalmatian towns such as Scardona, Narona, Epidaurum and Delminium. In fact, the entire province was laid waste except for the well fortified cities of Jadera and Tragurium. The population escaped either into these protected cities or to the islands along the coast.

By the end of the sixth century the imperial power in Dalmatia was reduced to practically nothing. The Avar and Slavic intruders pushed their luck so far that they were able to lay siege to the imperial capital itself, Constantinople. However, at this point (626), they suffered a severe setback. The Avars retreated to their land in the center of the Danubian plain, while their Slavic allies reinforced the defenses of the existing Slavic

15

population on the peninsula. At this time the Slavs were able to free themselves from the Avar subjugation.

*   *   *

The Avar-Slav devastations prompted Emperor Heraclius (610-641) to renew the old Roman practice of opposing barbarians with barbarians. Thus, he invited Slavic tribes from beyond the Carpathian Mountains to fight the Avars and their Slavic dependents. The Croats were among the first chosen by the Emperor for this task. Imperial emissaries journeyed to White Croatia, the land situated on the banks of the upper Vistula River and covering the regions of Silesia and Little Poland. The Polish city of Cracow is situated in this area today.

The Croats had a well-organized state ruled by twelve native chieftains (*zupan*). Upon imperial invitation, the twelve Croatian tribes began moving southward. On their way to Dalmatia, they crossed the territories of contemporary Bohemia, Moravia, Austria and the western part of Hungary. They settled along the Adriatic coast between the Rasa River in Istria and the Cetina River in Dalmatia. They recognized the supreme authority of the Empire, and paid tribute by sending delegations to Constantinople. Soon they established their domination over the Slavic, as well as the non-Slavic, elements already existing in the country. The only exceptions to their dominion were the populations of the imperial towns along the coast.

The Croats were undoubtedly a ruling people who imposed their political, social and military system on the existing population and ultimately gave to the land and people a common name: The land became Croatia, and the people became the Croats.

With the coming of the twelve tribes, Croatian settlement of the new land was complete. The Croats considered themselves imperial subjects, and the Emperor granted them free possession of lands on imperial territory. This grant was solemnly confirmed to a special delegation of Croatian chieftains sent to Constantinople in 678. At the same time the Papacy established a *modus vivendi* with them concerning the Christians in the coastal towns. In 680, Pope Agathon issued a document which stated that the Croatian chieftains agreed to respect the Christian religion and Christian practices in their territory.

*   *   *

Shortly after 670 the Empire fell once again into misfortune due to a new invasion by the Uralo-Turanian Bulgarians. These Bulgarians crossed the Danube and formed a powerful military state that straddled the river. The fortune of the Empire went further astray when, in 751, the Langobards brought an end to the Ravenna Exarchat, thereby evicting imperial authority from Italy.

Constantinople, therefore, undertook to save and reorganize what was left of imperial territory in the Adriatic. Venice emerged as an independent republic that was soon to dominate the Adriatic Sea. Dalmatian towns and islands were reorganized into the imperial province of Dalmatia and entrusted to the care of the imperial governor at Zadar. Dalmatia was now nothing more than an impoverished remnant of its former stature as a proud imperial province. It had been reduced to the towns of Zadar, Trogir, Split, Dubrovnik and Kotor, and the islands of Rab and Cres.

The Church, too, underwent reorganization. The former Archbishopric of Salona, destroyed during the Avar invasion, was reconstructed as the Archbishopric of Split. Various bishoprics were established or reestablished for the other towns as well.

As imperial authority, for all practical purposes disappeared from the country, the Croats fell more and more under the influence of either the Bulgarians in the east, or, more especially, the Franks, who were the new masters of Italy.

*   *   *

This period produced new political units among the Croats and the other Slavs in the neighborhood. Several tribes formed new, larger political units. Some of the most important were:

17

Croatia (*Hrvati, Hrvatska zemlja, Hrvatska, Bijela Hrvatska*),
along the Adriatic coast, covering the territory between the
Rasa, Cetina and Vrbas Rivers; Slavonia (*Slovinci, Slovinska
zemlja, Slavonska Hrvatska, Panonska Hrvatska*), between the
mountains and the Drava and Danube Rivers; Narentia (*Neretl-
jani, Neretljanska zemlja*), between the Cetina and Neretva
Rivers; Hum, between Narentia and Dubrovnik; Travunia, between Dubrovnik and Kotor; and Bosnia, in the mountains along
the upper Bosnia and Drina Rivers. The Serbs formed their own
political units, Rasa and Zeta, to the east of the Croatian lands.
The Slovenian Duchy of Carinthia was situated to the west.

CHAPTER III

THE RISE AND DECLINE
OF MEDIEVAL CROATIA

*From tribal to ducal organization — Slavonia — Croatia
— Between Byzantine and Frankish Empires — Duke
Ljudevit of Slavonia — Ascendancy of Croatia — Duke
Trpimir — Duke Branimir — Tomislav: Croatia becomes
a kingdom (925) — Stjepan Drzislav — Petar Kresimir
IV — Struggle between Latin and Slavonic clergy —
Dmitar Zvonimir — Extinction of the National Dynasty
An evaluation of Medieval Croatia.*

The Croats definitely appeared on the European historical
stage following the Frankish conquest of Istria and Italy in
the second half of the eighth century. At this time Charlemagne
also added to his empire the Duchy of Bavaria and its dependency, the Slovenian Duchy of Carinthia (788). Due to these
conquests, the Franks became the immediate neighbors of the
Croats.

Soon after moving next-door to the Croats, Charlemagne
launched his campaign against the Avars who were situated at
the center of the Danubian plains. He succeeded in breaking
their power and the Avar state vanished by 796.

Duke Vojnomir of Slavonia, a former Avar vassal, had fought
in alliance with the Franks against his former masters. After
the successful campaign, he merely changed overlords. The
Duke of Slavonia became vassal to the Emperor and submitted
directly to the rule of the Margrave of Friule. But when Mar-

grave Eric attempted as well to impose his rule on Duke Viseslav of Croatia, he met disaster at the Duke's hands in the battle of Trsat (799).

The coronation of Charlemagne as Emperor of the West on Christmas Day in 800 was received with general displeasure in Constantinople. It was considered an open provocation to imperial dignity and was followed by a long, tedious war. In the course of the war, the Franks conquered the Croatian lands situated between the Rasa and Drina rivers, but Byzantium successfully protected its Dalmatian possessions. The Peace Treaty of Aix-la-Chapelle acknowledged this new arrangement, giving Croatia as well as Slavonia to the Franks, while the Dalmatian towns of Zadar, Trogir, Split, Dubrovnik and Kotor, together with the islands of Krk, Cres and Rab, became the Byzantine Imperial Province of Dalmatia (814).

*　　*　　*

The establishment of any approximate date upon which the Croats might have accepted Christianity is still a matter for speculation. However, it is tempting to assume that the first converts were made due to the close proximity of the Latin and Christian towns in Dalmatia. This assumption becomes more than obvious when it is noted that the ancient Archbishopric of Salona was restored under the name of Split in 780. Moreover, restoration was preceded by an understanding between the papacy and the Croatian chieftains during the time of Pope Agathon (680) which enabled Christians to freely exercise their religion on Croatian territory. Furthermore, Frankish missionaries showed some activity in certain parts of Slavonia. Whatever the case, it is probable that by accepting Christianity, the Croats also accepted the Arian heresy, since it was the creed of the Goths who had previously settled in the country.

The first known Croatian duke of the Christian faith was Viseslav (800). Both he and his Slavonian contemporary, Duke Vojnomir, were vassals of the Frankish empire and were directly subject to the Margrave of Friule. When Louis the Pious suc-

20

ceeded his father, both of the ruling Croatian dukes, Borna of Croatia and Ljudevit of Slavonia, travelled to Paderborn to pay their homage to the new emperor.

The fact that Louis was a very inefficient ruler prompted the Frankish nobility to grab as much power as they possibly could. This tendency created general chaos in the Empire, which was followed by many abuses and oppressions exercised by some of the highest nobility. The Frankish overlord for Slavonia, the Margrave Kodolah of Friule, was particularly odious. His abuses prompted Ljudevit, the Duke of Slavonia, to visit the Emperor at Heristal in 818 in order to voice his protest, as well as to seek imperial protection. This action was of no avail. Subsequently Ljudevit united under his rule not only his Duchy of Slavonia, but also Slavic populations from Carinthia and Timok, in order to resist Kodolah. This resistance soon became outright revolt.

Ljudevit resided at Sisak and ruled the country situated between the Sutla River in the west and the confluence of the Sava and Danube rivers in the east, as well as between the Drava River and the Bosnian Mountains. But, the Croatian Duke, Borna, remained faithful to his Frankish master and waged war on Ljudevit.

Before engaging in open revolt, Ljudevit approached the Emperor and offered him complete submission if he would eliminate the Friulean Margrave intermediary. His offer was ignored. Soon after, Margrave Balderich invaded Slavonia and defeated Ljudevit's army. The Margrave then occupied the largest part of the country. But Ljudevit continued to resist from his fortified capital at Sisak. It was at this time that Borna joined the Franks and invaded Slavonia himself, but his army was badly routed by Ljudevit's forces.

Since the Friulean margrave was unable to subdue Ljudevit, the German Diet decided to invade Slavonia. Three armies were raised for that purpose. They began by completing the conquest of the Slovenian Duchy of Carinthia, which at this time lost its privilege of electing its own dukes from the local nobility. It was directly incorporated into the Duchy of Bavaria.

During this campaign, the Franks occupied all of the country except for Sisak, which was the stronghold for Ljudevit's continued stubborn resistance. But Ljudevit could not hold out long without help, and Byzantium, which would be his logical ally, was involved in a paralyzing struggle for its own continued existence. In fact, the Bulgarians had already defeated Emperor Nicopherus in 811, and laid siege to the city of Constantinople. Thus, when another Frankish army invaded Slavonia, Ljudevit sought refuge in Croatia. There, by order of Borna's uncle, Ljutomisl, Ljudevit was murdered. His death (828) brought an end to the revolt.

With Ljudevit's death and the Frankish conquest of Slavonia, the prime moving power of Croatian history passed into the hands of Croatia herself. Croatia was at this time headed by Duke Vladislav, who ruled the country as a Frankish vassal from 829 to 838.

* * *

The plight of Slavonia grew worse due to the Bulgarian conquest of its eastern section. With Bulgarian help, Duke Ratimir was able to establish temporary rule. However, when Margrave Radbold conquered Pannonia, Slavonia shared its destiny by being incorporated into the Empire as an adjacent tributary. The ruling Pannonian and Slavonian dukes, Pribina (861), Kocelj (861-896) and Braslav (880-896), were simply Frankish vassals.

* * *

The Bulgarians were a nomadic military alliance of tribes of Uralo-Altaic origin who appeared on the banks of the Danube River during the decline of both the Byzantine and Frankish Empires. There they easily conquered and devastated the province of Daciae, as well as parts of Pannonia and Moesiae, and founded a strong military state of their own. It was at this time that the eastern section of Slavonia fell into their hands while the western portion remained under Frankish rule.

The Eastern Empire declined even further due to its continued struggle for existence. Moreover, the instability of its authority permitted a series of civil wars which exposed it to the aggressions of the Arabs. The Arabs made themselves masters of Crete (826) and Sicily (827), and used these islands as stepping stones for an invasion of southern Italy. Their presence on the Italian peninsula would eventually bring them into conflict with the Franks who were established in northern Italy.

As Byzantine power practically disappeared from the Adriatic, its former dependency, the city of Venice, assumed all the proportions of a new, independent maritime power. Indeed, it gradually acted more and more as the natural heir to the Empire. Asserting its ambitions in this new role, Venice was immediately faced with a bitter challenge from Croatian pirates who, at this time of disorder, had become a dominant factor on the eastern shores of the Adriatic Sea.

*   *   *

In due time the Frankish Empire gave way to the organization of the new Kingdom of Italy. The Friulean Marches were abolished and the Croatian dukes submitted directly to the kings of Italy. These kings were occupied with other worries and were unable to pay due attention to the Croatian dukes, thus facilitating their tendency to assert their independence.

The early dukes resided at Nin, which was also the see of the Bishop of the Croats. Duke Mislav (835-845) moved his capital from Nin to Klis (in the proximity of Split) in order to put himself in closer contact with the imperial Dalmatian towns. He also tried to cultivate good relations with Venice. With this intention in mind, he signed a treaty of permanent peace with the Venetian doge, Peter Tradonigo (839).

Both the duke and the doge were prompted to sign this

treaty due to the newly created situation in the Adriatic brought about by the invasion of the Saracene fleet. Shortly after their arrival, the Saracene conquered Bari and used it as a point for further penetration. In 846, as they had done previously, they invaded unprotected Italy, conquering and plundering Rome and desecrating the Basilica of St. Peter. During the ensuing disorder on the Italian mainland, the Croatian pirates from Narentia plundered towns on the Istrian Peninsula and even made their presence felt in the Venetian lagoons.

Duke Trpimir (845-864) still formally acknowledged Emperor Lothar, but he was determined to assert more and more of his own independence. He organized his own ducal court along the Frankish pattern. It consisted of twelve *zupans,* who were representatives of the twelve tribes, and who were, in effect, the basis for the Croatian political organization. The court chamberlains and clergy completed the establishment.

In pursuing his political ambitions, Trpimir asserted his claim on some lands belonging to the Eastern Empire. This involved him in a war with Byzantium. The events of the war turned in his favor, and after routing the imperial army (846) he took possession of the new lands. In order to celebrate his victory and probably to establish good relations with Rome, he invited some Benedictine monks to settle in his country. Moreover, he built them a monastery and endowed them with rich lands. Upon this occasion (March 4, 852) he issued, in the full majesty of an independent ruler, the first preserved Croatian diplomatic document in which he proudly called himself, "by divine grace, Duke of the Croats" (*dux Chroatorum munere divinis*). Furthermore, he defeated the Bulgarians when they attempted to wrestle Bosnia from him.

Trpimir witnessed the first split between Rome and Constantinople, which occurred due to the conflict between Constantinople's Patriarch Ignatius and the counter-Patriarch, Fotius. Pope Nicholas sided with Ignatius, and Trpimir stood firmly with the pope. Consequently, the Croatian Bishop of Nin became a direct suffragan of Rome (864).

After Trpimir's death, Duke Domagoj (864-878) ascended the ducal throne in spite of Trpimir's direct heirs. This event caused some unrest in the country and prompted the Venetian doge, Ursus Patriciah, to invade the littoral. In the course of the invasion (865) he took numerous hostages.

Shortly after this Venetian invasion, the Saracene fleet penetrated the Adriatic and laid siege to Dubrovnik, blocking it from the sea. In its plight, the town asked for help from Constantinople. Consequently, after a long absence, the imperial fleet reappeared in the Adriatic and forced the Arabs to put an end to their siege.

The presence of imperial forces in Adriatic waters forced the Narentian pirates to submit again to imperial sovereignty. The ambitious Emperor, Vasilius Comnenus after re-establishing his power in Byzantium, formed an alliance with the German Emperor, Lothar II, in order to reconquer Bari and free southern Italy from the Arabs. The high hopes that Lothar held for this alliance were never justified because of Byzantium's reluctance to seriously carry through its part of the bargain. Consequently, the alliance failed to block Bari on its seaward side. Lothar then called upon his vassal, Duke Domagoj of Croatia, to use his own fleet to block Bari from the sea. Bari ultimately surrendered to Lothar in 870.

The result of the inoperative Franco-Byzantine alliance was a general deterioration of relations between the two powers, and ultimately an open enmity which provoked a series of wars. This newly created situation thrust Domagoj, a Frankish vassal and ally, into a hot contest with Venice, a Byzantine ally. The contest took the form of a naval war in which Domagoj achieved notable success. According to contemporary Venetian documents, Domagoj's treatment of Venice earned him the title, "the worst Slavonic duke" (*pessimus Sclavorum dux*), and it earned for his Croatian people the name of "worst Slavonic and Dalmatian people" (*Slavorum pessime gente et Dalmationorum*).

When Venice signed a peace treaty with the Franks, Domagoj was not included. This forced him to face, alone, both Byzantium and Venice. The Franks, also, joined the alliance against Domagoj. The ensuing war proved costly for both sides. Kocelj, Duke of the Pannonian Slavs, participated in the war against Domagoj as a Frankish vassal. He was killed, and his duchy was dissolved. The war finally came to an end with Domagoj's death in 876.

Domagoj's death was welcomed by Trpimir's heirs, who with Byzantine aid replaced Domagoj's successor, Duke Iljko, with Zdeslav. Zdeslav (878-879) inaugurated a time of subservience to Constantinople. This new policy was badly received in the country, provoking a conspiracy which resulted in Zdeslav's death.

Branimir (879-892) took possession of the throne and immediately terminated subservience to Constantinople. On May 21, 879, he sent a delegation to Rome. As a consequence of this new policy, the Croatian bishop was again freed of his connections with the Patriarchate of Aquilea and Constantinople and placed under immediate papal authority. The same year, by special agreement between Pope John VIII and Emperor Vasilius, Croatia was recognized as an independent country. Thus, Duke Branimir became the first completely independent ruler of Croatia.

During Branimir's rule, Methodius, Bishop of Moravia, visited Croatia on his way to Rome (882). His presence, and especially the presence of his disciples, reinforced the independent tendencies of the Croatian clergy and supported the use of the old Slavonic liturgy in church services.

After establishing his independence, Branimir imposed regular yearly taxes on Dalmatian towns for possession of lands in Croatian territory and for free navigation along the seacoast. (Split was taxed 200 Ducats; Zadar, 110; Trogir, 100; Rab, 100; Dubrovnik, 36; and Kotor, 36.)

Seeking free navigation along the eastern shores of the Adriatic, Venice soon challenged Branimir's independence. But in the ensuing naval war, the united Croatian and Narentian navies inflicted a crushing defeat upon the Republic. Venice was forced to sign a treaty (877) which imposed yearly taxes upon her for free navigation along the Croatian coast.

Branimir's successor, Duke Mutimir (892-910), preserved the strength and independence of the country and passed it intact to his heir, Duke Tomislav.

Tomislav (910-928) was at once faced with a new danger to his country. The Magyars, a new Asiatic invader, established themselves in the heart of the Pannonian plain. At first they were German allies against Duke Svatopluk of Moravia, but later they turned against their allies, destroying all German influence in what had originally been the Slavic Pannonian and Moravian duchies. From their new stronghold, the Magyars launched regular military expeditions into the very heart of Germany. They were finally stopped by Emperor Otto at the battle of Lechfeld (955).

The Magyars invaded Slavonia as well, bringing the rule of Duke Braslav to an end. But they met defeat at the hands of Tomislav, who then annexed Slavonia to his own duchy and in 925 proclaimed himself King of the Croats (*Chroatorum rex*). Thus Croatia became a kingdom.

The same year Tomislav joined the Byzantine Emperor, Romanus Lecapinus, as an ally in a war against the Bulgarian Emperor Simeun. After Simeun's defeat, Lecapinus granted Tomislav the title of Imperial Pro-consul in Dalmatia. By this act, Imperial Dalmatia fell under the authority of the King of Croatia, and Tomislav's rule stretched from Istria to the imperial territory. This fact re-established the territorial unity of the former Archbishopric of Salona by placing it under a single civil ruler.

At this time, the Archbishop of Split, as heir to the Archbishopric of Salona, endeavored, with the help of Tomislav, to establish his jurisdiction over the entire kingdom. Tomislav called a General Synod at Split into session (925) with the aim of estab-

27

lishing order and enforcing a necessary reorganization of the church within his country. Besides Tomislav himself, his court nobility, representatives of the twelve tribes, and delegates of Dalmatian towns, Mihajlo, Duke of Hum and Travunia, was also personally present.

The Archbishop of Split headed the Latin clergy, and Grgur, the Croatian Bishop of Nin, led the Croatian clergy. The two opposing views emerged at once. In the name of the Latin party, the Archbishop of Split insisted upon the establishment of church unity, under his jurisdiction, throughout the entire kingdom, as well as the exclusive use of the Latin language in the liturgy. The king, the court nobility and the representatives of the Dalmatian towns supported the Latin party (which also became known as the court party); while the tribal representatives gave their determined support to the national party. Before anything could be settled, Tomislav was faced with another Bulgarian invasion and the work of the Synod had to be postponed.

After a successful campaign in 928 Tomislav recalled the Synod. The second Synod established the primacy of the Archbishop of Split over all the territory of the kingdom, as well as over all bishoprics from Istria to Kotor. The Croatian bishopric of Nin was abolished, and its titular, Grgur, was appointed Bishop of Skradin. The old Slavonic liturgy was banned and the Croatian clergy was instructed to learn Latin as a condition for continuation of its spiritual vocation.

The Kingdom of Croatia earned an international reputation from Tomislav's victories over the Magyars and the Bulgarians. According to Constantine Porfirogenetus, Tomislav was able to put into the field an army consisting of 100,000 infantrymen and 60,000 cavalrymen, while his fleet could muster 80 large units and 100 smaller ones.

Trpimir II (928-935) and Kresimir I (935-945) maintained the country at the same level. However, *Ban* Pribina raised an insurrection against Miroslav (945-949) and a long civil war followed. During this period, Bosnia and Narentia detached themselves from Croatia; and the Republic of Venice, acting as a mandator of the Eastern Empire seized the opportunity to dominate Dalmatia.

The country was passed on, in this weakened condition, to Stjepan Drzislav (969-997), who was to prove to be one of the strongest medieval Croatian rulers. During this period, the new Emperor of the Eastern Empire, John Tzimisces, began rebuilding imperial power. Toward this end, he waged war against the Emperor of the Bulgarians, Samuilo. Drzislav joined Byzantium, and the coalition defeated the Bulgarians. As a token of recognition for his alliance, Emperor John awarded Drzislav the insignia of royal dignity, the sceptre and crown, and recognized him as King of Croatia and Dalmatia (988).

Venice, at this time, chose to ignore its former obligation to pay taxes for free navigation along the eastern coast of the Adriatic, and Drzislav was unable to enforce the agreement. Thus he left his throne to the joint rulership of his three sons, since his succession was not regulated. This created a bitter struggle among the brothers for sole possession of the throne. Svetislav Suronja (977-1000) was challenged by his brothers, Kresimir II (1000-1030) and Gojslav (1000-1020), and was thereby unable to oppose Venice effectively when the Republic, in full strength, appeared on the scene. Doge Peter Orseolo defeated the Croatian fleet, seized Dalmatian towns, and adorned himself with the title, "Duke of Dalmatia" (1000). Following contemporary customs, he returned to Venice with hostages, among them, Crown Prince Stjepan. It was during his stay in Venice that Stjepan took Orseolo's daughter, Hicela, in marriage.

The general disorder in Croatia prompted Emperor Vasilius to annex eastern Slavonia and to impose his domination on Croatia. To aggravate already existing difficulties, the simmering conflict between the Latin and Croatian clergy erupted again: Due to political changes in the Dalmatian towns and the precarious Croatian rule over them, the Bishop of Knin attempted to free himself from the jurisdiction of the Archbishop of Split. The conflict grew even more bitter after the definite split between the Roman Catholic Church and the Greek Orthodox Church (1056).

These were the conditions in the country when Stjepan I (1030-1058) attempted to re-establish order and deal with church affairs. He made himself master of Split and called another Synod into session there. This Synod was marked by an increasing papal interest in the state of the church in Croatia. This was the consequence of the Cluniac reforms, then prevailing in Rome. Rome dispatched a special papal delegate, John, who was to examine the activities, assess the fitness of both the Latin and Croatian clergy, impose strict discipline and establish church unity.

Stjepan's rule paved the way for his successor, the most powerful medieval Croatian ruler, Peter Kresimir IV (1058-1075). Due to his father's wise policy, Kresimir inherited a well organized country and was able to unite Croatian lands by establishing their boundary at the River Drina. Furthermore, he united Croatia and Dalmatia into a single kingdom. Following the pattern of the old Dalmatian towns, he built the Croatian towns of Sibenik and Biograd on the Adriatic coast and granted them the same rights and privileges held by the old Latin towns. He moved the capital to Biograd.

The most pressing problem of his rule proved to be the increasingly bitter conflict that separated the Latin from the Croatian clergy. The conflict came out into the open when Ulfo and Cededa, both supporters of the old Slavonic liturgy, blatantly challenged Latin supremacy. Consequently, Kresimir called another Synod at Split in 1060.

Due to the energetic intervention of Lovro, Archbishop of Split, and that of the equally uncompromising papal legat, Abbot Maynard, the Synod found Ulfo guilty of heresy. He was subsequently jailed and his disciples were dispersed throughout the country. Kresimir, the court nobility, and the magnates of the country wholeheartedly supported the Synod. But it was different with the small nobility and the representatives of the twelve tribes. They stood fast by Ulfo and his followers. Thus, what was originally a clerical squabble, soon assumed the proportions of a political struggle between the supporters of the court and those who supported the popular representatives. This struggle would ultimately exhaust the country and, after the extinction of the domestic dynasty of Trpimirovic, prove fatal to national independence.

To complicate the situation, the powerful new Kingdom of Hungary was becoming more and more involved in Croatian affairs. The Hungarian Arpad dynasty gave its full support to the younger branch of the Croatian royal house, which was established in Slavonia: moreover, it secured family ties with it. This relationship would be felt particularly when the Magyars emerged victorious in their contest with the Eastern Empire, replacing it as the dominant power in eastern Slavonia.

Hungary became even more preponderant when Dmitar Zvonimir, Duke of Croatia and *Ban* of Slavonia, married the Hungarian princess, Jelena Lijepa, sister of King Gejza. Kresimir, himself, recognized the special position of Zvonimir as Duke of Croatia and presumptive successor to the throne.

With the end of Kresimir's rule, Croatia found itself involved in a struggle between the Eastern Empire and the Normans, who were established in southern Italy at the entrance to the Adriatic Sea. The kingdom's troubles steadily multiplied due to religious and political dissensions within the country, as well as on account of foreign intervention.

Peter Kresimir IV's death left the throne vacant. Subsequently, the popular faction elected Slavac, Duke of Narentia, king. His rule was short-lived. It came to an end when the Norman Count Amico and his navy invaded Croatia, taking Slavac hostage.

Upon this occasion, the Normans conquered some Dalmatian towns and imposed a short-lived rule upon them. However, when the Normans were forced out of Croatian waters, their place was most actively filled by Venice, the successor to the Byzantine heritage. Byzantine diplomacy showed some interest in Croatian succession, but due to the general weakness of the Empire, its intervention was not strongly felt. Thus, for the first time, the Holy See emerged to play an ambitious and decisive part in the destiny of Croatia.

Pope Gregory VII (1073-1085), the most prominent representative of papal supremacy, had already established papal sovereignty over the Catalonian, Arragonian, Portuguese, Hungarian rulers and Norman dukes, who became kings of southern Italy. In fact, William the Conqueror had, himself, undertaken the conquest of England with similar papal blessings and obligations.

Gregory VII took the most active part in the settlement of the succession to the Croatian throne. Due to his intervention, the Croats recognized Dmitar Zvonimir as King of Dalmatia and Croatia. Zvonimir (1075-1089) was solemnly crowned by the Papal Legat, Abbott Gebizon. Upon this occasion, Zvonimir took an oath of fidelity to the pope.

Zvonimir was the last descendant of the House of Trpimir, which belonged to the branch established by King Svetislav and which was then ruling in Slavonia. Zvonimir was related by marriage to the Hungarian royal house of Arpad.

When Gregory VII, during the struggle for investiture, found himself involved in a series of wars against Emperor Henry IV, Zvonimir took part as a papal vassal. His participation in these wars proved damaging both to himself and to Croatia. In fact, Croatia lost some of its western territory.

Shortly thereafter, in support of papal policy, Zvonimir allied himself with the Norman Duke, Robert Guiscard, against the Eastern Empire and its ally, the Republic of Venice. At this time, Zvonimir successfully asserted himself as the sole ruler of what had been imperial Dalmatian territory.

The consequences of Zvonimir's policies as an obedient papal vassal were not altogether good for Croatia. The long warfare exhausted the country's resources, while the preponderant influence of the Latin faction in the royal court created general dissatisfaction within the popular faction.

During Zvonimir's rule, the first signs of the feudal system appeared in Croatia. The magnates of the royal court began to follow the general feudal pattern already established in western Europe. The consequences of these tendencies, together with those of the already existing general dissatisfaction, broke out into the open when Zvonimir, upon the invitation of Pope Urban II, convened the *Sabor* at Knin in 1089 for the purpose of calling his nation to arms on behalf of the Eastern Empire. Emperor Alexius had inherited a diminished Empire in Asia Minor following the battle of Manzikert (1071). Moreover, he was himself defeated on the Danube by the Patzinaks.

Pope Urban adopted the plan of his predecessor, Gregory VII, by preparing a general crusade for the liberation of the Holy Land. Thus the invitation to the Croatian king to participate fell into the general pattern. But the representatives of the tribal nobility were unwilling to follow the king. Consequently the *Sabor* was transformed into a bloody insurrection in which Zvonimir lost his life.

Zvonimir did not leave a child, since his unique son, Radovan, died at an early age. Thus the question of succession to the throne was once again open. The general disorder and confusion that followed led to a bitter struggle between the court and popular factions. Stjepan II (1089-1090), who was the last member of the House of Trpimirovic and who had been living the life of a monk, was brought forward from his monastery to resolve the dispute. But he soon died.

Upon Stjepan's death, the Court faction joined Zvonimir's widow, Jelena, in an offer of the crown of Croatia to her nephew, Ladislav, King of Hungary. A delegation headed by Petar of the Tribe of Gusic, representing the nobility, and Petar Kokauntov, Prior of Split, representing the Dalmatian towns, was sent to Hungary to extend the offer. Ladislav accepted, and at the head of a strong army crossed the Drava River and occupied Slavonia. His progress farther south was stopped short due to Croatian resistance.

While in Slavonia, Ladislav dispatched a delegation to Rome to ask papal recognition as ruler of Slavonia but he was still in Slavonia when the Cumanes, Byzantine allies, invaded his own kingdom. Thus he was forced to rush home to its defense. Before leaving, he passed his authority as ruler of Slavonia to his nephew, Almo, who assumed the title of King of Slavonia (1091-1095). Almo founded the Bishopric of Zagreb (1094), which was independent of Croatian ecclesiastical authority, as well as free from the jurisdiction of the Archbishop of Split.

Meanwhile, the Byzantine Empire once again became interested in Croatian affairs, which encouraged the popular faction to elect Petar as king (1093-1097). Petar ousted Almo from Slavonia. But the hapless Petar did not enjoy many quiet days: His country soon became exposed to the violence of the First Crusade. The Crusaders of Peter the Hermit, followed by those of Godfroy of Bouillon and Robert of Normandy, crossed the country from Varazdin to Zemun, leaving nothing but deserted lands behind them. Next, the expedition of Raymond, Count of Toulouse, passed, for several months, through Croatia along the Adriatic coast, fighting continually with the local populations. As a contemporary description put it: ". . . Raymond . . . marched forty days through the savage country of Dalmatia and Slavonia. The weather was perpetual fog; the land was mountainous and desolate; the natives were either fugitive or hostile, loose in their religion and government, refused to furnish provisions or guides, murdered stragglers, and exercised by night and day the vigilance of the count, who derived more security from the punishment of a few captive robbers than from his interview and treaty. . . ."

The Crusaders did not leave the country until Koloman, the new King of Hungary, invaded it in his own turn. Petar collected an army of his followers to face Koloman, but was

34

defeated at the battle of Gvozd Mountain (1097). Petar, himself, was killed on the battlefield. He was the last Croatian king of national origin.

* * *

From the ninth to the eleventh centuries, Croatia was organized into four duchies, viz. Croatia, Slavonia, Narentia and Bosnia, and then into a kingdom. The country was ruled by princes or kings, the latter belonging, by right of succession, to the House of Trpimir. There were exceptions to the rule by this house when the representatives of the twelve tribes of the nobility were called to elect dukes or kings at their *Sabor* or diet.

The primary task of the Croatian rulers was comprised in the need to transform the land and the half-barbaric population into a contemporary state which followed the pattern set up by the Frankish rulers, or which, more especially, followed the example of the superior Latin civilization preserved along the Adriatic shores. With this aim in view, the Croatian rulers would regularly seek the alliance of the Latin populations of the Dalmatian towns, granting them special favors, despite the fact that this undermined the traditional tribal organization and institutions of the country. This tendency brought the Croatian rulers into early conflict with their own kin and particularly with the clergy of the old Slavonic *glagolitic* church, while it simultaneously supported the ascendancy of the Archbishop of Split.

In the ensuing conflicts, the rulers and high court nobility sided with the Latins, forming the Latin or court faction. This faction opposed the popular or *glagolitic* faction. The bitter struggle between these two forces is considered one of the principal causes of the termination of national independence which followed shortly after the disappearance of the national dynasty of Trpimir.

The official name of the country was Croatia. From 925 it

was *regnum Chroatiae;* and after 988, *regnum Chroatiae et Dalmatiae.* Byzantine documents referred to it simply as Croatia, but the Holy See, as well as Venice, adopted the name of Slavonia. The name Slavonia was also generally accepted in western Europe. Thus the name, *Sclavonia,* and for its people, *Sclavi,* came into use in Venice to designate Croatia and the Croats.

Using the common denomination, Croats, the population was organized into a multitude of old traditional tribes, each called by the name, *plemenska zupa* (tribal county). Gradually the tribal system was penetrated by contemporary Frankish and Latin influences. Even at the time of the national dynasty and the establishment of the higher court nobility, the beginning of the feudal system could be observed.

The most influential Croatian tribal organization consisted of twelve tribes who were the bearers of Croatian statehood. They were Kacic, Kukar, Subic, Cudomiric, Svacic, Mogorovic, Gusic, Karinjani-Lapcani, Polecic, Jamometic and Tugomiric. Representatives of these twelve tribes ruled the country jointly with the king, and under special circumstances elected the new king.

There could also be found in Croatia many descendants of the ancient population who were, by that time, more or less Croatized. These people consisted chiefly of Latins, in the area that comprised the coastal towns and islands (Dalmatia), Latinized Illyrians or "Vlah" and "Cici," as well as many Avars, in the hinterland, Lika and Slavonia.

*   *   *

The Croats were among the first Slavic peoples to accept Christianity. This was due to their early and permanent contacts with the Latin and Christian civilizations on the Adriatic coast. As soon as they settled in their new land, Emperor Heraclius asked the Holy See to provide the Croats with suitable missionaries. Thanks to the influence exercised by the Latin towns as well as by the missionaries, the Croats became part of Christendom by 800. Previously their land was under Gothic domination. The Goths espoused Arian Christianity, thus it is reasonable to surmise that the Croats, at least in part, accepted the Arian heresy themselves. This was later to be used against them during their struggle for the use of the old Slavonic liturgy, a struggle in which the Latin hierarchy pitilessly persecuted them.

Besides the existence of old Latin bishoprics in the Dalmatian towns, new, purely Croatian bishoprics were formed at Nin, Skradin, Knin, Sibenik and Biograd. These towns were situated in territory where the old Slavonic liturgy was at least partially used, and in some cases used quite exclusively.

In time, the Bishop of Knin emerged as the most distinguished of the Croatian bishops. He eventually became the Chancellor of the Kingdom of Croatia. His dioceses spread from the Adriatic coast to the Drava River, and his official title was "Bishop of the Croats."

The Croatian clergy used the old Slavonic language in their worship services. The holy books were written in the *glagolitic* alphabet. This alphabet, which was used by the Croatian priests (*Glagoljasi*), is of unknown, but obviously Oriental, origin. It was subsequently attributed to the invention of the "Slavic apostles," Cyril and Methodus.

* * *

The old Croats were free men belonging to their respective tribes. They had no apparent social distinction except for the duties they performed. Some of them would lose their freedom as prisoners of war, criminal offenders and debtors, while foreigners in the same predicament were made slaves.

The country at this time did not have a fixed capital city. The dukes and kings resided at their own towns, which were any of the towns of Nin, Solin, Klis, Biaci, Knin and Biograd. Biograd, however, ultimately became the town for the crowning of the Croatian kings.

Besides dukes and kings, the principal magnates of the country were *bans,* and of the court, *zupans.* The *ban* was an official derived from an old institution of the Croatian political organization. He is first mentioned as a military commander of several tribal counties, and subsequently as a political assistant to the king in the function of duke; viceroy or governor. The name is of unknown origin, but could have originated from the Avar name *Bajan.* Yet it also could have come from the Croatian word *zupan,* as well as the Polish word *Pan,* since each of these words mean lord or master.

The king, dukes, *bans* and court *zupans* deliberated at the King's Council, while the representatives of the tribes and towns met at the *Sabor.* Sabor is an old Croatian word which means "diet," and it is still used to refer to the legislature today.

In order to cover the country's expenses, the king was entitled to collect special taxes from the citizens, including the nobility. These taxes were collected along with the customary taxes, customs, fines, revenues from royal lands, and regular taxes paid by the Republic of Venice for unhindered navigation along the eastern shores of the Adriatic Sea.

Croatian rulers did not mint their own coins, but, like the whole of contemporary Europe, used Byzantine currency.

The Dalmatian and Croatian towns of Sibenik, Biograd, Nin, Skradin and Knin were molded according to the pattern of Dalmatian towns in that they enjoyed a town autonomy based on the existing Roman law. A *prior,* assisted by a town council, headed the town government. The *prior* and bishop of the town were elected at a general meeting of citizens, which also appointed the town priests and judges.

The Croats were organized into traditional tribal counties whose chieftains gradually changed in status from tribal chiefs to nobility. The nobility authenticated their position by appealing to the right of succession, as opposed to demonstrating their talents as professional officials.

It is from this period that the oldest example of Croatian writing is preserved: The *Baska ploca* (Baska tablet) was written in about 1100 in a script based on the *glagolitic* alphabet.

In general, it is safe to say that Croatia, ruled by the national royal house, was, in its cultural development, an imitation of contemporary Byzantium as well as of the Frankish Kingdom of Italy.

Many elements contributed to the end of the medieval Croatian kingdom as an independent state under national rulers. In the first place, due to a lack of geographical unity, the Croats were seldom able to face a major crisis as an organized national unit. Moreover, religious unity in the country was never achieved because of the continuing bitter struggle between the Latin and Croatian churches. This religious disunity degenerated into blatant political conflict when the Latin church affiliated itself with the court to become the court faction, while the Croatian church sided with the popular faction.

But besides these matters that point to a general lack of unity in Croatia, the independent Croatian kingdom came to an end also on account of the brute mathematical fact that the Croats were simply outnumbered by their more aggressive neighbors. Furthermore, and this is perhaps the most decisive point of all, the national independence of the Croatian kingdom ended with the extinction of its national royal house, the House of Trpimir.

The Kingdom of Croatia, as an independent national state, came into existence in the border territory between the Eastern Empire and the Frankish Empire. These two empires were never able to keep this territory permanently under their control, although they continued to return there in hopes of permanent conquest. Thus, from the very beginning, Croatia was involved in the struggle between the eastern and western empires, and it was their mutual weakness that became the guarantee of Croatian independence. But when both empires were replaced by the numerically and militarily stronger and more aggressive powers, such as the Magyars of Hungary, the Normans in southern Italy and the culturally and economically more advanced Venetians, Croatian independence faced a tremendous challenge.

Croatian independence came to an end because of the loss of the national dynasty, internal disorder, and because it could not count on either German or Byzantine support. Byzantium was so disabled after the defeat at Manzikert (1071) that it had to request the support of the Croatian king, Zvonimir. Thus, for a time, Byzantium was not relied upon as a possible protector of Croatian independence. The German Empire, on the other hand, was at this time involved in the struggle for investiture, and its emperors were too preoccupied with preserving their power in Germany and Italy to pay any attention to the happenings in Croatia.

The Holy See, for its part, was involved in the struggle with the German emperors, when its popes were not busy preparing crusades. Thus, the papacy was only too willing to accommodate its vassal, the King of Hungary, when the latter presented himself as a candidate for the throne of Croatia.

Croatia was exhausted by incessant civil disorders, repeated Venetian assaults, and Norman incursions. The passage of the Crusaders through Croatia broke down her strength for resistance and facilitated Koloman's victory over Petar. However, even after his victory, Koloman was unable to secure the Croatian crown for himself, but was compelled to negotiate a treaty with the Croatian nobility in order to become King of Croatia. Croatia was too weak to preserve its national independence, but strong enough to prevent conquest and submission.

CHAPTER IV

CROATIA UNDER THE
HOUSE OF ARPAD

Pacta conventa — *Koloman* — *Byzantine intervention*
— *Introduction of the Feudal system* — *Golden Bull* —
Bela IV — *Tartar invasion* — *Foundation of the free
royal towns* — *New political order* — *Struggle for succession* — *An evaluation of the country under the House
of Arpad.*

Koloman, of the House of Arpad (1102-1116), became ruler
of Croatia on the basis of the family right of succession. He
was next of kin to the extinct Croatian Royal House of Trpimir.
His claims were based on an agreement with the Croatian nobility
arrived at by a free election, and they were realized by the
strength of arms.

After his victory over the hapless King Petar (1097), Koloman
ruled Slavonia and part of Croatia for a short period. He was
forced out of Slavonia following his unsuccessful war with the
Russians and Patzinaks in Galicia. Realizing his precarious situation in Croatia and the impossibility of maintaining himself
as an unwanted king, he decided to come to terms with the
Croatian nobility. The outcome was the *Pacta conventa*, a treaty
between the king and the Croatian nobility accepted in 1102.
According to this treaty, the representatives of the twelve tribes

41

of the Croatian nobility, as the bearers of national sovereignty, elected Koloman King of Dalmatia and Croatia. Koloman, for his part, took on the solemn obligations of observing the kingdom's rights, accepting a separate coronation for the kingship of Dalmatia and Croatia, and accepting a separate meeting of the Croatian *Sabor* in all matters concerning the national interest. Koloman also recognized the right of the Croatian nobility to possession of lands without taxation, while the nobility promised to serve at their own expense in the royal army in defensive wars conducted on Croatian territory.

After reaching this agreement, Koloman went to Biograd where, in a solemn ceremony, he was crowned King of Dalmatia and Croatia. On this occasion, Koloman formally guaranteed all of the public and state rights of Croatia. Hungary and Croatia would remain separate kingdoms connected only through the person of the king. His official title was to be the King of Hungary, Dalmatia and Croatia.

The royal rights resulting from the *Pacta conventa* and the coronation oath were: the appointment of the *ban*, or viceroy, the granting of rights and privileges, the confirmation of the laws voted on by the *Sabor*, the collection of taxes and customs duties, the full possession of royal lands inherited from the ancient Croatian kings, the supreme command of the Croatian army and navy, and the sole formulator of foreign policy.

All other internal, political, administrative, judicial, financial and military affairs fell within the jurisdiction of the *Sabor*. The *Sabor* was the diet of the Kingdom of Dalmatia and Croatia. It was convened and presided over either by dukes or *bans* and consisted of members of the nobility and representatives of the towns. The dukes of Croatia were usually the king's brothers or sons. If it happened that the oldest son and heir-apparent was the Duke of Croatia, he would be crowned King of Dalmatia and Croatia during the king's life-time.

With Koloman's rise to the throne, the political development of Croatia as an independent kingdom came to an end, with the exception of strictly internal affairs which were nevertheless strongly influenced by the political, economic and social trends prevailing in Hungary.

* * *

The first task imposed on Koloman as King of Croatia was to achieve the political and territorial unity of the country. This brought him into immediate conflict with Venice, which had come to occupy part of Dalmatia during the previous Croatian disorders. With the backing of a strong army, Koloman was able to force Venice to relinquish its hold on Dalmatia.

In order to assert himself as undisputed king, Koloman then called the *Sabor* at Zadar where he reaffirmed all of the ancient rights and privileges granted by Croatian kings to Dalmatian and Croatian towns. These rights dated back to Roman times and had been duly confirmed by the rulers of Croatia. On this same occasion, Duke Stjepan, the oldest son of Koloman, was crowned King of Dalmatia and Croatia (1107).

Thus, Koloman re-established the kingdom as it had existed during the rule of King Zvonimir, and thereby achieved the territorial unity of Croatia.

* * *

Following his father's death, Stjepan (1116-1141) ascended the throne to immediately face Venice which had promptly reappeared on the Dalmatian scene, laying pretentious claims against the towns there. After a prolonged war, Stjepan re-established his rule. But he was soon faced with another challenger.

The new and ambitious emperor of the Eastern Empire, John Comnenus, was endeavoring to rebuild the empire, reconquer some of its lost territory and re-establish imperial prestige. On this account, he took an active part in the struggle raging within the royal family. He gave his support to the king's opposition in order to weaken the latter's position in Dalmatia. Although Stjepan emerged as victor, his success proved costly.

Bela II, the Blind (1131-1141), secured the throne with im-

43

perial help. He was able to impose himself in Dalmatia, except for the city of Zadar, which fell into Venetian hands. After the weakening of imperial power in Constantinople and the subsequent Byzantine retreat from Bosnia, Bela brought Bosnia under his rule. He assumed the title of King of Bosnia (*rex Ramae*) in 1138, and thereby asserted his right over that province.

Since the rules of royal succession were not established, the question of the succession to the throne following Bela's death created bitter strife among his sons. Gejza's rule (1141-1180) was disputed by Stjepan, Duke of Croatia, and Ladislav, Lord of Bosnia. This conflict produced the awaited opportunity for another emperor, Emanuel Comnenus, to interfere in the dynastic struggle and establish his sway over eastern Slavonia, Bosnia, southern Croatia, and Dalmatia. Thus a substantial part of Croatia fell under Byzantine rule and remained there until Emanuel's death in 1180.

Emanuel's death created a new crisis in Constantinople which enabled King Bela III (1180-1196) to recover the lost territory. This territory was then added to the domain of Emerik, Duke of Croatia.

During the Byzantine rule, Bosnia enjoyed a certain amount of autonomy under *Ban* Kulin, who also subsequently acknowledged the suzerainty of the Duke of Croatia.

* * *

The first signs of nascent feudalism, introduced from western Europe, could already be detected in Croatia during the time of the last kings of the House of Trpimir. However, feudalism only came to be an accepted institution under the House of Arpad. The Arpadian kings appointed the *bans* of Croatia from the Hungarian nobility, which was already following the pattern of the German feudal system and which it began to introduce into northern Croatia, viz. Slavonia.

Feudalism also took root in Croatia proper where members of the most outstanding noble families gradually asserted themselves at the expense of their own clansmen. Thus the lords of

Krk, Frankopan, were subjects to the king and the honorary citizens of Venice at the same time, as were the lords of Bribir of the noble tribe of Subic, the lords of Cetina of the clan of Nelipic, and the lords of Omis of the clan of Kacic in Croatia. Meanwhile, the lords of Gorica of the clan of Babonic achieved the same preeminence in Slavonia.

*   *   *

During the rule of Emerik (1196-1204), the knights of the Fourth Crusade conquered the city of Zadar (1202) on behalf of Venice. The city was destroyed, the fortifications pulled down and the population dispersed. After their adventure at Zadar, these same knights performed a similar deed at Durazzo and crowned the whole affair with the conquest of Constantinople (1204). Emerik, himself, greatly raised his prestige due to the disorders resulting from the fall of Constantinople. He invaded imperial territory and assumed the title of King of Serbia (1202).

Emerik's successor, Andrija (1204-1235) an adventurer and an irresponsible ruler, made an effort to enhance his prestige at home and abroad by leading the motley army of the Fifth Crusade — including many of the Croatian nobility — to the Holy Land in 1217. His adventure ended in disaster. Upon his return, he found his treasury empty and his country in general chaos. In order to restore his finances, Andrija sold lands as well as the collection of taxes and customs duties to moneylenders. The magnates revolted, raised an army and compelled the king to accept their demands. These demands took the form of the Golden Bull (*Bulla aurea*) (1222).

*   *   *

The Golden Bull was a document written by the bishops and barons of Hungary and Slavonia and imposed on King Andrija. It contained thirty-one articles by which the king was obliged under oath to respect the privileges of the nobility, call a yearly session of the Court nobility, grant the nobility security from royal arbitrariness, refrain from collecting taxes only on the basis of royal authority, refrain from trespassing on the lands of the nobility, and commit the nobility to foreign wars only at royal expense.

The Bull also included articles of obligation for the nobility in which they were to participate in the kingdom's defense, refrain from holding double office (although this was allowed the king, queen, palatin of Hungary and *bans* of Croatia), refrain from granting titles or lands to foreigners without the consent of the royal council, allow the bishops taxes in the form of one-tenth of the nobleman's goods, refrain from using the promissory notes of the royal treasury longer than a year, refrain from employing Jews in the royal mints, salt mines and customs offices, pay the land tax (*kunovina*) in Slavonia according to the conditions accepted by Koloman in the *Pacta conventa* in 1102, and, finally, refrain from giving an entire comitat in fief and possession to a single magnate. The closing article of the Bull gave the nobility the right to use all legal as well as armed means to compel the king to observe the Bull.

The Golden Bull was a typical contemporary feudal compact beween king and nobility, but in the later days of feudalism it began to assume stature as the country's basic law. However, exaggerated significance was attributed to the Bull in the eighteenth century by nascent Magyar nationalism.

The Bull was signed by the king, and by twenty-one bishops who were headed by Stjepan, Bishop of Zagreb. It was introduced into Hungary, and with certain limitations, Slavonia. However, it was not introduced into Croatia.

* * *

During the rule of Bela IV (1235-1270), Bosnia became the cradle of a new religious movement called the Church of Bosnian Christians, or *Bogumili, Patareni* or *Cathari.* It was already professed by the first autonomous *ban,* Boric, and assumed considerable proportion during the rule of *Ban* Matej Ninoslav (1230-1250).

Since Bosnia submitted directly to the rule of Koloman, Duke of Croatia, Koloman, with the king's approval and the blessings of Pope Gregory IX, launched a crusading campaign against the Bosnian heretics. As soon as Koloman's army crossed into Bosnia, Matej Ninoslav and the Bosnian nobility declared themselves obedient sons of the Roman Catholic Church. Nevertheless, upon Koloman's return to Croatia, the obedient sons returned to their heretical practices. This game became a general rule for the Bosnian rulers and nobility, until their ultimate fall to the Ottoman Empire.

*　　*　　*

Bela IV was the first king to eliminate the separate coronation for the kingship of Croatia. But, although a single ceremony was used for both the Hungarian and Croatian crowns, Croatia and its dependency, Bosnia, were entrusted to the care of the king's brother, Koloman, Duke of Croatia. Koloman exercised full authority in the country.

Koloman found himself in the position to lead another campaign against the Bosnian schismatics. During this campaign he detached Bosnia from the jurisdiction of the Archbishop of Split and established a separate bishopric for Bosnia at Vrhbosna. Koloman granted rich lands from Bosnia, Usora and Soli, as well as from Slavonia, to Poza, the first Bishop of Bosnia. Shortly after, the bishop witnessed the decisive victory of the Patarens and was unable to maintain himself in the country. He thus retreated to Djakovo which became the see of the titular Bishop of Bosnia (1252).

From the outset, Bela's rule was not fortunate. Under Genghis Khan's successor, Khan Ogatai, the Tartars established their rule in Russia, and soon after, under the leadership of Batu Khan, they invaded Hungary. They routed Bela's army in a battle on the Saj River. The Croats took part in this campaign under the command of their duke, Koloman. Koloman was wounded on the battlefield and died when he returned to Croatia.

Bela escaped the pursuit of his enemies and ultimately found refuge in the court of Frederick of Babenberg, Archduke of Austria. Frederick used his hospitality to Bela to extort from him the cessation of three Hungarian comitats. The price was obviously too high, and Bela seized the first opportunity to escape from the care of his host. He settled in Zagreb.

Once in Croatia, Bela attempted to raise another army to go against the Tartars. But when Batu-Khan learned of Bela's new residence, he sent his commander, Kadan Khan, across the frozen Drava into Slavonia and Croatia (1242). There was practically no organized armed resistance and the Tartars brought general destruction to the country. On this occasion, a newly built cathedral in Zagreb was destroyed and only a few well fortified towns, chiefly located on the coast, successfully resisted the Tartar assaults. Bela ultimately took refuge at Trogir and Split which were defended by the lord of Bribir. The greater part of the country was laid waste and the population took refuge in the forests, or the inaccessible high mountains, or islands.

The Tartar invasion ended suddenly when their leaders received news of the death of their supreme ruler. The subaltern khans returned home to participate in the election of a new supreme khan. On their way home they destroyed what was left of Croatia, Slavonia and Bosnia. They returned to their Russian steppes through Serbia and Bulgaria.

After the Tartar destruction, Bela's primary concern was the establishment of order and the reconstruction of the country toward the end of preparing it for another possible invasion. The recent events clearly showed that only fortified towns could successfully resist the invaders. For this reason, Bela launched a program for the construction of fortified towns and castles. Castles were built at Medvedgrad (near Zagreb), Garic (in Moslavina), Okic, Lipovac (near Samobor) and Kalnik near Krizevci. Zagreb, known as Gric, built its own walls and towers for protection.

During the general reconstruction of the country, many foreign artisans, merchants and other professionals came to permanently settle in Slavonian towns on Bela's invitation. They were granted the rights and privileges of the free royal towns which were patterned after the free German imperial towns. Thus it occurred that many Germans, Hungarians, Italians and some Frenchmen settled in Varazdin, Zagreb, Krizevci, Bihac, Koprivnica, Samobor and Jastrebarsko.

*   *   *

As a result of the Tartar invasion, the ancient traditional tribal system known as the *zupa* disappeared in Slavonia and was replaced by larger units of comitats adapted from the Hungarian political organization. These were Bela's reforms and they brought Slavonia closer to Hungary. The new comitats were established at Zagreb, Varazdin, Krizevci, Virovitica, Pozega, Vuka and Srijem. With these reforms, the complete feudalization of Slavonia was achieved.

As soon as the country was secured against the Tartars, Bela opened a campaign against the Archduke of Austria in order to reconquer the three lost comitats. After a successful campaign, he turned his attention again to Croatia and the prospects of freeing the city of Zadar from the Venetians. This enterprise did not bring the expected result because a civil war, caused by the rivalry between the towns of Split and Trogir, was raging in Croatia. The Croatian nobility sided with one or the other of the towns, giving no support to the king's campaign. Stjepan Kotroman, *Ban* of Bosnia, seized this opportunity to achieve independent status by taking part in the civil war. Bela was finally able to impose a settlement only after several years of struggle.

Bela introduced several significant reforms in the political organization of Croatia. The Duke of Croatia was placed at the head of all Croatian lands. From this time on, what had been a single kingdom was split into two separate kingdoms, viz., the Kingdom of Croatia and Dalmatia and the Kingdom of Slavonia. Each kingdom had its own *Ban* and its own *Sabor*. Furthermore, the comitat at Pozega was separated from Slavonia and estab-

49

lished as the personal possession of the queen. The comitats of Vuka and Srijem were added to the newly created Banat of Macva (1260) in order to strengthen this borderland for resistance to foreign enemies.

The successors of Matija Ninoslav were established as the permanent rulers of Bosnia. However, Usora and Soli were detached from Bosnia and made separate units. Through this arrangement, the geographical and political unity of Croatia came to an end. Within this new situation, foreign influence was strongly felt, especially in Slavonia, where large land areas were granted to a foreign nobility which was chiefly of German or Hungarian origin. These new magnates endeavored to introduce into the country a legal and social order characteristic of their respective home-countries. Slavonia thus came closer to Hungary in its political institutions and social order. A similar process took place in Croatia, too, although on a much smaller scale and without the addition of the foreign element.

*　　*　　*

Stjepan (1270-1272) was a weak ruler unable to continue his father's policy. His successor, Ladislav (1272-1290), fared no better since general anarchy, caused by arrogant feudal lords, prevailed in the country. Royal power practically disappeared from both Croatia and Slavonia. The powerful lords of Bribir and Krk dominated Croatia's public life, while the lords of Babonic, Gut-Kelledy and Gising disputed for domination of Slavonia.

Due to the events in nearby Austria, the general situation in Croatia, as well as Hungary, became even more complicated. Following the extinction of the Austrian ruling House of Babenberg, succession was disputed by Otokar Przemysl II, King of Bohemia and Rudolph of Habsburg, Emperor of the Holy Roman Empire. Rudolph secured Austria as his family possession by defeating Otokar Przemysl in the ensuing war. From this time on, the Habsburgs never missed an opportunity to attempt to impose themselves on their neighbor's lands. They were prompted to do so by the prevailing conditions in Hungary, Bohemia and Croatia.

Ladislav was able to remain on his precarious throne due to the support of his mother's relatives, the Cumans. However, the Cumans used their presence in Hungary to intrigue against one another. These intrigues usually ended in bloodshed and ultimately cost Ladislav his head.

Ladislav's violent death left the Hungaro-Croatian throne vacant. This invited several interested candidates to compete for it. First to enter the contest was Andrija III, called the Venetian, who was the son of Ladislav IV and Maria Morosini (1290-1301). Rudolph of Habsburg challenged this candidacy on the basis that Andrija was not of the House of Arpad and therefore did not have title to the royal throne. Beyond this, Rudolph put forward his own claim which was based on the assertion that Bela IV placed himself under imperial protection while in German territory during the Tartar invasion. Pope Nicholas IV intervened in the dispute, claiming the right, as overlord of Hungary and Croatia, to dispose of their crown. Marija of Anjou, Queen of Naples and sister of Ladislav IV, joined the competition by declaring herself the only rightful successor to the crown and then passed her rights on to her son, Charles Martel.

The Pope sided with the Angevins and his legate crowned Charles Martel King of Hungary and Croatia at Naples (1292). In the meantime, Andrija won the support of the Hungarian nobility, and with their help, inflicted defeat upon Albrecht of Austria. Subsequently, Albrecht, in the name of the Habsburgs, renounced his claims and thereby brought peace to Hungary.

The situation in Croatia was more complex. There, the most powerful nobility of the country embraced the Angevin cause. In order to secure their support, Charles Martel had appointed Pavao of Bribir *Ban* of Croatia granting him the right of succession in his own family (1293). Meanwhile the Babonics in

Slavonia and the Kotromanics in Bosnia were trying to achieve the same status. But while the Angevin cause definitely prevailed in Croatia, Slavonia became the theater for a bitter civil war between the partisans of Charles Martel and those of Andrija. The feud was particularly bitter between the city of Zagreb, which supported Andrija, and its bishop who sided with Charles Martel.

Andrija did not have any children of his own. He therefore named his uncle, Albert Morosini, who was a Venetian nobleman, Duke of Croatia, with the right of succession to the royal throne. Albert, however, was unable to get himself properly accepted and his elevation to ducal dignity, as the first step to the royal crown, provoked new unrest. This unrest soon degenerated into a civil war which spread from Slavonia to Hungary itself. Charles Martel died during these convulsions, leaving his rights to his infant son, Charles Robert.

* * *

The Hungaro-Croatian kings of the House of Arpad inherited, with their ascension to the Croatian throne, all the problems that plagued the former Croatian rulers. This historical era was characterized by continuous struggle with Venice and the Eastern Empire for possession of Dalmatia.

Croatian lands were still called the Kingdom of Croatia and Dalmatia, but the Hungarian chancellery frequently used the name given to the country by the Holy See, i.e., Slavonia. In all official documents, the rulers used the full title, King of Hungary, Dalmatia and Croatia. Subsequently, the titles of Bosnia and Serbia were added.

Until the reforms of Bela IV, Croatia existed as a single territory. With Bela, it was split into two distinct political units, viz., the Kingdom of Croatia and Dalmatia and the Kingdom of Slavonia. Bosnia held a position apart. The Duke of Croatia represented the king, and as a ruler he was assisted by the respective *Bans* of Croatia, Slavonia, Bosnia and Macva. Macva was a border province in the northwestern part of present-day Serbia and the eastern part of Slavonia.

The dukes and *bans* ruled the country assisted by the *Sabors*, a diet of Croatian or Slavonian nobility. A duke or *ban* called the *Sabor* into session and presided over its deliberations. On some important occasions, the king, himself, called the *Sabor* into session and presided over it. In 1260, the hitherto unique Croatian *Sabor* split into separate Croatian and Slavonian *Sabors*.

Usually the Duke of Croatia was the king's son and heir presumptive to the throne. He was crowned King of Croatia during the king's lifetime. This ducal dignity was also granted to the king's younger brother. The dukes had their residences in Zadar, Knin, Bihac or Zagreb. They had a ducal chancellery at their service to issue official documents and to keep the ducal seal. The Croatian duke appointed *bans*, called the *Sabors* into session, granted titles of nobility, granted rights and privileges, collected taxes and customs, minted his own currency and acted as commander-in-chief of the Croatian army. When the ducal post was vacant, the *bans* assumed the same authority. The *ban* appointed *his* own assistant or vice-*ban*. The *Sabor* elected a chancellor (*protonator*) as sealkeeper and the *ban's* substitute in judicial matters.

According to the contract with King Koloman (1102), the Croatian nobility was free of land taxation, while in Slavonia the taxes imposed on the peasant household amounted to twelve *Denarii*. Nevertheless, Slavonia paid only half of the taxes imposed on the Hungarian nobility for war expenses.

*   *   *

The population of both kingdoms, Croatia and Slavonia, was essentially Croatian with an admixture of a few Croatized Illyrians and Vallachians (known as Cici or Morovallachians). The population of the Dalmatian towns during the last centuries of the period was completely Croatized, with a strongly emphasized Latin culture. After the Tartar invasion, special rights and privileges were granted to the free royal towns of Varazdin, Bihac, Zagreb, Krizevci, Koprivnica, Jastrebarsko and Samobor. These were the towns that brought in foreign artisans, merchants and other professionals who were chiefly of German, Italian, Magyar and, to some extent, French origin.

With the development of the free royal towns, feudalism simultaneously established itself according to the pattern prevailing in western Europe. In Slavonia, the rulers had granted huge land possessions to foreign magnates of German or Magyar extraction, who in turn successfully competed with the country magnates in ruling the country and shaping its destiny. They brought with them concepts of foreign order and customs hitherto unknown in the country. Nevertheless, Croatia remained a domain of local magnates where the old traditional social order continued to prevail.

Both the dukes and *bans* coined their own currency in Zagreb. It consisted of *Denarii, Oboli* (half a Denarii) and the *Bagat* (a small coin of silver mixed with copper).

The old coats of arms could be found on the face of these items of currency: Slavonia was represented by a martin between two stars, while Croatia had a half-moon against a star. The newer coat of arms for Croatia appeared during the fifteenth century and consisted of twenty-five silver and red squares. In 1406 Dalmatia's coat of arms became three leopard heads.

CHAPTER V

FROM ANGEVIN AUTOCRACY TO FEUDAL ANARCHY

Angevins — Ascendancy of the House of Bribir — Ljudevit the Great — Struggle for Ljudevit's succession — Marija and Sigismund of Luxemburg — Tvrdko of Bosnia — Beginning of the Turkish invasion — Hrvoje Vukcic Hrvatinic — Mathias Corvinus — Last Jagielones — Battle of Krbava — Battle of Mohacs.

Following the death of Andrija, the Croatian nobility, under the leadership of Pavao of Bribir, immediately recognized Charles Robert (1301-1342) as king. However, Hungary became the arena for the contests of several pretenders to the throne who had blood ties to the extinct House of Arpad. Veceslav, Prince of Bohemia, was the first to assert himself: He ascended the throne as Ladislav V (1301-1304). But he was unable to hold it against Otto of Bavaria (1304-1308).

Charles Robert was able to easily repulse the ousted Serbian ruler, Stephen Dragutin. With the intervention of the ambitious Pope Boniface VIII, his claim was finally recognized by the Hungarian nobility and he was crowned King of Hungary and Croatia (1310). But from the outset he had to face the powerful and arrogant Hungarian magnates. In order to overcome their opposition, he shrewdly pitted them against the Croatian nobility.

Pavao, Lord of Bribir, was granted lordship over Bosnia and the title of *Ban* of Croatia with familial right of succession. Charles thereby reconfirmed his father's donation. By the same token, Stjepan Kotromanic, *Ban* of Bosnia, recognized *Ban* Pavao as his feudal suzerain. This made Pavao ruler of all Croatian lands from Istria to the Drina River, except for Slavonia, and Zadar which remained under Venetian control.

In order to reconquer Zadar, Pavao declared war on Venice on his own authority. Before any result could be achieved, Pavao died, leaving his title to his oldest son Mladen. *Ban* Mladen was not his father's equal in dealing with the wealth of problems he inherited. His highhanded policy provoked his own brothers to conspire with the Croatian nobility, who deeply resented the power of the House of Bribir. A powerful alliance was formed to oppose his rule. It consisted of King Charles Robert; Pavao, Mladen's brother; the Republic of Venice; the Croatian nobility under Nelipic, Lord of Cetina; and Stjepan Kotromanic, *Ban* of Bosnia. When the royal army joined his local opponents, Mladen capitulated to the king. Charles Robert deprived him of all his titles, power and family possessions and took him to Hungary as a hostage where he fell into total oblivion (1322).

Following Mladen's fall, Ivan Babonic, *Ban* of Slavonia, also became *Ban* of Croatia, and Stjepan Kotromanic, *Ban* of Bosnia, was freed from his allegiance to the House of Bribir, becoming a direct vassal to the king.

When Charles Robert returned to Hungary, Ivan Nelipic of Cetina raised another armed insurrection against royal authority. The ensuing civil war played conveniently into the hands of the Republic of Venice. It established its ascendency over coastal towns seeking refuge from the prevailing anarchy. Moreover, Kotromanic seized the opportunity to annex for Bosnia Croatian territory situated between the Cetina and Neretva Rivers, as well as the counties of Imotski, Duvno, Livno and Glamoc. These latter were added as the province of Zavrsje.

*   *   *

Charles Robert brought to Hungary and Croatia the royal Italian glamor and luxury that he had been accustomed to in Naples. A beautiful royal palace was built for him in Zagreb. Moreover, to a certain degree, a royal serenity was established throughout the country: When Babonic proved to be unsuccessful in his dealings with the turbulent magnates, Mikac Mihaljevic assumed the position of *Ban* and established order.

*   *   *

Ljudevit I (1342-1382) was able to end the feudal disorders, but not without granting the nobility special privileges like the feudal familial rights of succession.

After establishing order in the country, Ljudevit decided to expel Venice from Croatia. The city of Zadar, which was the spearhead for the revolt against Venetian rule, appealed to him for help, and on this basis he declared war. He brought a strong army to Croatia and dislodged Venice from all towns except Zadar. In this campaign, Ljudevit deprived Juraj of Bribir (the last of this house) of his possessions in Croatia in exchange for the castle of Zrinj in the county of Zagreb. By this act the House of Bribir became extinct since each of the ruling descendants of Juraj assumed the title of Count of Zrinjski. Using similar methods, Ljudevit was able to deracinate many old established magnates whom he replaced by new nobility personally devoted to him and dependent on royal favors.

Without achieving any of his aims, Ljudevit was forced to abruptly end his campaign against Venice. He became involved in a situation in Naples created by the assassination of his younger brother, Andreas, King of Naples.

Andreas had been murdered on account of a conspiracy led by his own wife, Queen Joanna. Ljudevit invaded Naples in retaliation, defeated the conspirators and executed them. Joanna, however, escaped to safety and returned as soon as Ljudevit left for Croatia and Hungary. Unable to establish permanent rule in Naples, Ljudevit ultimately relinquished his right to the Neapolitan patrimony.

While Ljudevit was preoccupied in Naples, Stjepan Dusan, ruler of Serbia, took advantage of the general disorder prevailing in the Eastern Empire by assuming the title of Emperor of the Serbs, Greeks and Wallachs (1346). He invaded Bosnia, attempting to add it to his possessions. However, the invasion met spirited resistance from *Ban* Kotromanic who managed to hold the line until Ljudevit's timely return to the Croatian scene. During this campaign, Ljudevit married Elizabeth, daughter of *Ban* Stjepan Kotromanic. Shortly afterwards, Stjepan died and his nephew, Stjepan Tvrdko, succeeded him.

After consolidating his rule over Croatia, Ljudevit renewed the war against Venice for possession of Zadar. This war was fought chiefly in Friule and Dalmatia on both land and sea, and it ended in Ljudevit's favor. Consequently, Venice was forced to sign the Peace Treaty of Zadar in which it relinquished to Ljudevit's jurisdiction all its claims on Dalmatia, "from the middle of the Bay of Quarner to the city of Durazzo in Albania" (1358). By this treaty, Ljudevit was made master of all Dalmatia, the eastern coast of the Adriatic, including all islands, and the city of Kotor. Moreover, he became overlord of the Republic and City of Dubrovnik.

When the King of Poland, Ljudevit's uncle, Kazimir, died, the Polish Diet elected Ljudevit king. By his elevation to the Polish throne, Ljudevit became one of the most important European rulers of his time, exercising power from the Baltic to the Adriatic Seas. His influence was also felt in general in Neapolitan, as well as in Italian affairs. Toward the end of his rule, Venice once again challenged his supremacy but was decisively defeated and forced to accept the Treaty of Turin which reinforced the settlements of the Peace Treaty of Zadar (1381).

Ljudevit left two daughters, Marija and Jadviga, both minors.

Marija, while still a child, was betrothed to Sigismund of Luxemburg, Prince of Bohemia and son of Charles IV, who was for his part, Emperor of the Holy Roman Empire and King of Bohemia. On the other hand, her younger sister, Jadviga, inherited the Polish throne and subsequently married Ladislav Jagielo, Grand Duke of Lithuania.

* * *

For centuries the Croats, Serbs and Bulgarians had been attempting to raise up their own states and political organizations on the ruins of the Empire and, more specifically, according to the pattern of the Eastern Empire. They achieved temporary success, but their ambition for lasting achievement was rudely put to an end when the new and aggressive military power of the Ottoman Turks superseded that of the exhausted Empire. The Seldjuk Turks had already dealt a severe blow to the Empire at the battle of Manzikert (1071) and it never completely recovered, although the agony would last for an additional four and a half centuries.

Despite the prolonged invasions of the various crusades and the setbacks inflicted by the Mongols, the Turks were able to become undisputed masters of Asia Minor by the fourteenth century. The only exception to this rule was the Empire of Trebizond, which somehow managed to linger past its own time.

Osman was the leader of the Turks, assuming for himself the title of Sultan, and imposing the Moslem religion on his subjects. His son and successor, Orhan, moved the capital across the Bosporus to Brusa in order that it might face Constantinople itself. Moreover, Orhan took a most active part in the civil war created by the conflicts between the different aspirants to the imperial title and thereby greatly increased his influence in the Empire. On the invitation of one of the contestants, his son, Suleyman, crossed the Dardanelles and made himself master of the fortress of Zimpi (1352). This fortress was the first Turkish possession in Europe. Two years later, the Turks were in possession of the entire Peninsula of Galipoli.

Sultan Murad (1362-1389) consolidated under his rule what remained of the European portion of the Empire and moved his capital to Adrianople (1363). Constantinople, thus, became a Christian island in a Moslem sea and the last remnant of the glorious Empire.

The Turks were foremostly a militaristic nation which submitted to strict discipline. For centuries they had been famous for their light cavalry, but in coming into contact with the Empire they began to develop infantry and artillery as well. Special units were formed by means of a blood tax which expedited the recruiting of young Christian boys from the subjugated population. These boys were trained in the Moslem faith toward the end of becoming devoted and fanatical followers of Mohammed and, in the process, outstanding soldiers known as *Janitsars*. At first the Turks did not possess their own navy, but enlisted that of the Genovese which had hitherto been in the imperial service. Soon, however, they employed their Greek and Phoenician subjects to build their navy. Furthermore, they were first to make use of artillery in military operations in Europe.

The Bulgarian and Serbian feudal levies were no match for the well organized and disciplined Turkish army. It was only a matter of time before the Bulgarian and Serbian states fell under Turkish rule, and before it was Constantinople's turn to share in the fate of those around it.

*   *   *

At the time when Ljudevit's Hungarian and Croatian inheritance came to his twelve-year-old daughter, Marija (1382-1385), Turkish power was growing fast in the Balkans. During her minority, her mother, Queen Elizabeth, had assumed regency with the assistance of Nikola Gorjanski, Paladin of Hungary. But the rule of two queens became extremely unpopular among the Croatian nobility. Ivan Palizna, Templar Prior of Vrana, headed a conspiracy which aimed to detach Croatia from Angevin rule and invite Stjepan Tvrdko, King of Bosnia, to rule.

Upon learning of Palizna's conspiracy, the astute Gorjanski brought both queens, backed by a strong army, to Croatia. The conspiracy collapsed and Palizna escaped to Bosnia for his own safety. The queens received a royal welcome in Zadar and Marija presided over a session of the Croatian *Sabor* before her return to Hungary.

However, the newly established tranquility was short-lived. The Horvat brothers, Ivanis, *Ban* of Macva, and Pavao, Bishop of Zagreb, organized a movement to bring Marija's cousin from Naples to the Croatian throne. The cousin, Prince Charles of Durazzo, eagerly accepted Pavao's personal offer of the crown and journeyed to Croatia to take possession of it. After a year in Croatia, he proceeded to Hungary where, upon Marija's abdication, he was duly accepted as ruler. However he soon fell victim to a conspiracy masterminded by Queen Elizabeth, Gorjanski and Forgacs. In the aftermath of Charles's death, Marija ascended the throne for the second time (1386-1395).

The assassination of King Charles prompted Palizna and the Horvat brothers to join forces, raising the flag of insurrection. Gorjanski, attempting to repeat his former successful pacification, set out for Croatia with both queens and an army. His attempt miscarried. The army was routed by the Horvats, both queens were made prisoners, and Gorjanski and Forgacs were executed for the assassination of King Charles. The queens were taken to Palizna's stronghold, Novigrad on the Sea, where, at the insistence of Charles's widow, Elizabeth was executed.

*   *   *

When Sigismund of Luxemburg (1387-1437), who had married Marija while she was still a child, received the news of her imprisonment, he hastened to Hungary to take the crown for himself. The Hungarian nobility accepted him at once. His first and most important task was to free his wife from the Croatian insurgents. Toward this end he invaded Croatia with a strong army. Moreover, he made a bid for Venetian alliance, which was eagerly accepted. While the Venetian navy blockaded

Novigrad from the sea, Ivan of Krk, at the head of the Croatian loyalists, closed-in from the land. After a long siege Palizna accepted the conditions: free departure in exchange for the Queen's freedom. Meanwhile, Sigismund decisively defeated the Horvats who, following Palizna's example, sought exile in Bosnia under the protection of Stjepan Tvrdko.

During this period of unrest in Croatia the Turks dealt an ultimate blow to the Serbs in the battle of Kosovo, bringing to an end the last vestiges of Serbian independence (1389). The downfall of Serbia made the conflict between the Turks and the Hungaro-Croatian rulers inevitable.

* * *

The civil war in Croatia played into the hands of Tvrdko who, with Palizna's assistance, added all of southern Croatia to his patrimony, including the towns of Split, Omis, Trogir, Sibenik, Knin, Ostrovica and Klis. Subsequently he styled himself King of Croatia and Dalmatia (1390). After his death, however, Bosnia ceased to be a sanctuary for Croatian insurgents and his weak successor, Stjepan Dabisa, accepted Sigismund's suzerainty, delivering Croatian refugees to him. Ivanis Horvat was on this account executed, while his brother, Bishop Pavao, disappeared into the obscurity of a monastery. Meanwhile, Palizna had died, and with his death came the end of his family's rule. Thus the two prominent feudal families virtually disappeared from Croatian public life.

After the pacification of Croatia, Sigismund prepared a crusade against the Turks, partly to secure Constantinople and partly to lay claim to the imperial title of the Eastern Empire. A motley crowd of feudal adventurers gathered under his banner. The army went down the Danube to Bulgaria where at the Battle of Nikopolje it was completely routed by the Turks (1396). Sigismund escaped by the Danube to the Black Sea and ultimately to Constantinople.

The news of the catastrophe at Nikopolje stunned the country. No one had heard whether Sigismund was alive or dead.

Stjepan Lackovic, *Ban* of Slavonia, revived the party that had supported the Angevins of Naples, thereby calling Ladislav, son of Charles II, to the throne. While this intrigue was under way, Sigismund suddenly appeared in Dubrovnik. He called a general *Sabor* at Krizevci, allegedly to achieve reconciliation. But during the deliberation there his henchmen cut down Lackovic and his friends (1397).

The "bloody *Sabor*" at Krizevci gave the signal for a new conspiracy headed by Hrvoje Vukcic Hrvatinic, the most powerful nobleman of Croatia and Bosnia. On his invitation Ladislav of Naples came to Croatia where he was at Zadar crowned king (1403). Ladislav was able to establish his rule only over part of Croatia; Sigismund remained supreme in Slavonia and Hungary. While Ladislav, who had retained his Neapolitan crown, was in Croatia, a conspiracy against his rule was developing in Naples. He returned to deal with the situation. He left Hrvoje in power with the titles of *Ban* of Croatia, Duke of Split and Regent of the Kingdom. In short, Hrvoje emerged the strongest man of his time in whose hands the rulers of Bosnia were mere pawns.

Seeking to regain his lost territory, Sigismund led several military expeditions against Hrvoje (1405, 1406, 1407). Slavonia and northern Croatia were easily subdued, but Hrvoje maintained his sway in the south. The following year, in order to deal Hrvoje a decisive blow, Sigismund undertook a well-prepared campaign which he gave the pompous title of "the Crusade against the Patarens and other heretics in Bosnia, Dalmatia and Croatia." He received the special blessing from Pope Gregory XII for this campaign. After the invasion of Bosnia the nobility there submitted to Sigismund. He then ordered one hundred-fifty of them summarily executed. Realizing the futility of further resistance, Hrvoje came to terms with Sigismund, recognizing him as his sovereign. Stjepan Ostoja, King of Bosnia, did likewise.

Hrvoje continued to enjoy a great amount of independence,

ruling supreme in southern Croatia and western Bosnia. He was an avowed Pataren and sheltered his coreligionists from Sigismund and the church persecutions. Thus, in order to make himself absolute master, Sigismund led another crusade against him. Hrvoje was unable to resist this new onslaught and was forced to enlist the support of the Turks. As allies, Hrvoje and the Turks inflicted a humiliating defeat upon the invaders (1415). This was the first appearance of the Turks on Croatian territory. But Hrvoje did not enjoy his victory long because he died shortly thereafter, and his domain was distributed among his heirs.

*   *   *

Ladislav of Naples achieved general fame for his unscrupulous activities in both Neapolitan and Croatian affairs. Realizing the impossibility of retaining his possessions in Croatia and seeking to get himself recognized in Hungary, he entered into negotiations with Venice. After lengthy bargaining he sold to Venice all his rights as King of Croatia and Dalmatia for 100,000 Ducats. Moreover, he handed over the territories which were in his immediate possession. Thus the towns of Zadar, Novigrad and Vrana, and the island of Pag, passed into Venetian hands (1409). Subsequently, Venice was able to lay hands on the remaining Croatian coastline and islands, which then became known as Dalmatia. After twenty-six wars spanning five centuries, Venice ultimately and ironically took Dalmatia from Croatia in a commercial bargain. Dalmatia would remain under Venetian power until the Republic's demise under the heel of Napoleon (1797).

Sigismund half-heartedly attempted to regain this lost ground, but after an unsuccessful campaign in which Venice captured the towns of Sibenik, Ostrovica and Skradin, he turned his attention elsewhere.

After election as Emperor of the Holy Roman Empire (1411), Sigismund would only sporadically return to Croatian affairs. He devoted most of his time to imperial duties and to the

64

religious war raging in Bohemia. It was not until 1420 that he renewed his attempt to take Dalmatia from Venice, with the only result that the towns of Split, Trogir and Kotor, and the islands of Brac, Hvar and Korcula, fell into Venetian hands.

During Sigismund's rule all vestiges of royal power vanished from Croatia, Croatia became the contesting ground between two magnate families: the Count Celje dominating in Slavonia, and Frankopan of Krk holding sway in Croatia. Each of these men ruled according to his own peculiar whims and the country fell into general anarchy. Moreover, similar conditions prevailed in Hungary so that Sigismund had no recourse but to try to organize the defenses of Croatia against an attack from the Turks who continued to pose a threat from the east. The system of defense was conceived along the feudal pattern, imposing an obligatory levy on the church, magnates, smaller nobility and the free royal towns. Croatian territory along the Adriatic coast, which faced the Venetian possessions and comprised the City and Republic of Dubrovnik and also included the lords of Krbava, Cetina and Krk, was put under the military command of the *Ban* of Croatia. The territory of Slavonia which faced Bosnia and included the lords of Blagaj, the Bishop of Zagreb and the smaller nobility of upper Slavonia was put under the military command of the *Ban* of Slavonia. Finally, the territory of Usora facing Turkish Serbia and Bosnia was placed under the command of the *Ban* of Usora.

The period was marred by another civil war in Croatia caused by the succession of the House of Nelipic. Sigismund appointed Matko Talovac, a member of the Dubrovnik nobility, *Ban* of Croatia, who was ultimately able to establish order in the country.

* * *

Insofar as Croatian affairs were concerned, Sigismund proved to be a weak ruler. He was spendthrift, unstable and irresponsible. He got so entangled in immature plans and adventures that he was unable to protect his possessions in Croatia against either Venetian greed or Turkish conquest. Without an heir, he supported Albert of Habsburg in his candidacy for election to the Hungarian and Croatian throne and Albert duly became king (1438-1439).

The first task that Albert was faced with was the protection of Hungary from the Turkish invaders. The Turks besieged Smederevo, a fortress on the Danube, and Albert led an army to rescue it. This intervention resulted in a disaster in which Albert lost his life. Moreover, it led to a new crisis regarding succession to the throne.

Albert's wife, Elizabeth, was with child at the time, and a few months later gave birth to a male child named Ladislav Posthumus. The nobility, however, anxious to assert its right to elect the king, did not wait for the end of her pregnancy but proceeded to elect Vladislav Jagielo, King of Poland, to the throne (1440-1444). Although Elizabeth enjoyed the support of the two most powerful families in Croatia, viz. Celjski and Frankopan, the major part of the nobility sided with Vladislav. Consequently, civil war broke out. The unrest enabled Stjepan Vukcic Kosaca, Lord of Hum, to add what was left of Croatia between the Neretva and Cetina Rivers to his possessions, and Venice was able to occupy all the littoral around Makarska (1444).

The Turks laid siege to Belgrade which was the last Christian outpost south of the Sava River. Talovac, *Ban* of Croatia, offered a spirited defense of the town, while John of Hunjadi, Duke of Transylvannia, repulsed the Turkish attempts to invade Hungary.

Meanwhile, Queen Elizabeth put herself and her child-son, Ladislav, under the protection of her relative, Frederick III, Emperor of the Holy Roman Empire. He negotiated with Vladislav in her name. They agreed that upon Vladislav's death, Ladislav would inherit the Hungarian and Croatian thrones.

Subsequent to his agreement with Elizabeth, Vladislav prepared a major campaign against the Turks. At the head of a combined Hungarian and Croatian army his chief commander, John of Hunjadi, penetrated to the heart of the Balkans and inflicted a thorough defeat on the Turks. They signed the Peace Treaty of Szegedin (1444). Intoxicated with the successful campaign and encouraged by Cardinal Cesarini, the Papal envoy, Vladislav broke the peace and invaded Ottoman territory, hoping to aid beleaguered Constantinople. His march was stopped at Varna, on the Black Sea, his army defeated, and he, himself, killed (1444).

After the defeat at Varna, the nobility dutifully elected Ladislav Pothumus king (1445-1457). Since the king was a child, John of Hunjadi acted as Governor of the Kingdom (1446-1452). Hunjadi launched another campaign against the Turks, but was routed at the battle of Kosovo. On his flight from the battlefield, Djuradj Brankovic, despot of Serbia and Turkish vassal, detained Hunjadi by force, but released him after a few months and after having received a substantial ransom.

Croatia in turn was plunged into a bloody contest between *Ban* Talovac and the Counts of Celje. It ended only after the execution of Count Ulrich, the last of his family.

* * *

On May 29, 1453, the Turks made a final assault on Constantinople, bringing an end to the Roman Empire. Sultan Mehmed moved his capital to the conquered city, renaming it Istanbul and giving himself the honorific title *El Fatih.* From the moment of the fall of Constantinople, the Turks turned again to the west, again laying siege to Belgrade which was the key to the Hungarian plain and eastern Croatia. The city was successfully defended by Hunjadi and a special papal legate, Giovanni di Capistrano. But during the siege both of these leaders died of cholera which was plaguing the city. Hunjadi's oldest son, Ladislav, attempted to take his father's place, but a conspiracy of the king and the nobility brought about his execution. Yet Ladislav Posthumus did not enjoy his victory over Hunjadi for long. He soon died and brought an end to the first attempt to keep Austria, Bohemia, Hungary and Croatia under one rule.

Emperor Frederick III's attempt to ascend the throne was frustrated by the election of Mathias Corvinus, younger son of Hunjadi (1458-1490). Frederick bitterly disputed this election in a long war fought chiefly in Austria and Bohemia. While Mathias was occupied in the west, the Turks put an end to the Serbian autonomy, transforming it into the Belgrade *Pashalik*. The *Pashalik*, essentially a military organization, became a permanent threat to Hungary and Croatia and especially Bosnia.

For the last century Bosnia had been exposed to the punitive crusading invasions of the kings and *bans* of Croatia who intervened in the struggle between the Roman Catholic Church and the Church of Bosnian Christians (or Patarens). The authority of the King of Bosnia had practically disappeared. Thus, when the Turks invaded Bosnia (1463), no resistance was offered.

The fall of Bosnia forced Mathias to prepare the defense of Croatia. He led a partially successful campaign against the Turks in Bosnia and on liberated territory established two military provinces: Srebrnik in eastern Bosnia, and Jajce in southern Croatia and western Bosnia.

*　　*　　*

To bring their dispute to an end, Mathias and Frederick signed an agreement stipulating that in case Mathias should die without a male heir the right of succession to the Hungarian and Croatian thrones would pass to Frederick and his descendants (1463). This agreement did not, however, prevent Mathias from disputing with arms over Austrian possessions, nor did it stop him from taking part in the Husit War which, under the leadership of the Husit king, George Podebrad, was ravaging Bohemia. Because of Mathias's involvement in Austria and Bohemia, the Croats had to face the daily Turkish onslaughts from Bosnia alone.

Left to themselves, the Croatian nobles turned elsewhere for help, viz. to Venice or to the Empire. Mathias soon became suspicious of relations between his Croatian subjects and these foreign powers. He sent the newly appointed *Ban* Blaz Podmanicky to re-establish royal authority. Podmanicky carried his assignment to such extremes that Ivan Frankopan of Krk preferred to leave his island of Krk to the Republic of Venice (1480) rather than surrender it to the new *ban*. But, by this act Croatia lost her last Adriatic island.

Only at a late date did Mathias comprehend his alienation of the Croatian nobility. He tried to win them over by recognizing the right of the *Sabor* to elect the supreme commander of the Croatian army. He also re-established the political unity of his Croatian possessions by appointing Lovro Ilocki *Ban* of Croatia and Slavonia and by granting him the title of King of Bosnia (1472-1477). Subsequently he invaded Bosnia at the head of a strong army, penetrating to Sarajevo. But he was recalled from Sarajevo due to the renewal of hostilities in Austria.

Mathias Corvin was a typical ruler of the time of the Renaissance. He was independent, strong-willed and energetic. He was an avowed enemy of the arrogance and selfishness of the feudal nobility. And he was a protector of the burghers and peasantry who in turn preserved the memory of his rule by this simple saying: "Since King Mathias's departure, there is no more justice". His royal court in Buda became an important center for the Renaissance and for science. (At this time the first printing press was established in Croatia and the first book in the Croatian language was printed: *Glagolski Misal*, 1483.) Since Mathias did not leave a legitimate heir, he set his heart on securing the succession for his natural son, Ivanis. Toward this end he made him Duke of Croatia and *Ban* of Slavonia.

*　　*　　*

Mathias's death once again opened the fatal question of succession. Duke Ivanis had a certain amount of support in Croatia, but was facing an equally determined opposition in Hungary. Therefore, he did not press his claims. Besides Ivanis, three other candidates entered the contest: Vladislav Jagielo, King of Bohemia; his younger brother, Ivan Albert, King of Poland; and Maximilian, King of the Germans and son of Emperor Frederick III. The brothers Jagielo both based their claims on family ties with the former kings of Hungary and Croatia, while Maximilian pressed his claim on the basis of the treaty of succession signed by Frederick and Mathias. After lengthy bargaining, Vladislav II of Bohemia accepted the conditions imposed on him by the Hungarian Diet which made him virtually a toy in the hands of the aristocracy. He was thereby elected king, reigning from 1490 to 1516.

The Croatian nobility gave its support to Maximilian, with the exception of their two most powerful noblemen, Duke Ivanis Corvinus and Bernardin Frankopan. The two joined Vladislav's party. Subsequently Vladislav and Maximilian settled their differences by the Treaty of Pressburg (1490) which recognized the automatic succession of the Habsburgs upon the extinction of the House of Jagielo.

Vladislav's rule was characterized by a complete lack of royal authority and general feudal anarchy. There were continual disputes among the nobility regarding possession of lands and special rights and privileges. Duke Ivanis soon resigned as *Ban* and his successor, Mirko Derencin, became immediately involved in a struggle with the Frankopans for possession of the town of Senj and the littoral. The Bosnian Turks saw in this struggle their opportunity and, under the leadership of Jakub-Pasha, invaded Croatia. At the battle of Udbina they annihilated the army of the Croatian nobility and made *Ban* Derencin prisoner (1493).

With the battle of Udbina there began uninterrupted warfare between the Croats and the Turks, who were supported by the Moslems of Bosnia. Eventually the Croatians themselves began to exchange their Pataren faith for that of the Moslems.

Gradually the Turks were able to conquer all of eastern and southern Croatia. The Croatian nobility, feeling overwhelmed by fate and left to themselves, turned more and more to the Papacy and the Habsburgs for help. Resistance to the Turkish onslaught finally became effective under Duke Ivanis and especially under the new *Ban* Petar Berislavic. Berislavic imposed many setbacks on the Turks until he finally lost his life on the battlefield.

The situation was further aggravated when Sultan Suleyman, known as the "magnificent," and the most powerful Ottoman ruler, ascended the throne.

When Vladislav, who was an insignificant ruler, died, he was replaced by his ten-year old son, Ljudevit II (1516-1526). Ljudevit's advisors were recruited from the most unscrupulous magnates and they brought royal prestige to its lowest ebb. Furthermore, the Hungarian nobility split into two factions: one following the court and the other leaning toward John of Zapolja, Duke of Transylvannia. (Zapolja achieved fame when he defeated George Dosza's insurgent peasant army in 1514.)

Emperor Maximilian, for his part, renegotiated the treaty of automatic succession, giving it additional strength by arranging a marriage between his granddaughter, Mary, and Ljudevit. Moreover, he arranged a marriage between his grandson Ferdinand, Archduke of Austria, and Anna, Ljudevit's sister.

* * *

The Turkish attacks were crowned with the capture of Belgrade (1521) as well as all of southern Croatia (1523) except for the fortress of Klis. Thus Croatia's situation became desperate. The only help that Croatia received, either by way of soldiers, ammunition or money, was from Maximilian. Royal power, for all practical purposes, vanished from the country. The Turks had for years been besieging Jajce, a city-fortress a Croatian island in Turkish territory, and it was relieved for the last time by a military expedition headed by Krsto Frankopan (1525).

The general situation became desperate when the Turks, after the conquest of Belgrade, invaded eastern Slavonia. This conquest, due to the utter neglect of Ljudevit, prompted the *Sabor* deliberating at Krizevci to offer the crown to Archduke Ferdinand.

71

In the same year, the long-awaited blow fell on both Croatia and Hungary when Suleyman, an ally of Francis I of France, invaded Hungary to help Francis in his struggle with Charles V.

Ljudevit confronted the challenge wholeheartedly. Without waiting for the Croatian and Transylvanian armies, he led his Hungarian army against the Turks in the battle of Mohacs, but the result was a catastrophe (August 29, 1526). Ljudevit was drowned in a swollen creek while fleeing the battlefield; Hungarian independence came to an end; and the thrones of Hungary and Croatia were left vacant.

* * *

The Neapolitan Angevins based their claims to the Hungaro-Croatian crown on their family ties with the last kings of the House of Arpad. But they were able to realize their ambition only with the support, by election, of the Croatian nobility as well as by the nobility of Hungary.

The Angevins possessed their own philosophy of royal authority and the right of succession. As soon as he was established on the throne, Charles Robert applied this philosophy by skillfully attempting to reduce the importance of the very magnates to whom he was supposed to be thankful for his crown. He did this by granting the rights and privileges of these magnates to other less significant nobles or by elevating new ones whose importance and security depended exclusively on royal favor. These new magnates would prove to be valuable supporters when the king decided to settle accounts with the recalcitrant nobility of the old established families.

Feudalism, as it existed in Slavonia and to a lesser degree in Croatia prior to the Angevin period, was an imperfect imitation of the German and Hungarian pattern. The Angevins, in order to bind themselves more closely to the nobility, granted the latter the most complete application of the principles of feudalism, especially concerning the nobility's relationship to the peasantry. By giving sanction to the *Avicitat* law (1351), Ljudevit I granted the nobility the right of succession in the male line, complete peasant ownership, a defense for moving or for changing masters, choice of profession and complete jurisdiction. Thus absolute serfdom became a legal social institution, and consequently, many hitherto independent or free-holding peasants lost their freedom.

During this period the political and administrative organization of Slavonia also underwent significant changes. Instead of the former tribal counties (*plemenska zupa*), new larger administrative subdivisions, created along the lines of the Hungarian commitats, were introduced.

* * *

When the heavy hand of the Hungarian autocratic rulers who successfully controlled the feudal nobility disappeared, the crown became the object of bargaining between the royal candidates and the arrogant nobility. The country was exposed to a multitude of civil wars, disorders and general anarchy which ultimately led to Venetian occupation of Dalmatia, Turkish conquest, and the final catastrophe of Mohacs.

The loss of Dalmatia by the "shameful bargain" of Ladislav of Naples was the fatal blow to medieval Croatia. The essence of Croatia's independence, necessarily asserted in Hungary's direction, was based precisely on the possession of the Adriatic coast. It was through the coastal possessions that the country maintained direct contact with Italy and the Mediterranean world. When the loss of Dalmatia was followed by the Venetian conquest of its islands and the Croatian littoral, as well as by the Turkish conquest of Bosnia and southern and eastern Croatia, the kingdom was reduced to the western sections of Croatia and Slavonia. There the nobility was working toward closer ties with its Hungarian counterpart for common defense from the Turks, or for the imposition of its views on the newly elected rulers. These tendencies were reinforced by the fact that the kings were granting lands on Croatian territory to Hungarian magnates who would, in turn, cultivate close ties with their home country.

CHAPTER VI

MEDIEVAL BOSNIA

Origins — Contest for possession — Ban Boric — Ban Kulin — Church of Bosnian Christians — Kotromanics — Stjepan Tvrdko — Hrvoje Vukcic Hrvatinic — Turkish Conquest

At the time of the Slavic settlement on the Balkan Peninsula, Bosnia covered about one-fifth of what is now the Socialist Republic of Bosnia - Hercegovina. It was situated on the territory around the upper part of the River Bosnia and bordered by the River Drina to the east and the River Vrbas to the west. The origin of the name of the land, Bosnia, is obscure, but the name was mentioned for the first time in connection with other Croatian lands at the end of the eighth century. Since then it has shared in their destiny.

Following the signing of the Peace Treaty of Aix-la-Chapelle at the end of the Frankish-Byzantine War, Bosnia and the Croatian principalities of Croatia and Slavonia fell under Frankish domination (814). During the Frankish wars against Ljudevit, Prince of Slavonia (821-823), Bosnia supported Ljudevit. In subsequent years, Trpimir, Prince of Croatia, defeated Boris, Emperor of Bulgaria (855), and established his authority over Bosnia. At the beginning of the tenth century, possession of Bosnia became the subject of dispute between Simeun, Emperor of Bulgaria, and Tomislav, King of Croatia: Tomislav eventually

75

(925) defeated Simeun and established jurisdiction over Bosnia.

When the Kingdom of Croatia declined due to internal struggles, Caslav Klonimir, Prince of Rasa, acting as a Byzantine vassal, added Bosnia to his Serbian dominion (960). Following his death, Bosnia regained its doubtful status as a border land and was competed for by the Eastern Empire, the Bulgarian Empire, Croatia and Serbia. After a decisive Byzantine victory over the Bulgarian Emperor, Ivan Vladislav, Byzantium re-established its sovereignty for a time. But due to the victory of the Byzantine ally, Petar Kresimir IV, over the Bulgarians, Bosnia came back under Croatian rule (1060).

It was on the occasion of Bosnia's return to Croatian jurisdiction that the Bishopric of Vrhbosna was created as a suffragan to the Archbishop of Split. The administration of Bosnia was entrusted to a *Ban*, who was one of the heads of the nine provinces into which Croatia had been subdivided. From this time, until Bosnia became a kingdom, the office of *Ban* was a permanent political institution in the country.

In the turbulent situation in Croatia after the assassination of King Dmitar Zvonimir (1089), Mihajlo Bodin, King of Zeta, joined Bosnia to his kingdom for a time.

Bosnia emerged as a definite autonomous unit at the time of the conflict over who would possess it between Emmanuel Comnenus, Emperor of the Eastern Empire, and Bela II, King of Hungary and Croatia. In 1138, Bela emerged victorious and styled himself King of Bosnia (*rex Ramae*). He appointed his son, Ladislav, Duke of Croatia and overlord of Bosnia while the country was ruled by *Ban* Boric.

Boric was a Croatian nobleman whose family was established in the county of Pozega in lower Slavonia. Due to his Pataren leanings, he was forced to resign. He retired to his Slavonian estates and his relative Kulin assumed his position. In the dynastic disputes that followed Bela's death, Emmanuel returned in force, taking over Bosnia and a major part of southern Croatia. Kulin changed masters and ruled Bosnia as an imperial vassal who was simply waiting for the propitious moment to assert independence.

After Emmanuel's death in 1180, Kulin used the disorder prevailing in Croatia and Slavonia to add the territories of Donji Kraji, Usora and Soli to his patrimony. Although he continued to recognize the suzerainty of the Hungaro-Croatian king, he otherwise acted as an independent ruler by granting to the Republic of Dubrovnik free possession of Bosnian lands and trading privileges. Thus, it seems safe to assume that with the rule of *Ban* Kulin began the history of Bosnia as an independent political entity. But equally important to Bosnian independence was the emergence of the Pataren Christian sect.

*   *   *

The centuries-old struggle between the Latin and the old Slavonic liturgies in Croatia, as well as between the politically parallel "court" and "popular" parties, prevented a definitive organization of the church in the Croatian interior and therefore in Bosnia. The recent split between Rome and Constantinople created a fluid religious situation. Thus, the Balkans became exposed to the new creed for national and political reasons as well as for theological considerations.

The new creed, commonly known as Pataren or Bogomil, was of Oriental origin and could be traced to the Paulists or to the neomanichaen gnostics. It was brought from Asia to the European section of the empire by imperial soldiers. Due to the influence of Theophil, a priest active among the Bulgarians who took for himself the Slavic name, Bogomil, and who used the old Slavonic liturgical books, the new creed had some Slavonic characteristics.

The Patarens believed in God and accepted the trinity, but they did not believe that God created the world. God created the soul alone, and the devil or Satan created everything material. Christ was simply a supreme angel with an illusory body; therefore his death was illusory. Thus, the Patarens believed in the Zoroastrian concept of religious duality.

The Patarens rejected all sacraments and, from the New Testament, retained only the Lord's Prayer. They did not have a strictly established clerical hierarchy, except for the head who was a kind of supreme bishop (*djed*) and whose authority was recognized also by the Cathari sect in Italy and the Albigensi and Waldensi sects in France. A guest (*gost*) or teacher-priest regularly visited the religious communities. The various localities each had a dean (*starac*) and a keeper (*strojnik*). There were no churches or other visible religious structures; the liturgy was celebrated in simple rooms and consisted simply of the breaking of bread (a kind of communion) and the singing of hymns.

The Patarens who achieved perfection in the performance of their religious duties received the name of *perfecti*. In order to become perfect before death, the Pataren devotee had to renounce all of his wordly possessions, including his wife and family, and spend the rest of his life in solitude and fasting. The Patarens themselves took the simple name of "Christian", and their church was officially known as the Church of Bosnian Christians.

*   *   *

Ban Kulin not only favored the new religion but became an avowed member and powerful protector. From the administrative point of view, Bosnia belonged to the Archbishopric of Split. Thus Pope Innocent III instructed King Emerik to recall his vassal Kulin to the Roman Catholic Church as well as the Bosnian nobility and citizenry (1203). This papal policy toward the Bosnian schismatics was also accepted by the subsequent kings and dukes of Croatia who, on this basis, led a series of crusading campaigns against the Bosnian Patarens.

These crusading enterprises were characterized by the same cruelty and destruction found in every bigoted campaign. Due to the zeal of the Dominican monks who were entrusted with the task of eradicating the heresy, practically all the original written documents disappeared. These monks carried out their general policy according to the mood of the papacy as it was expressed in a letter to Stjepan Kotromanic, *Ban* of Bosnia:

> To our beloved son and nobleman, Stephen, Prince of Bosnia, knowing that thou art a faithful son of the Church, we therefore charge thee to exterminate the heretics in thy dominion, and to render aid and assistance to Fabian, our Inquisitor, forasmuch as a large multitude of heretics from many and divers parts collected hath flowed together into the principality of Bosnia, trusting there to sow their obscene errors and dwell there in safety. These men, imbued with the cunning of the Old Fiend, and armed with the venom of their falseness, corrupt the minds of Catholics by outward show of simplicity and sham assumption of the name of Christian; their speech crawleth like a crab, and they creep in sheeps' clothing, covering their bestial fury as means to deceive the simple sheep of Christ. . . .

> T. W. Arnold, *The Preaching of Islam: A History of the Moslem Faith* (London, 1913, p. 62).

After the "eradication," only a multitude of tombstones (*stecak*) that were artistically decorated with substantial inscriptions remained as witness to the turbulent Croatian and Bosnian history prior to the Ottoman conquest.

The reason for the easy spread of the Pataren faith in Croatia and Bosnia can be traced to several facts. Christianity seldom developed deep roots in the back-country; thus the established church, which was well-organized dogmatically, actually existed only superficially. Furthermore, it is reasonable to believe that with the acceptance of Christianity the Croats also accepted some aspects of the creed of the Arian heresy since it was the creed of the Goths who had inhabited the country for a time before the arrival of the Croats.

For nearly two centuries the followers of the old Slavonic liturgy bitterly fought against attempts of the church hierarchy to impose the Latin liturgy as well as strict Catholic discipline.

When they were defeated they retreated from the coast to the interior. Ultimately, the end of the Croatian national dynasty (the House of Trpimir) and the formation of the Hungaro-Croatian commonwealth, in which the established church played a most active part, prompted many Croatians to join a cause which was in opposition to the established spiritual and secular order. Thus the Patarens, who were persecuted elsewhere, found a receptive mood in Bosnia and in the Croatian interior in general and it was there that they sought refuge.

The source of the Pataren faith that found its way to Croatia and Bosnia is a matter for speculation. Well-organized Pataren communities existed in Split and Trogir and these certainly helped spread the faith to the interior. But, also, the Patarens by the names, Bogomils and Babunis, found their way into the Bosnian sanctuary following their persecution and extermination in Bulgaria and Serbia.

*   *   *

Bosnian rulers from the House of Kotromanic succeeded each other by the family custom of ancientry, i.e. the oldest or most notable member of the family replaced the departed ruler. Thus Stjepan succeeded Kulin (1204-1221). He was the first master of Bosnia to give the Patarens a free hand. His policy of protecting the Church of the Bosnian Christians provoked the First Crusade. This crusade was led by the King of Hungary and Croatia and was directed against the heretics of Bosnia. The spiritual leadership of the crusade was intrusted to Ugrin, the Archbishop of Kalocsa, under whose direction the over-zealous Dominican friars carried out a ruthless destruction of all the Pataren books and monuments that they could find. (1222).

After the invasion of Bosnia, Ugrin re-established the Bishopric at Vrhobosna and appointed the Hungarian, Posza, as its first bishop. The new bishopric received a rich donation of lands from Bosnia, Usori, Soli and lower Slavonia. By this act, Bosnia was severed from the Archbishopric of Split and added to the Hungarian Archbishopric of Kalocsa. However, the newly established order did not last long. As soon as the crusading army retired from Bosnia, the Patarens reappeared in full force and Posza was compelled to vacate his diocese. He took permanent residence at Djakovo in 1226.

The expulsion of Posza prompted Ugrin to lead another crusade against Stjepan's successor, Matej Ninoslav (1230-1250), who was an avowed Pataren. But despite all of its acts of cruelty, this crusade accomplished nothing durable. Subsequently, Koloman, the Duke of Croatia, assisted by the Dominican bearers of the Inquisition, invaded Bosnia. In the face of the powerful invading army, the Patarens either submitted or retreated to their mountain sanctuaries, leading Koloman to believe that he had been successful. But as a soon as order was established and Koloman returned to Croatia (1234), the Patarens retook the country and forced Koloman to lead another campaign (1237).

The campaign of 1237 was short-lived because Koloman was called by his brother, Bela IV, to assist him in stopping the Mongol invasion of Hungary. At the Battle of Shay River, Bela was defeated and Koloman received a severe wound which caused his death shortly afterwards. Consequently, the Mongols invaded Croatia and, even upon being recalled to their homeland in Asia, managed to plunder Bosnia on the way (1242). The Mongol invasion of Croatia was followed by a civil war between two Croatian towns, Split and Trogir, and Matej Ninoslav took part as an ally of Trogir.

Following the Mongol invasion, Bela IV undertook several far-reaching reforms aimed at consolidating his rule over his possessions. As a consequence, Bosnia was divided into three separate units, viz. Bosnia, and the newly created Usora and Soli.

During the dynastic struggles in Hungary and Croatia between the partisans of Andreas III of the House of Arpad and the followers of Charles II of Anjou of Naples, Pavao of Bribir, *Ban* or Croatia and leader of the Anjou faction, received Bosnia as his fief from Charles II (1293). Subsequently, *Bans* Prijezda,

Kotroman and Stjepan Kotromanic, rulers of Bosnia and descendants of Boric and Kulin, acknowledged Pavao, and Mladen his son and successor, as their overlords from 1293-1322. After Mladen's downfall, Stjepan Kotromanic, the *Ban* of Bosnia, changed allegiance by becoming a direct vassal to the king. His position grew strong, and with royal support the successfully resisted the attempt of Stephan Dusan, the powerful ruler of Serbia, to conquer Bosnia. Kotromanic's house gained new glory and privilege when Ljudevit I, the most powerful ruler of the time, married Jelizaveta, Stjepan Kotromanic's daughter.

* * *

Bosnia's status as an independent country was developed by Stjepan Kotromanic's nephew, Stjepan Tvrdko, who succeeded him as *Ban* (1353-1392). While his suzerain, King Ljudevit, was occupied in Naples, Austria, Bohemia and Poland, Tvrdko took the opportunity to proclaim independence (1363). However, his brother, Vuk, remained faithful to the king, and with the king's support was able to force Tvrdko to accept him as co-ruler. But Ljudevit's death permitted Tvrdko to realize his ambitions for independence and to further enlarge his domain by adding Hum, Podrinje (1374), and Travunja (1376).

At this time, the Kingdom of Serbia was falling to pieces on account of the death of the last king of the House of Nemanjic. Tvrdko seized the opportunity to present his claim on the basis of succession in the female line, and he assumed the self-proclaimed title of King of Bosnia, Serbia, Primorje, Hum, Donji Kraji, Zapadne Strane, Usora, Soli and Podrinje (1377). Simultaneously, he took an active part in the struggle for succession to the Croatian throne in which Ljudevit's daughter, Marija, opposed Charles of Durazzo. Tvrdko first gave his support to Ivan Palizna. Later he supported the Horvat brothers which enabled him to become master of all southern Croatia, adding to his title that of King of Croatia and Dalmatia (1390).

After his untimely death, the throne passed to his nephew, Stjepan Dabisa (1391-1398), who proved to be an extremely weak ruler. He soon recognized Sigismund's suzerainty and surrendered the Horvat brothers, who were the leaders of the Croatian rebellion, to him. The remnants of the Horvat party rallied around Ladislav of Naples who came to the country and was crowned King of Croatia and Dalmatia in Zadar in 1403. However, unable to establish his claims on the Hungarian throne and seeking to get his rule accepted in Croatia, Ladislav returned to Naples, leaving Hrvoje Vukcic Hrvatinic, the most influential Croatian and Bosnian nobleman, to rule as Duke of Split and *Ban* of Croatia. Hrvoje completely dominated the weak rulers of Bosnia, Stjepan Ostoja (1395-1404) and Stjepan Tvrdko II (1404-1409).

In order to establish his rule over Bosnia and Croatia, Sigismund waged a succession of wars against Duke Hrvoje (1405, 1406 and 1407), but without any decisive success. Prompted by Pope Gregory XII, he assembled a huge army and penetrated Bosnia, calling this invasion a crusade against the Bosnian heretics. Following victory, he ordered the summary execution of one hundred-fifty captured noblemen. Only Hrvoje preserved his independence, ruling supremely over Split, Omis Cetina, Neretva, Korcula, Brac, Hvar and his own Bosnian land of Donji Kraji.

Sigismund could not tolerate Hrvoje independence and launched another campaign against him which resulted in his submission. The submission was, however, more apparent than real. As soon as Sigismund and his army left Croatia, Hrvoje re-established his independence. These were often-repeated tactics, and Sigismund was prompted once again to attempt to decisively conquer this elusive duke. Forced into a tight corner, Hrvoje made an alliance with the Turks and was thereby able to rout the Hungaro-Croatian army (1415). Following this victory, the Turks invaded Croatia itself, for the first time, and their advance troops even penetrated as far as Celje in Styria, carrying away numerous slaves.

Under the weak rulers, Stjepan Ostojic (1418-1421) and Stjepan Tvrdko (1421-1443), Bosnian independence grew more and more illusory. This dissipation was due to the contest between Sigismund and the Turks whose sporadic invasions of the country prompted Bosnian rulers to seek Sigismund's protection. As a consequence of the lack of any strong central power, Stjepan Vukcic, ruler of Hum, detached his land from the king's rule and styled himself Duke (*Herceg*), thereby giving to his patrimony the present-day name of Hercegovina. Meanwhile, Hrvoje's former possessions of Omis and Poljica fell under Venetian domination (1444).

* * *

After the conquest of Constantinople (1453), the Turks felt bound to reconstruct the Eastern Empire. Seeking to bring the former imperial Balkan dependencies under their domination, they carried out one military campaign after another. The Bosnian ruler, Stjepan Tomas (1443-1461), and his successor, the last independent king Stjepan Tomasevic (1461-1463), were unable to seriously resist the Ottoman onslaught. Thus when the Turks invaded Bosnia, the great majority of the country's nobility, Pataren and Catholic alike, followed the example set by the people who were attached to the Turkish concept of equality: They joined the Islamic faith. Meanwhile, the unfortunate king, attempting to hold out at his fortress, Kljuc, was betrayed by his own captain, Radak. He was captured, and by the Sultan's order, executed.

The fall of Bosnia due to complete lack of organized resistance, left the memory in the people that "Bosnia fell by a whisper." But Hum, or Hercegovina, under the rule of the independent *Herceg* would nevertheless continue its precarious existence until 1482.

* * *

The fall of Bosnia prompted Mathias Korvin to undertake a campaign to liberate it from the Turks. His campaign was partially successful and he established his rule over all of northern Bosnia. There he organized two military *banovinas*: Jajce in the west, for the protection of Croatia, and Srebrnik in the east, for the protection of Slavonia and Hungary.

However, especially in southern Croatia, the Turks continued their conquests. In the aftermath of each of their campaigns they carried away thousands of slaves. King Mathias renewed his efforts against this Turkish danger by strengthening the political organization of Croatia. He gave the title of King of Bosnia to Lovro Ilocki, who was already *Ban* of both Croatia and Slavonia. Thus, for a time, all Croatian lands again formed a single administrative unit.

The primary task of Ilocki was the retaking of Bosnia from the Turks. This, however, proved to be beyond his ability. Thus, Bosnia as an independent unit disappeared from the historical scene in fact as well as in name.

CHAPTER VII

THE REPUBLIC OF DUBROVNIK

Greek Epidaurum — Latin Ragusa — Croatian Dubrov-
nik — Part of the Empire — Venetian domination —
Protectorate of the Hungaro-Croatian kings — Ottoman
allegiance — Golden Age of the Republic — Decline
and fall.

The origin of Dubrovnik can be traced back as far as the beginning of the Greek colonization of the Adriatic coast and islands. From the island of Korkyra, the Greeks penetrated the Adriatic Sea in the fourth century B.C., establishing colonies on several islands and along the coast. Among these colonies was Epidaurum located at what today is the small town of Cavtat.

Like the other Greek settlements, Epidaurum passed under Roman control: According to Roman sources, it was recognized as a Roman colony at the time of the struggles between Caesar and Pompeus (47 B.C.). During the Roman period, the colony received its drinking water from a huge aqueduct or *canalis* and it was from this word that the Croatized name, *Konavle,* was derived and given to the surrounding area.

Epidaurum shared the destiny of the imperial province of Dalmatia, being destroyed by the invading hordes of Avars and their Slavic allies in 614. The population escaped a few miles to the north and on the rocky peninsula broke ground for their new town. This new town was well protected from the mainland and assumed the Latin name of Ragusa. In the beginning, its population was exclusively Roman, but in the following centuries the Slavic or Croatian element gradually asserted itself until it attained a definite Croatian character in the fourteenth century.

From its foundation, Ragusa (renamed Dubrovnik by its Croatian population) was part of the Byzantine Empire as were the towns of Zadar, Split and Trogir, and the Adriatic islands of Cres and Rab, all of which made up the Imperial Province of Dalmatia.

With the renewal of the political and religious life after the destruction of the Avar invasion, the Archbishopric of Split was established as successor to the former Archbishopric of Salona; and Dubrovnik, as well, received its own bishopric (780).

During the eighth and ninth centuries, Dubrovnik had to pay taxes to the Slavic princes of Hum and Travunia for unhampered possession of lands on their own respective territories. When Tomislav, who was the first King of Croatia, received Dalmatia as his imperial proconsul, Dubrovnik also came under his rule. Thus Dubrovnik was represented in a series of church synods in Split held under Tomislav's jurisdiction. At this time, the Archbishopric of Split was established as supreme in all Croatian territory, including the Bishopric of Dubrovnik (928).

During the civil war in Croatia, the Venetian doge, Pietro Orseolo, invaded the Adriatic coast and imposed Venetian rule on several towns and islands. He assumed the title of Duke of Dalmatia and was recognized as such by the Byzantine authorities. Dubrovnik became a Venetian dependency at this time (1000), and henceforth began shifting its allegiance from Venice to Byzantium, or from the Norman rulers of southern Italy to the rulers of Croatia.

The city, however, maintained a great amount of independence and even had enough freedom to sign international treaties with the *bans* of Bosnia, who were the masters of Travunia and Hum in the immediate vicinity of Dubrovnik. Essentially a maritime power, Dubrovnik maintained regular trading relations with Constantinople and, above all, with the prominent Italian city-republic of Venice and its Adriatic dependencies. It also traded with Pisa, Amalphi, Ancona, etc.

When Venice came into possession of Zadar during the Fourth Crusade and, after the Latin conquest of Constantinople, became virtual heir to the Eastern Empire, Dubrovnik fell under the Republic's influence and accepted its suzerainty. A duke was appointed for a period of two years to represent the Venetian government in Dubrovnik. Under his supervision, the tasks of the government were carried out by vice-comes selected from the local patricians. (At this time the territorial extension of the Republic of Dubrovnik included the Peninsula of Peljesac, purchased from the ruler of Bosna, as well as the islands of Mljet and Lastovo.)

As the sailors of Dubrovnik engaged themselves in an active and lucrative maritime commerce in the Mediterranean, which included trade with Tunis, Egypt, Syria and countries in the area of the Black Sea, the influence of Venice waned. The country signed commercial treaties with the rulers of Bosnia, Serbia, Bulgaria and Byzantium and maintained a busy commerce with Venice, Ancona, Florence, Naples and Sicily. Throughout all of this economic activity Dubrovnik functioned as an intermediary agent in the east-west exchange that had developed according to the pattern dictated by the more important Italian city-republics.

After losing the war to Ljudevit I, King of Hungary and Croatia, and signing the Peace Treaty of Zadar (1358), the hegemony of Venice came to an end. Subsequently, Dubrovnik acknowledged the suzerainty of the Hungaro-Croatian king and accepted the immediate authority and supervision of the *Ban* of Croatia. But for all practical purposes, Dubrovnik was an independent city-republic ruled by a Great Council, which was a legislative patrician assembly, and a Senate (*consilium rogatorum*). The Senate met twice a week to prepare bills and motions to be presented to the Great Council, as well as to settle pending judicial issues. A Council of Solicitors was composed of members of the Senate; and it selected members for a Small Council from its ranks. The Small Council was an executive body which consisted of seven members, one of whom was appointed as the supreme official of the Republic and given the title of duke. The duke, whose position was more representative than executive, was provided with a special red robe and insignia and served for one month.

At the time of the Hungaro-Croatian protectorate (1358-1526), Dubrovnik reached the zenith of its power and glory. The Republic had some forty thousand inhabitants and a fleet of some three hundred ships. Moreover, its navigators participated in naval enterprises from the Levant to Spain and England; even Columbus used some of its sailors on his trans-Atlantic expeditions. The Republic enjoyed an enviable economic prosperity: It had a flourishing naval commerce, a practical monopoly on overland trade on the Ottoman territory of the Balkan Peninsula and it developed industries producing textiles, colors, soaps, silver products, armaments, church bells and ships. General prosperity enabled its population to follow the example of contemporary Italy in developing its own literary renaissance as well as in adorning its city with many beautiful churches and buildings, such as the Ducal Palace.

*   *   *

With the downfall of independent Hungary and Croatia (1526), the Republic exchanged protectors. It approached the Ottomans and accepted them as its protectors, paying on that account a regular annual tribute. This new situation gave Dubrovnik the opportunity to further develop its interests in the Balkan Peninsula, since this peninsula was now firmly in Ottoman hands. The merchants of Dubrovnik established permanent depots on former Croatian, Bosnian, Serbian and Bulgarian territories and reached such distant outposts as Sofia, Trnovo, Plovidiv, Adrianapolis and Istanbul.

Dubrovnik enjoyed an exceptional position on the Balkan Peninsula. During the centuries of warfare that engulfed the ancient civilizations and political organizations of the Greeks, Bulgarians, Serbs, Croats and Byzantines, Dubrovnik remained such an oasis of peace and freedom that Ivan Gundulic, the most outstanding poet of the Republic, was moved to sing a proud ode to liberty in his pastoral drama, *"Dubravka."*

*   *   *

Due to several factors, these favorable conditions suddenly changed. One of the most important of these factors was the discovery of America which provoked a shift in the center of economic activities from the Mediterranean to the Atlantic. Just as with the more glorious Italian city-republics, Dubrovnik gradualy lost its prosperity and glory. Moreover, a catastrophic earthquake (April 16, 1667) which destroyed many buildings and churches and killed some four thousand people served to hasten Dubrovnik's general decline.

Although it was never able to attain its former glory, the Republic was able to renew its existence in a modest way even after the earthquake. Its end came as a consequence of events begun in the French Revolution and culminating in the Napoleonic campaign against Austria and Russia.

In the Peace Treaty of Pressburg, Austria ceded to Napoleon her momentarily-held and formerly Venetian possessions of Dalmatia and Boka Kotorska. In order to establish territorial unity for his newly acquired lands, Napoleon ordered General Lauriston, who had already entered the city on May 25, 1806, to extend his occupation to the territory of the Republic of Dubrovnik as well. On January 31, 1808, Napoleon decreed, by a special proclamation, the end of the Republic of Dubrovnik as an independent unit. Its territory was subsequently incorporated into the Illyrian Provinces.

When Napoleon fell, the Austrian general, Milutinovic, occupied Dubrovnik. Henceforth, until the ultimate dissolution of the Habsburg Monarchy in 1918, it was part of the Austrian Province of Dalmatia.

CHAPTER VIII

THE HABSBURG ERA

*Election of Ferdinand I — John of Zapolya — Turkish
conquests —* Reliquiae reliquiarum *— Peasant revolt —
Military Border —* Uskoks *— Protestantism — Zrinjski
and Frankopan conspiracy.*

On August 29, 1526, the Turks defeated Louis II's army
before either the Croats or the Transylvannians could join it.
The Croatian levies received the news of the Mohacs catastrophe
on their march from Zagreb to the River Drava. Since the
bans of both Croatia and Slavonia, Franjo Bathiany and Ivan
Tahi, were with their respective contingents at Louis' camp,
the command of the Croatian army was left to Krsto Frankopan who had the reputation of being the most experienced
military leader of his country at the time. Upon hearing of the
disaster at Mohacs, Frankopan called a *Sabor* into session at
Koprivnica (September 23). The necessary measures for the
country's protection were effected and Frankopan was named
"tutor and protector of the Kingdom" in the absence of the
king.

Soon the news of the Mohacs catastrophe reached Vienna,
provoking Ferdinand of Habsburg, Archduke of Austria, to proclaim himself successor to the unfortunate Louis. He sent his
delegates to the *Sabor* at Koprivnica for the purpose of "deliberation on matters of common interest." He had already made

93

overtures to the Croatian nobility for immediate recognition as king in accordance with the ancient treaties of succession signed in 1491, 1505 and 1515 by his ancestors and the then ruling kings of Hungary, Bohemia and Croatia. While Bohemia's nobility acknowledged the validity of these treaties and acclaimed Ferdinand King of Bohemia on October 23, the Hungarian nobility elected John of Zapolya, Grand Duke of Transylvannia, King of Hungary at a Diet on November 11. However, Ferdinand had the support of the Court faction which gathered around his sister, Queen Mary, who was also, fortuitously, the widow of the late Louis. This faction met at Pressburg and proclaimed Ferdinand King of Hungary on December 16.

When the delegates failed to achieve their aim at the *Sabor* at Koprivnica, Ferdinand sent new emissaries to Croatia to further his cause. Their leading member was a Croatian nobleman and captain in the Habsburg army, Nikola Jurisic. An agreement was finally reached after long and tedious bargaining over the country's defense against the Turks and after certain rights were granted to the nobility of southern Croatia. The *Sabor* then met at Cetin where the nobility, "entirely of their own accord and free from foreign influence, elected Ferdinand King of Bohemia and Archduke of Austria, King of Croatia (January 1, 1527).

The action of the *Sabor* at Cetin established Ferdinand as King of Croatia despite the abstention of the nobility of Slavonia. Krsto Frankopan, a prominent member of the nobility and, on account of his previous service in the imperial army, a longtime supporter of the Habsburgs, instigated this abstention. He switched allegiance, securing for Zapolya the support of Simun Erdody, Bishop of Zagreb. Consequently a counter-*Sabor* gathered at Dubrava near Zagreb and elected John of Zapolya King of Croatia (January 6, 1527). As it turned out, Zapolya not only gained the support of most of the Hungarian and Croatian nobility, but also the official recognition of several foreign powers, viz. the Papacy, France, Poland and Venice.

The rivalry between Ferdinand and Zapolya produced a bloody civil war: Zapolya rewarded Frankopan for his support by appointing him *Ban* of Croatia, while Ferdinand gave the same office to Ivan Karlovic of Krbava. Both *bans* attempted to grab supporters from each other by means of persecution and reward. But it happened that when Frankopan besieged the town of Varazdin in retaliation for its support of Ferdinand, he was mortally wounded. His death shook the Zapolya cause to the point that when a *Sabor* met at Krizevci it voted an address to Ferdinand, confirming the election at Cetin. Simultaneously it declared Croatia's independence from Hungary, insisting that ". . . After the death of Zvonimir, our last king of fond memory, we joined the holy crown of Hungary by our own free will, just as we do now, the rule of your majesty" (October 6, 1527).

The anarchy produced by the civil war left the country defenseless against the Turks, who proceeded to conquer all of southern Croatia, including the towns of Obrovac, Udbina, Jajce and Banja Luka. (This territory would later be known as Turkish Croatia.) The Croatian line of defense was pushed back to the River Una and the fortress of Klis, near Split, was totally isolated. In this precarious position, the fortress stimulated a number of fierce enemy assaults which the garrisons, under the command of Captain Petar Kruzic, valiantly resisted.

In 1529, a new invasion brought the Turks to the gates of Vienna as French allies and supporters of Zapolya. Suleyman the Magnificent led the Turkish army to the rescue of Francis I who was prisoner of Charles V. As the Turkish army passed through Croatia and Hungary it encouraged the partisans of Zapolya to push the country into a renewal of the civil war. The plight of the country was desperate after three years of general misery, and Suleyman moved another army toward Vienna. But he was stopped outside the fortified town of Kosseg in western Hungary by defensive forces commanded by Nikola Jurisic. Unable to subdue Kosseg's garrison and threatened by approaching winter, Suleyman returned home by way of northern Croatia. He left a trail of destruction and pillage, capturing numerous people to be sold in the slave markets of Asia Minor (1532).

When Charles V and Francis I signed one more of their many truces, Ferdinand was able to enlist his brother's support for the reconquest of Hungary and Croatia. He sent an army under the command of General Johannes Katzianner to Croatia where, after an initial success, it was finally defeated by the Turks. This defeat permitted a gradual Turkish advance through all of eastern Slavonia and ultimately moved the Turkish frontier into the immediate vicinity of Zagreb.

Meanwhile Ferdinand reached an agreement with Zapolya that put an end to the civil war in Croatia. Zapolya agreed to relinquish all his rights, as well as his title of King of Croatia, to Ferdinand in return for the retention of his title of King of Hungary.

* * *

As soon as Ferdinand was firmly established on the throne he employed a policy of personal rule over his possessions which concentrated all affairs in a strong central government at Vienna. In keeping with this policy, but without success he repeatedly invited the Croatian nobility to take part in the deliberations of the Royal Council in Vienna. Nevertheless, for the defense of Croatia, as well as his Austrian lands, Ferdinand felt justified in installing central offices for military and financial affairs. These greatly curtailed the rights of the Croatian *Sabor* and thereby endangered the country's autonomy. Thus, the trend toward centralization inspired considerable opposition and resistance from the Croats, but they fought a losing battle.

Ferdinand's son and successor, Maximilian (1564-1576), carried the policy of centralization even further. But besides inheriting this more or less gratifying task from his father, he also received the heritage of a long and bitter war with the Turks which took the form of a new campaign launched against him by Sultan Suleyman in his old age. But this new march of the Turkish army toward Vienna was impeded by the resistance of the fortified town of Sziget in southern Hungary. Sziget's defender was Count Nikola Zrinjski, a former *Ban* of Croatia and a man renowned for his past military success over the Turks.

Suleyman's chief adviser, Grand Vizir Mehmed Sokolovic, suggested that Sziget might be defeated by bribing Zrinjski with the offer of the rule of Croatia. When Zrinjski refused, the town was surrounded and eventually conquered, but not before Zrinjski had heroically perished leading his garrison in an attempted sortie (1566). Ironically, Suleyman himself had died a few days before Sziget fell, but Sokolovic had kept this a secret to prevent an abrupt end of the campaign that customarily occurred upon the Sultan's death. Nevertheless, the capture of Sziget was followed by the withdrawal of the Turkish army and it therefore marked the end of the campaign. Two years later, in the Peace Treaty of Adrianople, the existing boundaries were simply reconfirmed.

* * *

The long, drawnout war with the Turks which resulted in the loss of Croatia's most important territory also reduced the size of the country to an all-time low. The surviving inhabitants of the territories that fell to the Turks either converted to Islam or were sold into slavery. Many fled to the west and north. But the heaviest burden of the war was born by the peasants who were the country's only taxpayers, soldiers and builders of fortifications. Yet this fact did not prevent the nobility, which was seeking compensation for the loss of its estates to the Turks, from imposing itself even more oppressively upon these people.

In 1514 the Hungarian peasantry had found itself in a similar plight and was led by George Dosza in insurrection. They were defeated and paid dearly for their daring. The nobility imposed a strict status of serfdom on them in the *Code Tripartitum* which was drawn up by Stephen Verboczy, the Notary of the Kingdom, and effected by the Hungarian Diet. This law levelled free peasants, tenants and the fixed land tenants to the lowest form of serfdom. Hungarian noblemen who had lands in Croatia automatically applied the same rule to their Croatian subjects in total disregard for local rights and the existing system. The Croatian magnates were quick to follow suit. During the first half of the sixteenth century the lot of the peasants was one of abuse and humiliation, since they were left to the arbitrary rule of their masters. Voicing the general dissatisfaction of the peasantry, the Croat Antun Vrancic, Bishop of Vesprem, complained in a letter to Emperor Maximilian that the Croatian magnates ". . . treated their subjects worse than cattle. . . ."

The situation was no better for the Croatian lands and islands that passed under the rule of the Venetian Republic. Their traditional institutions were replaced by a Venetian legal and social order which resulted in the introduction of serfdom. Under the leadership of Matija Ivanic, the inhabitants of the Island of Hvar staged a revolt against the new order which consisted of both Venetian and local nobility. After a few years and some bloodshed it was quelled by an army that had been dispatched to the island. Ivanic and some of his close friends were hanged on galley masts and a large number of insurgent peasants were condemned to the galleys (1516).

These various revolts as well as the recent Peasant War in Germany set the pattern for the organization of massive resistance by the Croatian peasants. The center for the conspiracy was the estate of Ferko Tahi at Dolnja Stubica near Zagreb. Tahi was the leader of the Lutheran faction in Croatia. He was deeply resented for the odious way in which he dealt with his subjects for he freely interpreted and applied Luther's pamphlet attacking the peasantry. These peasants had protested to the *ban* for years and had even fruitlessly tried to appeal to the Emperor. During the winter of 1572-1573 they were determined to act. After prolonged deliberation they decided to fight for the restoration of the ancient order that had existed before serfdom. According to their own confessions the peasant leaders intended to abolish the existing political and social order, retaining only the authority of the king under whose governance equality and personal freedom for all men would be introduced. Moreover, they wanted equal taxation and the organization of an efficient defense from the Turks.

Their immediate goal was to make themselves masters of the countryside and then storm Zagreb where they would establish a national government. Matija Gubec was chosen to lead. He was a peasant from Stubica who had served in the army and who had a little experience in reading and writing. Ilija Gregoric, a man who had achieved some fame in the wars against the Turks, was appointed Gubec's military assistant, as were the twelve captains who were directly in charge of the insurgent peasant army. The revolt was centered in Hrvatsko Zagorje but had ramifications over all of northern Croatia between the Drava and Kupa Rivers. Moreover, attempts were made to enlist the support of the population in the Military Border as well as the Slovene peasants of Styria and Carniola.

Military operations began at the end of January. But due to betrayal and the strategic superiority of the opponent, the revolt was crushed by the first part of February. The last battle was fought at Donja Stubica on February 9, 1573, where the *ban* sent an army under the leadership of Gaspar Alapic to rout the peasants. Many peasants died on the battlefield, but others upon their capture were summarily executed by the vengeful noblemen. Gubec was taken prisoner and brought to Zagreb where he was found guilty of treason. To set an example that would be a lasting deterrent, Count Juraj Draskovic, Bishop of Zagreb and acting *Ban*, ordered him ". . . crowned with a white-hot iron cow muzzle symbolizing a peasant king (he allegedly intended to proclaim himself king) and seated on a white-hot iron harrow as upon a peasant throne". Gubec was duly executed according to these instructions on February 15, Carnival-Sunday. The persecution of the peasants continued until an imperial decree restored some semblance of order.

Due to this internal unrest the Turks were able to move the Croatian border from the Una River to the immediate vicinity of Zagreb along the Kupa River. Bihac, which was the former place of residence of the Duke of Croatia, was surrounded by Turkish territory and became the last Croatian outpost on the Una. In an effort to rescue this beleaguered town, General Herbert Auersperg led an Imperial army on an ill-fated campaign. In a surprise attack by Ferhat Pasha, Auersperg lost his army and his life (1574). Bihac held out until 1592 when the Turks finally became its masters.

Maximilian's successor, Rudolph (1576-1608), who resided in Prague, was too preoccupied with astronomy and alchemy to exercise his prerogative as ruler. He left the defense of Croatia to his cousin Charles, Archduke of Styria. In order to protect Croatia and his Habsburg lands of Styria, Carniola and Carinthia, Charles established a new territorial unit in Croatia called the Military Border. The territory, situated along the Turkish border, was taken from the authority of the *ban* and the *Sabor*. The archduke administered it via his appointed generals who commanded the garrisons on the border.

The Military Border was divided into two generalities. The Slavonian Generality was situated between the Drava and Sava Rivers and was supposed to protect northern Croatia. It received its support from Croatia and the Diet of Styria. The commanding general of the Slavonian Border resided first at Varazdin, then Koprivnica and ultimately at Bjelovar. On the other hand, the Croatian Generality extended from the Kupa River to the Adriatic Sea, covering the southern part of the country. The Diet of Carniola was partially responsible for its financial support. The commanding general resided at Karlovac which was a fortress built at the confluence of the Kupa and Korana Rivers. This fortress was named after its founder, Archduke Charles Karlovac, or, in German, Karlstadt. In the foundation of this fortress nine hundred Turkish heads were

100

immured to commemorate a military victory over the Turks
(1592).

With the establishment of the Military Border, Croatia was
better prepared to resist any new Turkish assaults. Thus, when
Hasan Pasha of Bosnia, invaded Croatia, he met defeat at the
hands of Tomo Bakac, *Ban* of Croatia, in the Battle of Sisak
of June 22, 1593. The battle of Sisak marked the high tide of
Turkish penetration into Croatia and was followed by a stab-
ilization of the eastern border which lasted for several years.

*   *   *

Emperor Rudolph's negligence and passivity permitted state
affairs to sink into political and religious license not only in
Germany, but also in Hungary, Bohemia and Croatia. His
policy of tolerating the German Protestants became the guide-
line for his co-ruler and successor, Mathias (1608-1619).

Mathias was duly recognized as King of Hungary, Bohemia
and Croatia during his brother's lifetime. In order to prevent
religious disorder in Hungary, Mathias granted religious freedom to all the lands entrusted to his care. The Croatian *Sabor,*
however, meeting in Zagreb, refused to accept Mathias's policy
and voted in a law authorizing the Roman Catholic Church as
the only religious institution of the country (1603).

Rudolph reached an agreement with the Sublime Porte which,
through the Peace Treaty of Zitva-Torok (November 11, 1606),
recognized their respective possessions and thus put an end to
the long war. The conditions of the settlement greatly mortified
the Hungarian and Croatian nobility since it left the major
parts of their respective countries under Ottoman rule. In
Croatia's case the treaty functioned merely as a truce since
fighting and raiding continued on the Croatian-Bosnian border.

*   *   *

Weary of the century-old war and the more recent Turkish
conquests of Bosnia, Hercegovina and major parts of Croatia
and Slavonia, some of the population refused to accept Turkish
rule and retreated westward. They formed special military units

101

to fight the Turks known as *Uskoci*. After the fall of their stronghold at Klis (1530) they moved farther to the north, settling in Senj and its vicinity.

The *Uskoci* struggle against the Turks coincided with the Venetian-Turkish wars, thus they became valuable allies to the Venetians, fighting the Turks on both land and sea. But when Venice came to terms with the Turks, the *Uskoci* were not included. They continued their habitual forays into Turkish possessions. Since Venice had assumed responsibility for the protection of Turkish navigation on the Adriatic Sea, she found herself in conflict with her former ally. The *Uskoci* pirates soon disregarded the distinction between the Turkish and Venetian ships. Their depredations compelled Venice to seek Imperial intervention. Baron Joseph Rabatta, Governor of Rijeka, was appointed Imperial Commissary with the special task of dealing with the *Uskoci* problem. He entered Senj at the head of imperial troops and proceeded to spectacularly execute several *Uskoci* leaders. His ruthless policy provoked a *Uskoci* revolt that cost him his life.

When the Habsburgs became involved in another war with Venice, the *Uskoci* regained their lost favor with Vienna and, with renewed vigor, and instigated attacks on the Republic's possessions and ships. In 1617 the Peace Treaty of Madrid put an end to the war between the Habsburgs and Venice. Consequently, the *Uskoci* were expelled from their stronghold, Senj, and began to settle around Otocac and Zumberak, which eventually to become incorporated into the Military Border.

*   *   *

The Protestant Reformation spread to Croatia from its neighboring Habsburg possessions. Although the Croatian nobility and clergy resisted the Protestant trend, by the end of the sixteenth century there were many noblemen and burghers who followed the teaching of the new creed. The chief contributor to the development of Protestantism was the former *Ban* of Croatia, Baron Christopher Ungnand, a Styrian nobleman who emigrated to Würtemberg, Germany, and there reunited around his person the various leaders of Croatian and Slovenian Protestantism. He bought a printing press and began to print Protestant books in the Croatian and Slovenian languages, using both Latin and Glagolitic characters for the Croatian books, but only Latin characters for the Slovenian books. The chief editors, writers and translators of these books were Primoz Trubar, a Slovenian priest, and the Croatian priests, Antun Dalmatin and Stjepan Konsul Istranin. They justified the more extensive publication of these books in the Croatian language by their conviction that Croatian was spoken to the very doorstep of Istanbul.

The most outstanding Protestant leader of Croatian origin was Matija Vlacic (Mathias Flacius Illyricus) although he did not belong to the Ungnad circle. His places of activity were the universities of Erfurt, Jena and Regensburg where he emerged as the leader of the radical wing of Protestantism which was in bitter opposition to the moderate, Philip Melanchton.

The books published in Germany found their way to Croatia due to Emperor Maximilian's toleration of the new religion.

Some of the Croatian nobility such as *Ban* Petar Erdody, *Ban* Nikola Zrinjski (the "hero of Sziget") and particularly his son, Juraj Zrinjski (who established a Croatian printing press at Nedelisce in Medjumurje in order to print Protestant literature), as well as Franjo Tahi, joined the new religion. Furthermore, the new religion found many sympathizers among the citizens of Zagreb, Varazdin, Koprivnica and some localities situated along the Adriatic coast. The most attractive aspects of the new religion were the use of the Croatian language and the permissibility of marriage for the priests. Even Mark Anthony De Dominis (Marko Antun Gospodnetic), former Bishop of Senj and Archbishop of Split, joined the Protestants. He made the court of James I of England the center of his activities for a period of time.

Protestant successes eventually alarmed the remaining clergy

103

and nobility and prompted Simun Bartulic, Bishop of Zagreb, to tender an invitation to the Jesuit Order to establish itself in Croatia. Furthermore, the *Sabor* voted a law into existence by which only the Roman Catholic religion was permitted in the country.

When the Hungarian Diet attempted to foster the spread of Protestantism in Croatia, as it already had in Hungary, the Croatian nobility resisted the move most vehemently. *Ban* Tomo Erdody expressed the feelings of the Croats this way: ". . . We shall extirpate this pest with sword in hand if ever it appears at our doorstep; we still have three rivers, the Drava, Sava and Kupa, from which we shall give drink to these unwelcome guests. . ."

Jesuit activities and the uncompromising attitude and energetic activities of the *Sabor* put an end to the attempt to spread Protestantism. As a consequence of Jesuit activities, a *kajkavska* literature developed in northern Croatia, while similar literatures developed elsewhere in the *stokavski* and *cakavski* dialects.

* * *

Emperor Mathias did not have children, thus the Habsburg title passed to the younger Styrian branch represented by Archduke Ferdinand. His father, Ferdinand, already was encouraging the Catholic counter-reformation and he instigated a relentless persecution of the Protestants living in his domain. Young Ferdinand received his education from the Jesuits and naturally continued his father's policy of hostility toward the Protestants. The prospect of having such a determined foe on the imperial throne made the Protestant leaders uneasy. Although Ferdinand was duly acknowledged as Mathias's successor and was crowned King of Bohemia in 1617, and King of Hungary and Croatia in 1618, his actual ascent to the throne provoked the Bohemian Protestant nobility to challenge his rule, thus starting the famous Thirty Years War. The Protestant leader of Hungary, Gabor Bethlen, Grand Duke of Transylvania, immediately joined the Bohemian nobility and challenged Ferdinand's right to rule Hungary.

The peace established along the Turkish border permitted Ferdinand to enlist the support of Croatian units for the German theatre of operation. Contemporary chroniclers record many atrocities committed against the population of Magdeburg after its downfall. Gustavus Adolphus, the "lion of the north," met death at the hands of Croatian troops at the Battle of Lutzen (1632). Croatian troops, consisting chiefly of light cavalry, were recruited by the young count, Juraj Zrinjski, who was suspected of being a Protestant. After his premature death (he was poisoned, allegedly by Wallenstein), these troops served under various professional soldiers such as Pappenheim, Isolani, John Werth, and Walter Leslie all of whom were international adventurers and mercenaries in either Wallenstein's or the Emperor's service.

*   *   *

The major part of the Croatian lands in Ottoman possession were left devastated and depopulated by the Turkish war. The new masters brought an enslaved Christian population, chiefly of the Greco-Orthodox faith, from Thrace, Macedonia and Serbia to settle on the vacated lands as *raja* or serfs. This population also was the source for irregular recruits who served in the border wars and who were known as *bashibozuk*. As they began plundering the countryside of Croatia they instilled terror in the hearts of the people.

The Habsburg generals were not long in recognizing the advantage in using the same methods against the Turks. Upon their invitation, this pillaging population moved across the vacated Croatian territory. They submitted directly to imperial authority and were granted special privileges, e.g. in religious practices, and were included in the military system established for the Military Border.

The Croatian nobility, on whose lands the new-comers settled, vainly attempted to assert its authority. The *Sabor* protested and complained to the Emperor, but ineffectually. In fact, Ferdinand II went even further by issuing a special charter which formally created the Military Border as a special territorial unit exempt from the authority of the *ban* and *Sabor* and under direct control of the imperial government in Vienna. The population of the Military Border was granted the right to elect its own local authorities and judges and, to satisfy the Greco-Orthodox population, was guaranteed religious freedom. This latter guarantee was an explicit contradiction to the decision of the Croatian *Sabor* (October 5, 1630).

As long as the Thirty Years War lasted, the Habsburgs were scrupulous in observing the stipulations of the Peace Treaty of Zitva-Torok with the Turks. The situation on the Croatian border, however, was exempt from these stipulations. The *bans* of Croatia and the *pashas* of Bosnia continued to exchange blows. It was during this period that the office of the *ban* became the exclusive privilege of the House of Count Zrinjski. The Zrinjskis, belonging to the oldest Croatian nobility, were rich, cultured and proud. They often exercised authority without Vienna's sanction. Thus clashes between the imperial generals in Croatia and the *bans* became inevitable.

Ferdinand III (1637-1657), while still involved in Germany, attempted to secure automatic succession for his son, Ferdinand IV. Toward this end he was able to enlist the support of the Hungarian and Croatian nobility in getting him recognized as king (1647-1654). Ferdinand died before his father and thus the royal title was of little meaning. His younger brother, originally destined for priesthood and thereby educated by Jesuits, succeeded the elder Ferdinand to the imperial throne as Leopold 1 (1657-1683).

Under Leopold's rule, the centralistic tendencies of the Viennese court predominated. Because he was bigoted and under the complete influence of his educators, Leopold surrounded himself with a camarilla and paid little attention to the wishes of his subjects. Moreover, he was constantly preoccupied with his relations to Louis XIV of France and the problem of Spanish succession. He did not have an adequate training in politics, but he had the good fortune of having the finest military leaders of Europe at the time in his service who corrected the disastrous effects of his policies.

When the Turks reopened hostilities over the Transylvanian issue, Raymond de Montecucculi, the imperial general, immediately achieved the upper hand. It was during this war that Count Nikola Zrinjski, *Ban* of Croatia, and his brother, Petar, won special military fame. But after Montecucculi's brilliant victory over the Turks in the battle of St. Gothard, Leopold unexpectedly signed the Peace Treaty of Vasvar which affirmed the status quo (1664). This act created great dissatisfaction among the Hungarian and Croatian nobility who expected the victorious war to be continued until all the territory under the Turks had been liberated.

As imperial policy aimed more and more to reduce the status of Croatia to that of Bohemia, i.e. to make it simply a Habsburg possession, it created additional dissatisfaction and unrest. Similar sentiments prevailed in Hungary as well. Moreover, the vexation prevaling in Croatia because of the highhanded policy of the imperial generals on the Military Border, as well as because of the unfulfilled hope of Zrinjski to become *ban* and commanding general of the Military Border simultaneously, form the background for what became known as the Zrinjski conspiracy.

In the beginning, the members of the Zrinjski conspiracy tried to impose on the Emperor observance of Article 31 of the *Golden Bull,* viz, respect for the constitutional rights of the nobility and for the territorial integrity of the country. *Ban* Nikola Zrinjski assumed the leadership of the movement. Although he was a Croat by origin and conviction he had become a leading poet in contemporary Hungarian literature. His second in command was his brother, Petar, who was an outstanding military leader and Croatian poet and writer in his own right. Petar's wife was Katarina, a Frankopan and also a poet; while her brother, Marquis Fran Krsto Frankopan, was the last member of the once famous and powerful lords of Krk, and a poet and translator of Moliere. The Hungarian nobility was represented in the conspiracy by such prominent personalities of public life as Francis Wesselenyi, Palatin of Hungary; Francis Nadasdyi, Supreme Judge of the Kingdom; and George Lipay, Archbishop of Estergom. Count Erasmus von Tattenbach represented the Styrian nobility.

The conspiracy remained within the constitutional bounds drawn out by the *Golden Bull.* It received a serious blow to its ambitions by the sudden death of Nikola Zrinjski whose cool head and clear judgment had kept it under control and in touch with reality. Nikola's brother, Petar, was duly appointed *Ban* of Croatia, but his expectation of also receiving the post of commanding general of the Military Border was unfulfilled. Thus he was ready to renew the conspiracy.

Petar was less experienced and more impetuous than his late brother. He grossly misjudged the international situation and was soon involved in a series of international intrigues that paved the way to his doom. By the intermediary of Louis XIV's ambassador in Vienna he established contact with the French king and offered him the crown of Croatia. When he did not receive an answer he turned to Michael Wisnievicky, King of Poland, who was at that moment courting Vienna for the hand of one of the Habsburg princesses. Wisnievicky politely declined to become involved in Petar's scheme. Moreover, Petar's attempt to enlist Venetian support for his plan proved futile. Finally, he sent his personal emmissary, Captain Franjo Bukovacki, to his old foe, the Turks, to secure the Porte's support in the event of military insurrection. Vienna was soon informed of Bukovacki's activities in Istanbul.

The overly optimistic Bukovacki had led Petar to believe that the Ottomans were ready to accept his proposal. He, therefore, with the help of his brother-in-law, Frankopan, began the ill-fated preparations for the insurrection. The imperial government forestalled his plan and dispatched an army to invade Croatia. This invasion was supported by the units of the Military Border. Petar discovered how precarious his situation was only when it was too late to rectify it. He decided to throw himself on Leopold's mercy. In the company of Frankopan, he set out for Vienna. At the same time, Leopold issued in the Croatian language a proclamation to the Croatian people which outlawed Zrinjski and Frankopan. It read in part: ". . . Count Petar Zrinjski had become a traitor to our crown by starting a rebellion with the aim of taking over our Kingdom of Croatia, Slavonia and Dalmatia. . ." Thus Zrinjski and Frankopan were intercepted by imperial order, put on trial for high treason, found guilty, had their possessions confiscated, and their families dispersed. On April 30, 1671, they were beheaded at Wiener Neustadt. Katarina Zrinjski was interned in a monastery in Graz where she died two years later.

The executions at Wiener Neustadt brought an end to the two most outstanding feudal families of Croatia. For centuries the Lords of Bribir (who were the later Counts of Zrinjski), and the Lords of Krk (who were the later Marquis of Frankopan), had played decisive roles in Croatian history. For a long time, members of their families held the position of *ban* as a family right. Their extinction brought an end not only to the independent magnates, but also prevented any attempt toward independence that the Croatian nobility could conceive. Moreover, there was no other single noble family of Croatia that could be compared to either the family of Zrinjski or Frankopan as representative of feudal Croatia. Thus the country's autonomy was undermined and the post of *ban* was left vacant for a decade. When a new *ban* was finally appointed, he was (as were his successors) selected from the Hungarian magnates who settled in Croatia. Therefore he was lacking in the spirit of independence and was thoroughly subservient to the wishes of Vienna.

CHAPTER IX

THE ERA OF HOPE FOR REVIVAL

*Peace Treaty of Karlovci — Pavao Ritter Vitezovic —
Pragmatic Sanction — Maria Theresa — Joseph II —
Beginning of the Hungaro-Croatian conflict — Impact
of the French Revolution.*

One of the primary causes of the Zrinjski conspiracy, i.e.
the war for liberation directed against the Turks, incidently
became the policy of Vienna. While Leopold had the war
with Louis XIV on his hands, Louis's ally, Sultan Mehmed IV,
invaded the Habsburg Empire, by sending his Grand Vizir Kuprili
to besiege Vienna. But due to the timely intervention of an
imperial army under Charles, Duke of Lorraine, as well as
that of the Polish army, under King Jan Sobiesky, the Turks
were decisively turned back at the gates of Vienna (1683). This
Christian victory was the turning point in the centuries old
struggle between the Habsburgs and the Ottomans. The Habsburgs turned from defensive action to an offensive aggressive-
ness that pressed the Ottomans into retreat. This dramatic
reversal brought about a general liberation of Hungarian territory, although at the same time there was only a partial liberation of Croatian lands.

When the imperial armies invaded the Turkish Empire, those
Croats of the Christian faith who had been living under Moslem
domination joined cause with the invaders. The leadership of

the insurgents fell to the local clergy. Luka Imbrisimovic, a Franciscan friar, carried out the liberation of Slavonia, while Luka Mesic, a parish priest, did likewise for Lika county in Southern Croatia.

When Prince Eugen of Savoy invaded the Balkans, the Serbian population responded enthusiastically to his call to them to rise up against their masters. However, he was soon recalled from the Balkans due to complications arising from the problem of Spanish succession. Thousands of Serbs, following their spiritual leader, Arsenije Carnojevic, joined the retreating imperial army rather than wait for the Turks to return. They eventually settled in parts of recently liberated eastern Croatia and Slavonia, as well as the southern part of Hungary (1690). These military operations were finally brought to an end with the Peace Treaty of Karlovci signed on January 26, 1699. At this time a new boundary along the Danube, Sava and Una Rivers was established.

During the campaign, the Croatian army, under the command of the *ban*, carried out successful operations in southern Croatia, but was later compelled by the Karlovci settlement to relinquish the liberated territory either to the Turks or to the Republic of Venice. Thus, while practically all of Hungary was liberated, the major part of the Croatian territory was left to Turkish and Venetian domination.

The successful war against the Turks raised new hopes in the Croats for complete liberation and reconstruction of Croatia. These hopes were expressed in the writings of Pavao Ritter-Vitezovic (1652-1713). He published a book in Zagreb (1700) called *Croatia rediviva* (Croatia revived) which was addressed to Leopold and suggested that he liberate all the Croatian lands: White Croatia, covering the territory situated along the Adriatic coast from the River Rasa in Istria to the town of Bar on the Albanian border; Mountain Croatia, covering the territory of Bosnia and Hercegovina, and Slavonia, the country situated within the boundaries of the Drava, Danube and Sava Rivers. He pointed out that the historical and geographic terms, Illyrian and Slavonian, are mere synonyms for the term Croatian. A few years later in *Bosnia Captiva* (Bosnia captive) he argued that Bosnia was historically simply a part of Croatia.

* * *

Joseph I (1705-1711) inherited not only the War of Spanish Succession from his father, but also a Protestant rebellion in Transylvania headed by Francis Rakoczy, Zrinjski's grandson. After Rakoczy's defeat, freedom and equality for both the Catholic and Protestant religions was granted to the territory of Hungary by the Peace Treaty of Szatmar (1711). The liberation of Hungary brought unexpected good fortune to the Hungarian nobility. When the Moslem landlords were expelled, their estates passed into the hands of the Hungarian magnates. Upon achieving this economic prosperity, these magnates began to re-establish the ancient rights and privileges they had enjoyed prior to the Turkish conquest of Hungary.

The Croatian nobility did not share the good fortune of the Hungarian magnates. The major part of what had formerly been Croatian territory continued to be controlled by either the Turks or the Venetians. Even the territory that had been liberated was not restored to the control of civil authority, but was absorbed into the Military Border. Moreover, the generous land grants in eastern Croatia were not returned to the descendants of the original Croatian owners, but given to foreign magnates most of whom were of Hungarian and German origin. Since many of these magnates had received similar land grants in Hungary, it was natural that they began making common cause with the Hungarian aristocracy.

The intrusion of those foreign magnates on Croatian soil soon produced a conflict between the Croatian *Sabor* and the Hungarian aristocracy, which dominated the Hungarian Diet. Even as early as 1708 the Hungarian Diet passed a bill with a provision that prohibited the Croatian *Sabor* from enacting laws that contradicted existing Hungarian laws. The Croats demurred and the Emperor supported them by refusing to sign the bill. (The issue in question was that of religious freedom established in Hungary by the Treaty of Szatmar, but rejected by the Croatian *Sabor*.) On this same occasion, the *Sabor* pressed its imperial advantage by requesting that the Bishopric of Zagreb be elevated to the status of an archbishopric.

Following Joseph's death, his brother, Charles III (1711-1740), renounced his claim to the Spanish throne in order to assume the imperial title. Charles was preoccupied with the problem of regular succession to the throne from the very beginning of his reign. Since he had no male heir, he kept busy attempting to secure succession for his daughter, Maria Theresa. Toward this end he sought the support and official recognition of the various legislative bodies of his kingdoms.

Even before Charles's coronation, the *Sabor* came forward in support of his ambition by voting for the *Pragmatic Sanction* which stated that Croatia ". . . would accept as her rulers members of a female branch of the Austrian House who would reside in Austria. . ." The *Sabor* declared further that ". . . Croatia as a kingdom was joined with Hungary, but without establishing common citizenship. We were not compelled by force to join Hungary. We accepted only her king and not the kingdom. We recognize the King of Hungary only if he is also the ruler of Austria and we have no intention of following Hungary's policies; we are free citizens and subjects to no one. . ."

The *Pragmatic Sanction* was effected by vote on March 11, 1712. Charles would use it to induce the diets of the lands of the Habsburg family to accept female succession as law. But when Charles attempted to secure this legislation from the Hungarian Diet it demurred, making the point that the Hungarian Diet alone had the right to decide on the question of succession (1715). Meanwhile Venice found herself involved in another war with the Turks. Charles was now free from his European entanglements and joined Venice. His army won the Battle of Petrovaradin under the leadership of Prince Eugen (1716), and a year later won the Battle of Belgrade. The Croatian army, whose operations were directed by the *ban*, liberated the larger part of western Bosnia. The Turks were forced to sign the Peace Treaty of Pozarevac on July 21, 1718. As a consequence, Austria received Belgrade, some territory in northern Serbia and all of northern Bosnia situated along the Sava River.

Charles turned once again to the question of succession. The *Pragmatic Sanction* was accepted by his possessions and, through diplomatic recognition, by various European powers. Hungary alone demurred. But after prolonged bargaining, the Hungarian Diet finally accepted it in 1722.

With his daughter's succession secured, Charles once more faced the Turkish problem. The last peace treaty proved to be merely a truce. A new war started. But Prince Eugen was dead and his successors piled one blunder upon another until they were defeated. Charles had to sign the Peace Treaty of Belgrade in 1739 in which he ceded Belgrade and all the territory south of the Danube and Sava Rivers to the Turks.

By virtue of the *Pragmatic Sanction,* Maria Theresa (1740-1780) followed Charles as Queen of Hungary, Bohemia and Croatia. For the time being, however, her husband Francis, Duke of Loraine, was denied the imperial title although it eventually was conferred on him (1745-1765).

Maria Theresa's rule began under unfavorable auspices. Although Frederick II of Prussia had accepted the *Pragmatic Sanction,* he seized the opportunity to invade the Austrian province of Silesia. This action resulted in a general war for Austrian succession from which Frederick emerged victorious (1741-1748). The Croats, who were loyal subjects of the Queen, were actively involved in this military operation. They participated as recruits for the regular army, or as the famous *Granicari* units from the Military Border, or as special irregular troops known as *Panduri* and recruited by the adventurer Baron Franjo Trenk. As Trenk's *Panduri* achieved general fame for their military and especially non-military exploits, Maria Theresa was forced to dissolve them due to general complaints, and, moreover, to commit their commander to life imprisonment in the Spielberg fortress in Moravia.

In her struggle with Frederick, Maria Theresa needed all the support she could get. In order to win additional support from the Croatian nobility she restored the civil authority of *ban* over three Slavonia *commitats* (Virovitica, Pozega and Srijem) and over the city and port of Rijeka. Simultaneously, she proceeded to reform the Croatian and Slavonian Military Border. It was put under the command of the general residing in Zagreb and was divided into eleven regiments (Lika, Otocac, Slunj, Ogulin, Petrinja, Glina, Krizevci, Djurdjevac, Novagradiska, Brod and Petrovaradin). Strict military discipline became the rule. Every male subject within the confines of the Military Border, from sixteen to sixty, was placed in the military organization. The usual capacity of the population toward the end of supporting this military project was 50,000 men.

However, in her treatment of Hungary and Croatia, Maria Theresa continued her father's policy which had been detrimental to the Croats in the distribution of land grants and in the establishment of civil authority over liberated territory. While nearly all of the liberated territory of Hungary was returned to civil authority, the largest part of the Croatian territory was absorbed by the Military Border.

A series of Habsburg wars directed against both Turkey and Prussia, placed a particularly heavy burden on the peasant population in terms of blood and money. Thus, several bloody insurrections occurred in the vicinity of Zagreb and Varazdin, and it was not without cruelty that the authorities were able to put them down. But when the unrest spread to the peasantry of the adjacent Military Border the central government in Vienna became seriously alarmed. Maria Theresa enacted several *Patents* and *Urbars* regulating the status of the serfs in Croatia and Slavonia. Moreover, she introduced some social and economic reforms into the government of the Military Border.

After the bitter disappointment of the Seven Years War, the Empress devoted her attention to the general political reorganization of her patrimony. The ultimate aim of these reforms was the transformation of the congregation of her kingdoms and lands, each with its special historical background, institutions, constitutions, and customs, into a modern and singularly centralized state. Due to her constant preoccupation with the conflict with Prussia, and the clash of interest among her different subject nationalities, she was compelled to move cautiously. The most outspoken and powerful opposition to her reforms came from the Hungarian nobility which was also the most conscious of its national and historical rights and privileges. The Croatian nobility followed the Hungarian example. In order to win them over, Maria Theresa created the Order of St. Stephen and the College of *Theresianum,* both reserved exclusively for the Hungarian and Croatian nobility. Furthermore, in order to flatter Hungarian pride, she added the expression "the Apostolic King of Hungary" to her title in 1758.

After Emperor Francis's death, Joseph II (1765-1790) assumed the imperial title and thereby became his mother's co-ruler. His rule was empty of all content although it carried the imperial title, since Maria Theresa retained full control over the Habsburg lands as well as Hungary and Croatia. In pursuing her reforms, Maria Theresa replaced the traditional Croatian government with a Royal Council consisting of a *ban,* six councelors and two secretaries, all directly appointed by the Queen (1767). Due to Hungarian opposition this experiment was short-lived. The Croatian Royal Council was abolished and Croatian affairs were joined to those of Hungary and thereby put under the supervision of the Hungarian Royal Council (1779). Thus, for the first time, Croatia was subject to the control of the Hungarian government.

Although Joseph II became his mother's co-ruler, she did not trust his advanced thinking about government and kept him from making any decisions about policy. As Emperor, he was for all practical purposes powerless and had to bide his time until his mother's death when he became King of Hungary, Bohemia and Croatia, and ruler of the Habsburg family lands (1780).

Joseph possessed an engaging personality, a powerful mind, and a sense of humor and satire. He liked to think of himself as an enlightened despot. His idea was to emulate his older contemporary, Frederick II of Prussia, and after his fashion become "the first servant of the country." In following the tradition of his family, he was bound to practice the policy of unlimited Imperial power. This was possible only by transforming the age-old and complicated diversity of his kingdoms and lands into a single highly centralized and unique country. Following the contemporary trend, he did away with the traditional Latin language as the official language of his possessions and replaced it with modern German. His foremost task, then, was to impose the German language on his non-German subjects. But besides this, he had traveled extensively in his future domains during his mother's lifetime and he had at that time become acquainted with the most pressing problems and needs of the populations. Consequently he prepared a long list of political, religious, cultural, social and economic reforms that he would set as goals for his reign.

When Joseph ascended the throne, he forewent the traditional ceremony of coronation and ordered the Crown of St. Stephen, i.e. the crown of Hungary and Croatia, to be placed among the family jewels. At the same time, he published a decree of religious tolerance, granting to the Jews, among others, complete freedom for their religious practices as well as the rights of full citizenship. However, he did impose on them the use of the German language instead of their own Yiddish or Hebrew and he compelled them to germanize their names (1781).

Joseph carried out such an extensive reformation of the Catholic Church on his domains that he became known as a "sacristan". By these Josephinian reforms, the church achieved considerable independence from Rome and the Emperor himself asserted the right to appoint all church dignitaries strictly on the basis of their "merits and spotless morality." This reform prevented the highest posts in the church hierarchy from continuing to be the exclusive privilege of the well-born. Moreover, since the Society of Jesus was already dissolved by papal order in 1773, Joseph decided to dissolve all ecclesiastical orders and monasteries that were not actively engaged in education or health and hospitalization services. This decree applied to the Order of St. Paul with its famous monasteries at Lepoglava and Remete as well as to the monastery of Clarissa in Zagreb. For centuries, the monastery at Lepoglava was a leading center for learning and the arts. Its Paulian university and library were transferred to Vienna by Imperial order. Eventually, the monastery buildings were transformed into a modern penitentiary.

The Imperial *Patent* of 1784 introduced the German language as the only official language of the monarchy. The assemblies of the Croatian *commitats* protested vehemently against this act and refused to comply with it. Already the germanization sponsored by Maria Theresa and especially by Joseph's latest act was bringing abuot a revival of national spirit among the different non-German nationalities of the empire. The Hungarian nobility set the pace and was soon followed by the Croats. Both became particularly outraged when Joseph simply abolished all existing constitutional institutions and divided Hungary and Croatia into ten administrative circles. The Croatian *commitats* formed a circle that was administered from Zagreb by a *ban* who served as an Imperial commissary; the Slavonian and Hungarian *commitats* formed a circle that was ruled from Pecs.

Joseph was careful to appoint some of the younger enthusiasts who shared his ideas to the highest positions of his administration. Baron Franjo Balassa, the former head of the *Commitat* of Zagreb, was appointed the new *ban* and Maksimilijan Vrhovac, an enlightened young clergyman, received the post of Bishop of Zagreb.

Joseph had nurtured his ideas for a long time and was now in a hurry to apply them. One *Patent* followed another in stupendous speed. The Imperial *Patent* of August 25, 1785, abolished serfdom altogether in the entire territory of the Empire. The measure was so hastily drawn up that it failed to provide the liberated peasants with land and therefore created the climate for a multitude of conflicts and insurrections. But the most far-reaching reforms involved the general area of justice and the judicial system. The medieval concept of justice with its use of torture and its frequent recourse to the death penalty was replaced by the modern concept which abolished torture altogether and retained the death penalty for only a few major crimes.

Too impatient to prepare the ground for his reforms, Joseph neglected to win over a substantial part of the privileged classes and their representative institutions. Dissatisfaction and a readiness to resist spread throughout the country. When, on the question of education, Joseph provoked the resistance of the clergy in Belgium, they joined the nobility in general opposition to his reforms. In order to get rid of this troublesome Belgian problem and achieve better geographic unity for his possessions, Joseph tried to exchange Belgium for Bavaria. However, this incursion into the field of international policy was unsuccessful because of French and Prussian opposition. He therefore turned his attention to the Eastern Question.

During his visit to Catherine II of Russia, Joseph negotiated the division of the European territory of the Ottoman Empire with her. Thus he began a war with Turkey in 1787 in order to implement this preconceived plan. However, his army did not function according to his expectations, and the Turks' strength exceeded his calculations. What had been anticipated as a short skirmish deteriorated into a long, disastrous war. The fact that Joseph was suffering from bad health, involved in a hopeless war and faced with general unrest at home, i.e. the conspiracy of the clergy and the nobility and the resistance of the different nationalities to his enforced germanization, forced him on his death bed to revoke all of his reforms, except for the one granting personal freedom to the serfs.

*　　*　　*

Joseph's brother and successor, Leopold II, had achieved a deserved reputation as an enlightened despot when he was the Grand Duke of Tuscany, but he was more cautious than his late brother. His short rule (1790-1792) was initially faced with a very difficult situation both at home and abroad. The disaster of the Turkish war and the spectre of the French Revolution prompted him to attempt a policy that would pacify his subjects as quickly as possible. He nullified the *Patent* freeing the serfs, despite its manifold consequences. He called into session both the Hungarian Diet and the Croatian *Sabor*, neither of which had convened under Joseph's rule.

The Hungarian nobility immediately initiated an attack. In reaction to Josephinian germanization, they produced a frenetic propaganda for Magyar nationalism. At the sessions of their Diet developed an extremist program of Magyar nationalism that declared that there was ". . . one God, one King, one Magyar nation, one Magyar national language covering all the territory from the Carpathian Mountains to the Adriatic sea. . ." This territory included Croatia. Thus the Magyar aim was the transformation of the existing Hungaro-Croatian commonwealth into a single and united Magyar Kingdom with the Magyar language as the only official language.

The Croatian legates at the Hungarian Diet protested against the program and the Croatian *Sabor* answered the Magyar pretensions by implementing Latin as the official language of their country. However, the Croatian position was weakened by the earlier decision of Maria Theresa, as well as the earlier attitude of the Croatian nobility, in establishing closer ties with Hungary for the resistance of Vienna's germanization policy. Thus, when the *Sabor* met on May 12, 1790, under the presidency of the *ban*, Count Ivan Erdody, it voted a resolution favoring the establishment of separate governments for Hungary and Croatia in order to compel respect for tradition and the law: ". . . the common government would last until the ultimate liberation of Croatian territory from Turkish and Venetian rule at which time Croatia would have her own government; until such a time, the Croatian authority and *commitats* are willing to accept the direction emanating from the Hungarian government. . ." By this resolution, the Croatian nobility virtually sanctioned Maria Theresa's act of 1779 which had put Croatia under the control of the Hungarian government. (The territory to be liberated, referred to above, was the so-called "Turkish Croatia," i.e. western Bosnia to the Vrbas River, the Sava River Valley in northern Bosnia, western Hercegovina to the Neretva River, and the Venetian Province of Dalmatia which included the Adriatic islands.)

The *Sabor* elected two legates to represent it in the upcoming Hungarian Diet and to assist the *ban* in dealing with this self-interested administration. In the first session, a bill was introduced making the Magyar language the only official language in both Hungary and Croatia. Another bill requested the establishment of religious equality for both Catholics and Protestants in Croatia. A resolution was presented aiming at the direct incorporation into Hungary of the three Slavonian commitats, i.e. Virovitica, Pozega and Srijem. The Croats resisted all Hungarian demands and *Ban* Erdody attempted to nullify them with the statement: ". . . *regno regni non prescribit leges. . .*" (One kingdom does not make laws for another.)

The Hungarian Diet had met, as dictated by tradition, at Pressburg and it was characterized by conflicts between Leopold II and the Hungarian nobility. Seeking the Diet's support,

Leopold tried to salvage some of Joseph's reforms, but the nobility stubbornly resisted. It based its opposition, as it had its attempts at magyarization, on the traditional feudal system and the Hungarian constitution. The Croats, however, while accepting Hungarian rule for common affairs, emphasized their demand for Hungarian respect of their autonomy in all domestic affairs.

When the *Sabor* met again in 1791, it capitulated to the Hungarian demands by voting for a resolution showing its willingness to introduce the Magyar language as a non-compulsory subject in the Croatian schools. But this resolution was never put into practice.

Emperor Leopold was at the time facing problems created by the French Revolution and was prompted to end his war with Turkey. On the basis of *status quo ante bellum*, he signed the Peace Treaty of Svistova (August 4, 1791).

Leopold's son and successor, Francis I (1792-1835), had little in common with his enlightened father. He was conservative by education and a firm believer in the principles of Imperial absolutism, beliefs that were reinforced for him by the excesses of the French Revolution. He despised the aristocracy and was a staunch supporter of Roman Catholicism. Taciturn, serious, inflexible, hard working, conscientious, but of limited intelligence, he became more and more the sworn enemy of revolutionary ideas. He used every means to combat them.

As enlightened ideas began to take root among the former subjects of Francis's uncle, Joseph, some of the more zealous recipients attempted to carry then through to their ultimate conclusion. One such zealot, Abbot Ignjat Martinovic, professor and erudite, formed a secret society whose activities had ramifications in both Hungary and Croatia. The government put a swift end to this society, trying Martinovic and his associates for high treason and executing them.

* * *

Austria was soon involved in the long wars of the French

Revolution and with the subsequent wars with Napoleon. Croatia was involved in a substantial share of these conflicts. As Imperial soldiers in the regular army, and especially as *Granicari,* the Croats found their way to all European battlefields. For instance, they were present at Dego and Arcole, where Napoleon took the first victories that ultimately led to the signing of the Peace Treaty of Campoformio on October 17, 1797. This treaty was to have profound influence on the future of Croatia.

By the stipulations of the Treaty of Campoformio, Austria exchanged her possession in the Netherlands, i.e. Belgium, for the former Venetian provinces of Istria and Dalmatia, both ancient Croatian lands. Upon receiving the news of the departure of the Republic of Venice from Istria and Dalmatia and the annexation of these provinces to Austria, a special delegation of Dalmatian Croats consisting of Count Draganic Vrancic, Archbishop Cippico, Bishops Blaskovic and Dorotic, the Greco Orthodox Bishop Zelic, and a score of other prominent personalities, went to Vienna to request the reunification of Dalmatia with Croatia. This request was renewed once Austria came to virtually occupy Dalmatia.

The occupation of Dalmatia was entrusted to General Matija Rukavina who was a Croat. He recommended the reunification of Dalmatia with Croatia, but Count Thugut, the Imperial Chancellor, had other ideas. He deprived Rukavina of all political authority in civilian matters. Then he appointed a special civil governor for the province whose task was to win the Italian minority over to his policies at the expense of the sentiments of the Croatian majority. The Italians, although representing no more than five percent of the population, were in a dominating position; therefore it was to the Austrian authority's interest to secure their support.

Following the Battle of Austerlitz, Francis signed the Peace Treaty of Pressburg in which he ceded Dalmatia to Napoleon (1805). French troops under General Molitor replaced the Austrian occupiers. However, Russia was still at war, and the

Russian fleet was in possession of Boka Kotorska and the Island of Korcula. In order to approach Boka Kotorska, the French had to cross the territory of the Republic of Dubrovnik. General Lauriston, the commander of the expedition, presented an ultimatum for free passage through the Republic. The Grand Council which was the governing body of the Republic had no choice but to yield. Consequental to this French intrusion, Napoleon published an ordinance decreeing the end of the Republic (May 26, 1806). After centuries of an independent and oftentimes glorious existence, it ceased to exist entirely and its territory was incorporated into the French Province of Dalmatia and later into the Illyrian Provinces. The French ousted the Russians from Boka Kotorska, but since the French had no navy, the Russians retained Korcula until the Peace Treaty of Tilsit deprived them of it (1808).

After taking Dalmatia, the Republic of Dubrovnik and Boka Kotorska, Napoleon put them under the authority of a single governor. Marshall Augustin Marmont, his favorite, became governor, assuming the title of Duke of Raguse (Dubrovnik). Marmont set out at once to provide for a modern government. Toward this end he introduced the French legal system and form of administration as they had developed out of the French Revolution. Immediately upon taking his position, he issued a public proclamation written in the Italian and Croatian languages announcing the beginning of French rule.

Marmont assigned the task of organizing the civil administration to Vincenze Dandolo, a Venetian nobleman who was imbued with the Jacobin spirit. He began by publishing a weekly paper in both Italian and Croatian under the name of *Il regio Dalmata — Kraglski Dalmatin*. The first issue appeared on July 12, 1806, and thereby became the first periodical ever published in the Croatian language.

Dalmatia was directly incorporated into the Empire and her administration was put under the supervision of Eugene de Beauharnais, the Vice-Roy of Italy. The new authority immediately introduced the French administrative, legal and social system. Serfdom was abolished and a subsequent legal equality instituted. A general educational system which employed the Croatian, Italian and French languages was introduced. Dalmatia was the first of the Croatian lands to enjoy these and other fruits of the French Revolution. The French initiated the construction of public buildings, schools, hospitals, roads, canals and the drainage of marshes. They also conducted the digging of water wells in the stony and dry backcountry.

But while Dalmatia was benefiting from the French administration, civil Croatia was struggling under the weight of magyarization. The Croatian nobility resisted stubbornly, clinging to the Latin language as a symbol of the country's independence and equality.

Meanwhile, Austria was involved in a disastrous war. Napoleon occupied Vienna and from that vantage point was able to dictate the harsh conditions of the Peace Treaty of Schoenbrun (October 14, 1809). By the terms of the treaty, Francis I was compelled to cede to Napoleon all of southern Croatia to the Sava River and, in fact, to the very doorstep of Zagreb, as well as the provinces of Istria, Gorizia, Gradisca, Carniola, Carinthia and the City and Port of Trieste. Napoleon then formed a new political unit called the Illyrian Provinces with the capital city of Ljubljana. Marshall Marmont, Duke of Raguse, was appointed governor. The territory was divided into these six provinces: Croatia, Dalmatia, Dubrovnik, Littoral, Carinthia and Carniola. A special unit, Military Croatia, was made from the territory of the Military Border.

The French policy for the Illyrian Provinces was similar to that already in effect for Dalmatia. Legal equality, compulsory general education in the national language and many economic and social reforms were introduced. Napoleon, however, retained the Military Border for himself, using its military capacity in many of his exploits. During the invasion of Russia, Croatian units from the Military Border achieved considerable distinction in his Grand Army. This was particularly true during the retreat, when, with the Swiss units, they were Marshall Ney's rear guard at the crosssing of the Berezina River.

With Napoleon's collapse in Russia, Austria once again joined the Great Coalition, and her army proceeded to occupy the Illyrian Provinces. This occupation was duly legalized by the Congress of Vienna. Austrian authorities put an end to French reforms, but did not revert to the ancient political order. Francis I used his domination of the Illyrian Provinces as a pretext to add the name of King of Illyria to his title. It was not until 1822 that the Croatian part of these provinces was returned to its mother country.

Following the Congress of Vienna, the Austrian government embarked on a policy aimed at preventing the recurrence of liberal political agitation within her various subject nationalities. The main tools of this policy were the strict supervision of education and a stringent press censorship. As a consequence, neither the Hungarian Diet nor the Croatian *Sabor* were called into session.

*   *   *

Croatia suffered fateful changes during the Habsburg era, i.e. the years from 1527 to 1815. Through the election of a *Sabor* at Cetin, the Habsburgs ascended the Croatian throne. From the beginning of their rule they sought to reduce Croatia to the status of a family possession. This tendency became more obvious with time. Croatia was gradually, but certainly, losing the characteristics of a separate political body. By the end of the eighteenth century, her autonomy was so restricted and reduced that it was virtually annihilated. In fact, Croatia became at this time a virtual dependent of Hungary.

Because of Turkish and Venetian conquests, Croatian territory dwindled from some 30,000 square miles to 5,000 square miles, a fact which caused the Croatian *Sabor* to sadly call its homeland the *reliquiae reliquiarum*. Furthermore, a considerable portion of the country was exempted from Croatian rule and integrated into the Military Border which was being administered directly from Vienna. The liberation of Slavonia only slightly improved the territorial extent of the country.

The nobility and the orders, which were the substance of the political life, had already paid a heavy price at the Battle of Krbava, a price from which they never recuperated. The remnant of the battle was expelled from Turkish lands and impoverished, and thereby never again attained any significant influence in public affairs. The role of the magnates became preponderant. When the two most powerful Croatian noble families, the Zrinjskis and the Frankopans, were rendered extinct by the execution in Wiener Neustadt in 1671, even the post of *ban,* which hitherto had been more or less the right and privilege of these families, lost its luster and substantial meaning. This position fell to those who were the supporters of Vienna's policies, practically all of whom were of Hungarian origin. It was, therefore, natural that for a century and a half, the *bans* paid only limited attention to the exercising of Croatian political will. When they did so, it was always in intimate relation to the attitude of the Hungarian nobility of which they were a part.

After the liberation of Slavonia, the influence of the Hungarian nobility increased, since the large estates were granted to them or to German aristocrats to whom the Habsburgs were indebted in one form or another. In political issues, the lesser nobility followed the example of the magnates.

The middle class was numerically insignificant. Its population was limited to five or six free royal towns and a considerable percentage of it was of foreign origin. It consisted of Germans in Slavonia and of Italians, or at least the italianized, in Dalmatia and on the Littoral.

Since the Protestant movement was short-lived, the announced renewal of the general use of the Croatian language did not materialize. The Catholic counter-reformation brought several gymnasiums and a university to Croatia (1699), but these institutions were of a cosmopolitan character.

Roman Catholicism was the official religion of the country, but its hierarchy was dominated by members of the nobility who were often of foreign origin and who therefore did not significantly contribute to the preservation and development of a genuine national culture. Nevertheless, the cultural contribution of the Croats outstripped the political stagnation. (See the chapter dealing with literature and the arts.)

In spite of the official status of the Roman Catholic Church, the Serbian Orthodox Church enjoyed special rights and privileges in the territory of the Military Border, and became the bearer of Serbian nationalism.

The destiny of the peasantry was particularly tragic. From the fourteenth century, when serfdom received legal status, the situation of the peasants became increasingly aggravated. They were frequently driven to despair, and in their despair they frequently revolted. But none of these revolts could be compared to the revolt of Matija Gubec in the sixteenth century. The Habsburgs were finally forced to intervene to alleviate the unbearable condition of the peasants. Joseph II went so far as to abolish serfdom in his attempt to rectify the situation, but this attempt was short-lived. The same thing happened to the Napoleonic reforms in the Illyrian Provinces when the Congress of Vienna re-established the ancient order.

The Croats entered the nineteenth century divided into several political bodies, viz. Croatia, Slavonia, the Military Croatian and Slavonian Borders, Dalmatia and Istria, all of which were under Austrian rule. Bosnia and Hercegovina still languished under the Turkish yoke. Nevertheless signs of new ideas and tendencies which would bring about the renewal of national identity manifested themselves here and there.

CHAPTER X

NATIONAL AWAKENING

Impact of the French Revolution — Revival of historicism — Metternich system — Magyar nationalism — Croatian reaction — Illyrian movement.

The Napoleonic armies spread the spirit of the French Revolution over all of Europe and awakened the various European nationalities to the new concept of public and national life known as nationalism. This general awakening occurred for the numerous nationalities under the Habsburgs as well. Following the example of the Italians and Germans, the Magyars were among the first to assert their own national identity. They had already done so in their opposition to Emperor Joseph II's reforms and his attempted centralization and germanization. At that time the Hungarian nobility based its opposition on the historic rights and constitutional privileges granted to them by the *Bulla aurea*.

The Hungarian nobility was the only nobility within the Habsburg realms that developed a spirit of independence combined with sufficient economic backing. It was determined to assert and preserve its exclusive political right in Hungary. Moreover, it insisted on becoming the nation itself. Thus, at the beginning of the nineteenth century the nascent modern Magyar nationalism assumed the aspect of a confusing mixture of an historically founded aristocratic exclusivism together with the romantic verbiage of modern liberalism. The extremists proposed the goal of a single Magyar nation stretching from the Carpathian Mountains to the Adriatic Sea. This was their proclamation: "There is one God in heaven, there is a single Kingdom of Hungary, and there is a single Magyar nation." The nationalities associated with Hungary, i.e. the Croats, Germans, Slovaks, Serbs, Rumanians and Ukrainians, must lose their identity and become Magyars pure and simple, even though they outnumber the Magyars. In a somewhat free interpretation of historical and jurisdictional facts and recent political events, the Magyar nationalists included the "sisterly Kingdom of Croatia, Slavonia and Dalmatia" in the projected Magyar kingdom, denying the Croats the same rights they claimed for themselves. It is natural to expect that Croats would react to Magyar pretensions.

* * *

The beginning of Croatian nationalism can be traced back to Pavao Ritter Vitezovic (1652-1719). The French occupation of southern Croatia and Dalmatia and the subsequent formation of the Illyrian Provinces revived the dormant spirit of national consciousness. But the militant Croatian nationalism of the nineteenth century was the direct answer by the lesser nobility and the educated younger generation to Magyar pretensions toward Croatia.

Since the destruction of the Zrinjski and Frankopan families, Croatia was left with practically no national aristocracy. The existing higher nobility was either of foreign origin or cosmopolitan in outlook and did not embrace the cause of Croatian nationalism in the same spirit that the Hungarian aristocracy had embraced the Magyar cause. The Croatian nobility entered the ensuing bitter contest greatly handicapped. Its numbers were limited and poor and it believed that its best defense was the preservation of established institutions and the Latin language. The Magyars insisted on replacing the Latin with their own language.

Croatia's situation in comparison to Hungary's was extremely weak and precarious. While Hungary achieved liberation and geographical and political unification (by the Peace Treaty of Karlovci in 1699), Croatia was still split into different sovereignties and regimes. The central Croatian lands, i.e. Turkish Croatia, were the part of Bosnia under Turkish rule, while Dalmatia and Istria had been simply incorporated into Austria as Habsburg family provinces. Croatia, or the Kingdom of Croatia and Slavonia, lost nearly half of her territory in the creation of the special political unit known as the Croatian-Slavonian Military Border. The territory put under the civil authority of the *ban* consisted of the *commitats* of Zagreb, Rijeka, Varazdin, Krizevci, Virovitica, Pozega and Srijem. Especially in the last three of these lands, the Hungarian nobility received considerably large land grants, and while residing on them forwarded claims on the territory in the name of Magyar nationalism.

During Napoleon's rule and with the establishment of the Illyrian Provinces, the use of the ancient geographical term, Illyrian, (still used by the Roman curia) emerged. Thus in the vocabulary of the French, not only the Illyrian Provinces, but also Habsburg Croatia and Ottoman Bosnia, were included under this name. Some of the young Croatian intellectuals who were educated in the Illyrian Provinces accepted the term with a ready understanding of its liberal and revolutionary implications. The term was eventually accepted by the Croatian nationalists. By this acceptance, the Croats inaugurated a confusing and dangerous gamble of systematic de-croatization in favor of, first of all, Illyrianism, then Pan-slavism, and ultimately Yugoslavism.

The Croatian situation was very difficult indeed. Thus there is little wonder that the ephemeral political leaders were undecided about the direction the country's policy should take. The official attitude and practice of Vienna contributed greatly to this dilemma.

Francis I (1793-1835) had not called either the Croatian *Sabor* or the Hungarian Diet into session since 1811. The basis for his government was the army, diplomacy, the secret police, the Catholic hierarchy and the aristocracy. Education was placed under the strictest control in which the study of such innocent topics as music and singing was encouraged to the neglect of history, philosophy and political science. An equally strict censorship of the press prevented the publication of dangerous politically democratic and liberal ideas. Thus, for all practical purposes the political or public life of the entire empire was brought to a complete standstill. Absurdly enough, despite his absolute power, the emperor was unable to raise new recruits for the army without the approval and active cooperation of the Hungarian and Croatian *commitat* assemblies.

When the liberal insurrections took place in Italy and Spain in 1820, the emperor needed 30,000 additional recruits which were to be drafted from Hungary and Croatia. The *commitats* demurred, pointing out that only the Hungarian Diet, or the Croatian *Sabor,* could order them to proceed with the enlistment of recruits. As the international situation became pressing, Francis had no choice but to call the Hungarian Diet into session (1823). The politically minded Hungarian leaders seized the opportunity to press their demands for the magyarization of Hungary by voting to replace the Latin with the Magyar language as the official language of the entire territory. The special delegation of the Croatian *Sabor* at the Hungarian Diet supported the Magyar demands and expressed its desire for the introduction of the Magyar language into Croatian schools, as well as for a non-compulsory class which would enable the young generation to learn that language. The Croatian *Sabor* duly acknowledged this wish. By this vote the Magyar nationalists achieved their greatest success in Croatia, and this with the consent of the Croats themselves.

Although it appeared that the Magyars had achieved a decisive triumph over the resistance of the Croatian nobility, which was protecting the Latin language, they still had to face the more determined challenge of nascent Croatian nationalism. The leaders of the new Croatian nationalism were generally mem-

134

bers of the younger generation who were educated in the French ideas at the Zagreb Academy of Law. Also, some of them were university students from Graz or Vienna.

For several years these young Croatians witnessed the revival of national consciousness among the Germans, Italians, Magyars and Czechs, and such examples attracted them with irresistible force. When the Magyars came out with their ultimate nationalistic program which consisted of the transformation of Hungary into a national Magyar state, an equally radical nationalistic movement among the Croats was the inevitable answer. These tendencies received additional fuel from the July Revolution in France (1830) which inspired currents of national, liberal and democratic ideas all over Europe. Both the Magyars and the Croats passed from limited and private intellectual squabbles to public and explicitly political agitation.

However, the Croats did not have an outstanding personality to assume the leadership of the movement. Thus, the lead fell to Ljudevit Gaj, a student of law at the universities of Graz and Budapest, since he was the most ambitious and active of the Croat nationalists. While studying in Prague, Gaj fell under the influence of the Slovak, Jan Safaryk, who was a Lutheran minister. Safaryk was educated in the school of Johann Gottfried Herder, the German philosopher of the romantic *Sturm und Drang* period who, on the sidelines, was something of a "father" to modern Pan-slavism.

Safaryk became the friend of Vuk Stefanovic Karadzic, a self-educated Serb, collector of folklore, and official of the Austrian censorship. Through Safaryk, Gaj became acquainted with the popular poetry of the Serbs and Croats that Stefanovic had collected. This gave him a sense of pride in his native tongue. With several of his student friends at the University of Graz, he formed a cultural association by the name of the Illyrian Club. The moving spirit of the club was Gaj himself, and his position became even more prominent when in 1832 he published a pamphlet in

Budapest called *Kratka osnova* (A short exposition of the foundation of the Croatian and Slavonian language).

In his pamphlet, Gaj proposed the introduction of new spelling rules for the Croatian language based on the adoption of diacritic signs for the Latin alphabet, a reform similar to that introduced into the Czech language. Furthermore, he advocated exchanging the term, Croatian, in favor of Illyrian. With the publication of this pamphlet, Gaj became the undisputed authority among his friends in the field of linguistics. That same year another member of his circle, Ivan Derkos, wrote a pamphlet entitled *Genius patriae* which proposed the adoption of a single literary dialect for all the Croatian lands, viz. Croatia, Slavonia, Dalmatia and Istria.

Gaj's circle was an exclusive association of younger men, chiefly students. The only member of the older generation to join the movement was Count Janko Draskovic, a scion of an old Croatian aristocratic family. He was educated in the spirit of the French Encyclopedists and had received his political baptism in his younger years as a student in the Paris of the French Revolution. He was known by the Austrian police agents in Zagreb as a "Jacobin".

Draskovic wrote the first modern Croatian political program in the form of a pamphlet entitled *Disertacija* and addressed it to the members of the *Sabor's* delegation to the Hungaro-Croatian Diet. Opposing the Magyar nationalists who wished to transform Hungary into a single national Magyar kingdom, he advocated the reassertion of the independent Kingdom of Croatia with its own independent government combined with the introduction of Illyrian as the official language. He also put forward his idea for the general reorganization of the Habsburg Empire into a federation which would grant to all its nationalities independent and equal status.

Like many of the European liberals of the time, Draskovic was a great admirer of British parliamentarian institutions and thought they should serve as the example for future constitutional and political development in his native country.

For many politicians of the time *Anglia docet* became a favorite panacea for all the ills afflicting humanity, and in the case of Draskovic, especially for those afflicting his homeland.

* * *

The Magyar nationalists were celebrating the easy victory over the conservative element among the Croatians (it had accepted the Magyar language for the Croatian schools), when the new *Sabor* brought the premature jubilation tumbling to the ground. It nullified the previous decision and accepted the general outline of Draskovic's program. This new spirit became even more manifest when General Juraj Rukavina, the newly elected Captain of the Kingdom, delivered his acceptance speech to the *Sabor* in the Croatian language. This was the first speech delivered in the Croatian tongue; heretofore all speeches and records were in Latin.

Following Rukavina's election, the *Sabor* elected its delegation to the Hungaro-Croatian Diet: Draskovic was elected delegate to the Upper House and Herman Buzan and Antun Kukuljevic were elected delegates to the Lower House. Furthermore, in case of the Diet's unwillingness to accept the *Sabor's* requests, the *Sabor* voted special instructions to the delegation. They were to leave the Diet and return home immediately, for ". . . the Kingdom of Croatia will be able to assert its rights by its own will . . ."

The Croats followed the example of the French Revolution in forming different political and cultural clubs. Draskovic presided over the foundation of one such club in 1838. It was a literary association called *Citaonica*. This association would gradually develop into the *Matica Hrvatska,* a patriotic society for the publication and dissemination of books written in the Croatian language.

From the economic point of view, Croatia was dominated

by both Vienna and Budapest. In order to promote an independent economic development for the nation, in 1838 Draskovic sponsored the formation of the *Gospodarsko drustvo* (Economic Society) whose aim was to promote economic development in the country, especially in the area of agriculture. This was just one more way in which Draskovic assumed responsibility for prodding awake national consciousness and spreading it among all of the populations covered by the mystic Illyrian name.

But the more radical popularization of the idea, with an appropiate political and social organization, fell to the younger and more ambitious Gaj. He wrote the patriotic poem, *Jos Hrvatska nij propala* (Croatia has not yet perished), which for a time served as the rallying anthem for the Croatian patriots.

*   *   *

Following Emperor Francis's death, his son Ferdinand V (1835-1848) ascended the throne. By nature, Ferdinand was of limited intelligence, easy-going and unable to exercise imperial and royal prerogatives. Thus, a special imperial regency was created. It was presided over by Ferdinand's brothers, Archduke Ludwig and Archduke Francis Charles, but the dominating personality was Prince Metternich.

The Hungaro-Croatian Diet was still in session when the change of rulers occurred. At this time the Hungarian representatives voted in a law introducing the Magyar language into Croatian schools despite the most energetic opposition of the Croatian delegation. The Croats immediately protested to the King. Following Metternich's advice, Ferdinand refused to sanction it. In the bitter and tumultuous deliberations that ensued, Buzan, speaking in the name of the Croatian delegation, declared his country's determination to use all available legal means to maintain Croatia's national identity. Henceforth, maintained Buzan, the Croats would fight, not for the use of the Latin language, but for the introduction of the Croatian language as the official language of Croatia's public life.

At the close of the session of the Diet (May 2, 1836), the

Magyar and Croatian nobilities separated as bitter enemies for the first time in nearly seven centuries of close cooperation within the Hungaro-Croatian Commonwealth.

* * *

Vienna was watching the Magyar and Croatian conflict with great amusement, giving support from time to the weaker party. Metternich was willing to listen to the advice of the conservative Croatian aristocracy which was opposed to the overbearing Magyar nationalism and inclined to help the struggling Croatian nationalists. By the intermediary of these aristocrats, Gaj was able to secure royal permission from Metternich to publish in Zagreb a political paper and a literary magazine in the Croatian language. This permission was granted on June 15, 1834, despite the opposition of the Hungarian government. Consequently, on January 1, 1835, the first issue of the *Novine Horvatzke* (The Croatian Gazette) and the literary magazine, *Danica Horvatzka, Slavonska i Dalmatinska* (The Croatian, Slavonian and Dalmatian Morningstar) appeared in Zagreb. For the first year, both publications used the local *kajkavski* dialect which was spoken in Zagreb and northern Croatia. But the next year the *stokavski* dialect was adopted because it was common to the majority of Croats and Serbs as well. The name was then changed from Croatian to Illyrian.

* * *

The next Hungaro-Croatian Diet (1839-1840) became the theater for another violent Magyar assault on Croatia, with the Croatian legates resisting with equal fervor. Vienna again showed sympathy for the Croatian cause. After the Diet closed, the Croatian *Sabor* convened and voted for a law introducing the Croatian language as the official language for all of its schools and gymnasiums as well as for the Zagreb Academy.

The Magyaro-Croatian conflict brought about the formation of the first political parties in Croatia. Part of the Croatian

139

aristocracy leaned toward closer ties with Hungary. Its representatives were the first to act. Under the leadership of Baron Levin Rauch and his brother, Juraj, the first Croatian party was formed and given the name the Croatian-Hungarian Party. The followers of Draskovic and Gaj answered by forming the Illyrian Party which advocated the formation of an independent Kingdom of Croatia through the unification of all Croatian lands within the Habsburg Monarchy, viz. Croatia, Slavonia, Dalmatia, the Military Borders, the city and port of Rijeka, and the Croatian districts of Istria. As an instrument to bring about this unification, the Croatian language would be official. Moreover, the Illyrians were seeking closer ties with the Croats in Bosnia and Hercegovina with the ultimate and romantic aim of forming a unique Illyrian nation together with their Slavic kin, the Serbs, Slovenes and Bulgars. However, the Serbs, Slovenes and the Bulgarians showed no tendency whatsoever to become part of this Croatian dream.

The newly formed political parties entered the bitter campaign at once, accusing each other of all imaginable crimes, including high treason, and then going on to instigate violence in the streets. *Ban* Baron Franjo Haller of the Hungarian nobility proposed to Vienna that the use of the name Illyrian be forbidden since he thought it was the major cause of the disturbances. Moreover, the Illyrians did not limit their activities to Austrian territory alone, but agitated among the Croats of Bosnia and Hercegovina as well, so that finally the Ottoman government complained to Vienna. The Hungarian government joined in the protest. Thus it was easy for Ferdinand to forbid further use of the Illyrian name for any political, cultural or general public purpose.

The name of the language should have been changed from Illyrian to Croatian. However, the Imperial prescription insisted upon complete freedom for the national Croatian language and on its use in all the country's institutions. The Vienna decision also supported the free development of Croatian municipal institutions (January 11, 1843). Consequently, Gaj was compelled to change the title of his publications: The Gazette became simply the *Narodne novine* (The National Gazette) and the magazine assumed the name *Danica* (The Morningstar). The Illyrian Party changed its name to the National Party.

CHAPTER XI

THE MAGYARO -- CROATIAN
CONFLICT

*Language issue — Revolutionary 1848 — Ban Jelacic —
First elected Croatian* Sabor *— End of serfdom — Croato-
Magyar war — Bach absolutism — October* Diploma *—
February* Patent *— Ban Sokcevic — Emergence of the
new political formations*

The Hungarian Diet was called into session in the spring
of 1843. The Croatian *Sabor* met in advance to elect its delegation to the joint session. Herman Buzan was elected to the
Upper House, while Karlo Klobucaric and Metel Ozegovic were
elected to the Lower House. All three men were representatives
of the National Party. The *Sabor* instructed these representatives
to use the Latin language exclusively in the proceedings of the
joint session. In accordance with the proposal of Ivan Kukuljevic, the *Sabor* also voted to introduce the Croatian language
as the official language for all affairs of the country (May 2,
1843).

The Magyaro-Croatian conflict reached its climax at the session of the Pressburg Diet. Because the Magyar representatives
insisted on the sole use of the Magyar language, the Croatian
delegates walked out in accordance with the *Sabor's* instructions. Both parties appealed to the king. By attempting to please
both sides, Ferdinand only managed to create an ambiguous
situation. While supporting the Magyar demand for the use

of their language in the sessions of the Diet, he also sanctioned the *Sabor's* decision to introduce the Croatian, or Illyrian language, as the official language of Croatia (January 3, 1845).

The political strife in Croatia created a self-perpetuating violence that resulted in open bloodshed during the elections of the officials for the Zagreb *commitat*. On this occasion, soldiers opened fire on the demonstrators, killing several of them (July 29, 1845). Consequently, the *Sabor*, which was entirely in the hands of the National Party, voted an address to the king which presented demands for the re-establishment of the independent government of Croatia, the elevation of the Zagreb Academy to the status of a university, and the raising of the Bishopric of Zagreb to the rank of an Archbishopric.

Meanwhile, Hungary was undergoing profound changes. The relatively moderate and conservative elements were pushed aside by the intransigent nationalistic movement which had been styled in the liberal and democratic fashion under the leadership of Louis Kossuth. Kossuth clamored for the establishment of a single centralized Kingdom of Hungary and a single Magyar nation stretching from the Carpathian Mountains to the Adriatic Sea. In his enthusiasm, he was uncompromising and absolutely intolerant of the other nationalities under Hungarian rule, i.e. the Croats, Serbs, Slovaks, Rumanians, Ukrainians and Germans. In his arrogant way of dealing with the Croatian opposition he is credited with such exclamations as, ". . . where is Croatia? I cannot find it on the map!" This kind of attitude produced an equal stubbornness among the Croats.

When the new Diet was called into session, the Croats were prepared to face Kossuth and his followers. The *Sabor* re-elected Buzan to the Upper House, while Ozegovic and Josip Bunjik went to the Lower House. It also passed a resolution which, by the *Sabor's* own authority, ". . . raised the Croatian language to the honor, valor, and position hitherto enjoyed by the Latin language in the territory of the Kingdom of Croatia, Slavonia and Dalmatia. . ." (October 23, 1847). In another resolution, the *Sabor* called for the reunification of the Military Border, Dalmatia and the city and port of Rijeka to the mother country. This *Sabor* of 1847 was the last representative body of medieval Croatia and thus the last to have the nobility and the orders represented.

The sessions of the Pressburg Diet started with dark forboding for the Croatian legates. Kossuth immediately introduced a law aimed at the complete elimination of Croatian autonomy, refashioning its *commitats* into Hungarian *commitats* pure and simple. While this project was being introduced, the Diet, and all of Europe as well, was taken by surprise by the events of the French Revolution of February 24, 1848, a revolution whose reverberations were to rock the established order all over the continent. Spurred on by these Parisian events, Kossuth sponsored an address to the king requesting the immediate formation of an independent government for Hungary and royal sanction for all bills of reform prepared by the Diet.

In the meantime a revolutionary situation was emerging in Vienna. As a consequence of popular demonstrations, the camarilla succeeded in forcing Metternich's dismissal. He then went into exile in London. Subsequently, Ferdinand promised the various Austrian nationalities their own constitutions as well as freedom of the press. Press censorship was abolished at once. Having been under pressure from the Viennese events since March 13, Ferdinand, after some delaying tactics, finally agreed to the demands of the Hungarian Diet.

Archduke Stephen, Palatin of Hungary, brought a special Hungarian delegation to Vienna to present the Diet address to the king. On this occasion, Ferdinand named Count Louis Bathyany president of the independent Hungarian government (April 7, 1848). The most influential members of the new Hungarian cabinet were Kossuth himself, who was Minister of Finance, Prince Paul Esczterhazy, Minister of the Royal Court, and Francis Deak, Minister of Justice. Moreover, Ferdinand sanctioned all bills presented to him by the delegation. These bills were aimed at the establishment of the exclusive Kingdom of Hungary and a united Magyar nation. This decision by the king appeared to be the decisive victory of Magyar nationalism over the Croats.

However, the Croatian leaders did not await these events with folded hands. Baron Franjo Kulmer, the leader of the Croatian conservative element and a man who enjoyed a certain amount of influence in the Habsburg Court, counteracted the Magyar move by suggesting to Archduke Louis, Ferdinand's brother, that Baron Josip Jelacic, colonel of the Military Border, be appointed to the post of *ban*. Even before the Hungarian delegation could present its demands, Jelacic was promoted to general and then duly appointed *ban* (March 23).

In this topsy-turvy situation, the leaders of the National Party called a general meeting in Zagreb. The meeting was presided over by Ivan Kukuljevic and it voted to send a special delegation to the king to present the Croatian demands. The gist of these demands was as follows: the election (sic!) of Jelacic as *Ban* by the *Sabor;* the unification of all Croatian lands within the boundary of the Monarchy, i.e. Croatia, Slavonia, the Military Border, Dalmatia and Rijeka; the appointment of an independent government of Croatia; a permanently elected *Sabor;* and the abolition of the last remnants of serfdom and class privileges.

The Imperial Court was obviously badly split over the issue of Hungaro-Croatian relations. Thus Vienna pursued a two-faced policy: A faction favored the Magyars and another the Croatian cause. When Jelacic's appointment to the post of *ban* and to the equally important post of commanding general of the Military Border became public the crisis broke out into the open. Jelacic was personally responsible for this. He hastened the severance of all relations between the Hungarian and Croatian governments by ordering all authorities in Croatia not to receive any communications emanating from the Hungarian government and to act only on instructions issued from Zagreb.

146

This order, which was published on April 19, virtually brought to an end all the existing common affairs of both kingdoms.

Jelacic went even further by composing a new ordinance calling for the election of members to the Croatian *Sabor* from all the territory of Croatia and the Military Border. The *Sabor* elected on May 18 was the first political body in Croatian history which represented the people according to the contemporary concept. It convened on June 5 and after electing its officers it confirmed the previous act of *Ban* Jelacic of April 25 in which he abolished serfdom. With the abolition of serfdom a law for equal taxation followed, as well as its corollary, the end of the feudal system in Croatia. Next, the *Sabor* dealt with the problem of the general reorganization of the Habsburg Monarchy. An address to the king was voted as a result of this deliberation.

The *Sabor* advocated the reorganization of the Monarchy along the lines of the Swiss confederacy. The Monarchy would be limited according to federalistic principles with the responsible governments of each nationality having a central parliament in Vienna in common as well as a central governing agency for common affairs, such as the army, finance, commerce and foreign relations.

*   *   *

The breach between Hungary and Croatia was confirmed. This ugly turn of affairs prompted Archduke John to advise the Hungarian and Croatian conservatives to try to reach common ground. A meeting between the two heads of government was organized. But neither Bathyany nor Jelacic were able or willing to come to an understanding. When separating, Bathyany challenged Jelacic with these words: ". . . All right then, *Ban*, we shall meet at the Drava. . ." (The Drava River was a boundary between the two countries.) To this challenge Jelacic retorted: ". . . I shall look for you first at the Danube. . ." (Budapest, the capital of Hungary, is situated on the Danube River.)

Jelacic returned home from the meeting with a firm belief in the inevitability of an armed conflict between Hungary and Croatia. Upon his return to Zagreb, he proceeded with the organization of his government, creating these five departments: The Department of Justice, internal administration, culture and education, army and finance, economics and commerce. This organization of the government and the appointment of departmental heads was carried out with the cooperation of the *Sabor*.

At this time Jelacic was also appointed to the governorships of Rijeka and Dalmatia. With these positions combined with his position as *Ban* of Croatia and Chief commander of the Croatian and Slavonian Military Border, he practically completed the unification of Croatian lands within the Habsburg Monarchy. The one exception was Istria. Upon the completion of governmental reorganization, Jelacic was granted full power by the *Sabor*, and he thus began to make military preparations for a campaign against Hungary. But the military resources of the country were greatly depleted because the bulk of Croatian soldiers from the Military Border were under the command of Radetzky in Italy.

Meanwhile, the Hungarian government was not idle in dealing with the other nationalities of Hungary who attempted to assert their own independent spirit. The Magyar nationalists answered by hanging some young Serbian nationalists. This convinced Jelacic all the more to move against Budapest. To the amusement of later historians, Jelacic declared war on Ferdinand V, King of Hungary, in the name of Ferdinand V, King of Croatia. At the head of an army of 40,000 men, he crossed the Drava River near Varazdin, initiating an invasion of Hungary (September 11). After crossing the river, he issued a proclamation for the return of Medjumurje, which had been detached from Croatia at the time of the Zrinjski conspiracy (1671). He then advanced by way of Nagykanyysza and Szekesfehervar in the direction of Budapest.

Jelacic's declaration of war provoked a crisis in the Hungarian government. The ministry of Count Bathyany resigned, and the Hungarian parliament entrusted to Kossuth the task of creating a new government for the national defense from which all conservative and moderate elements were to be excluded (September 16). The formation of the radical Hungarian government marked the beginning of the Hungarian Revolution. Kossuth immediately organized an army and sent it to meet Jelacic. The two armies clashed in a battle that had no definite victor at Velence and Pakozd, southwest of Budapest. Although Jelacic achieved a certain tactical advantage, he did not exploit it. Receiving a pressing invitation to come to the rescue of Vienna, which was in the full swing of revolution, he turned his back on Budapest and moved in the direction of Austria.

The Austrian Revolution broke out on October 6, forcing the Imperial Court to flee to Olumec in Moravia. The Constituent Assembly, which was meeting in Vienna, followed the Court. The government ordered General Windischgraetz, who had suppressed the Czech Revolution in Prague not too long before, to join with Jelacic in the advance on Vienna.

With the hope of giving insurgent Vienna a helping hand, the Hungarian army followed close at Jelacic's heels, but Jelacic outmaneuvered it and decisively defeated it on October 30 at the Battle of Schwecht. As a consequence, insurgent Vienna surrendered to Prince Windischgraetz. But under the pressure of revolutionary events and court intrigues, Ferdinand was induced to abdicate in favor of his brother, Francis Charles, who in turn abdicated in favor of his son, Francis Joseph I, on December 2, 1848.

* * *

The day Francis Joseph I (1848-1916) ascended the throne he issued a solemn proclamation addressed to all his people expressing his wish to rule according to the principles ". . . of the complete equality of all the nationalities of the Monarchy, the equality of all citizens before the law, and the participation

of the people's representatives in the legislation. . ." This proclamation accepted, more or less, the principles of the constitution which had been effected by the Olumec Assembly. On the
same occasion, Francis Joseph confirmed the appointment of
Jelacic as governor of Rijeka and as civil and military governor
of Dalmatia. Baron Franjo Kulmer was named the Croatian
Minister without portfolio in the central government formed by
Prince Felix Schwarzenberg.

*　　*　　*

The Hungarian parliament reacted violently to the change on
the throne. It voted a resolution in which it rejected ". . . any
change without receiving, acknowledging and consenting to the
appropriate information, being the only body to decide on a
change on the Hungarian throne. . ." It therefore invited the
citizens of the country to disobey anyone who did not recognize and respect the country's ". . . law, constitution and parliament. . ." This resolution was tantamount to an open revolt
against the new ruler. Thus the central government ordered
its generals, Windischgraetz and Jelacic, to suppress the revolt
with armed forces. Following a series of local victories, the
combined Bohemian and Croatian armies entered Budapest
(January 5, 1849).

Kossuth retreated with his government and the rump parliament to Debreczen. There, on the basis of Kossuth's motion,
the parliament declared the expulsion of the Habsburgs from
the Hungarian throne. It also declared itself a republic and gave
Kossuth full power to make war against invading armies. Kossuth proceeded with the organization of the Magyar army, placing
it under the command of the Polish generals, Bem and Dembinski.

Windischgraetz defeated Dembinski at the Battle of Kapolna
in February. This defeat created the impression in Vienna that
the Hungarian revolt was ended, prompting Schwarzenberg to
proclaim a constitution which bypassed the document voted by
the Olumec assembly. The new constitution established Austria

150

as a single empire consisting of mutually independent political units. It recognized Croatia as a single unit consisting of the Kingdom of Croatia, Slavonia and Dalmatia, as well as the city of Rijeka, but not the Military Border. At the same time it formed Serbian Vojvodina out of the eastern districts of Croatia and the southern districts of Hungary. But the new constitution created a general dissatisfaction in Croatia. The Croats insisted on royal sanction for decisions voted by the *Sabor*.

Revolutionary Hungary answered the constitution in a most radical way. The Hungarian throne was declared vacant, the Habsburg dynasty was ousted from the throne, and national independence was proclaimed. Kossuth was elected president-governor of the country (April 14, 1849). The new Hungarian army headed by the young general, Georgey, expelled the Austrian army from a major part of the country.

In this new and precarious situation, Vienna addressed an appeal for help to Nicholas I of Russia whose forces had recently put an end to the Polish insurrection. Under General Paskiewicz, the Russian army crossed the border into Hungary, joining the Austrians in the suppression of the Hungarian Revolution. Faced with an overwhelming foe, Kossuth and his principal collaborators escaped to Turkish territory, leaving General Georgey and his army to surrender to the Russians at Vilagos on August 13, 1849. The Austrian general, Haynau, surnamed the "Hyena of the Revolution," took revenge. Count Bathyany, former President of the Hungarian government, and thirteen generals were summarily hung. The military courts inflicted severe penalties on the other insurgents.

* * *

With Russian help, the Habsburg government defeated insurgent Hungary. This victory ended a two year revolutionary period in which the ancient order of the Austrian Empire was destroyed. Thus, at the beginning of his rule, Francis Joseph was faced with a dilemma: Should he attempt to restore the

151

ancient order or try a new approach to the problems of the empire? Being of limited intelligence and mediocre political ability, the answer to this dilemma for Francis Joseph depended a great deal upon the capabilities of his ministers. Prince Felix Schwarzenberg, the new, as well as last, Chancellor of the Empire, was too preoccupied with the Austrian position in Germany to pay much attention to the pressing problems of the Habsburg realms. This task was left to Alexander Bach, the Minister of Interior, who proceeded to experiment with it according to his own political ideas. Since he was formerly a German nationalist with a liberal disposition, his approach was essentially revolutionary. He used his exceptional rights and power as supreme arbitrator in dealing with the problems. Historical rights, constitutions and privileges were utterly ignored. Everything had to be organized along the lines of a strictly centralistic and generally germanistic pattern.

Although Croatia, due to Jelacic's policy, had been loyal to the Habsburg cause during the time of crisis, it lost its autonomous government and *Sabor*. Jelacic would remain in the office of *ban* until his death in 1859, but the office was reduced to an empty, ceremonial title. A single Austrian system of administration was imposed on the country. It was run by a host of German, Czech and Slovenian officials who replaced the local administration. The German language was introduced as the official language for the administration and for education. The new officials, foreign in origin and language, were nicknamed the "Bach hussars."

The ancient feudal system of an autonomous and elective administration was replaced by a new administration which was bureaucratic and foreign in spirit, origin and language. The new Austrian legal system, civil code, criminal justice, and economic policy (as well as the consequential taxation system) were imposed on the country without due preparation. This new system also wiped out all remnants of serfdom and imposed new regulations concerning land ownership and the use of so-called

152

common lands and forests. Although many of the measures were greatly beneficial to Croatia, they were bitterly criticized and rejected by the political opinion of the country simply because they were imposed from above by foreign and unpopular officials. A cynically-minded Hungarian aristocrat remarked to a friend of his that, in a way, Croatia was rewarded for its loyalty to the Habsburgs in the same way that Hungary was punished for its disloyalty.

The constitution of 1849 did not last long. A *Patent* issued on December 31, 1851, established Francis Joseph as an absolute monarch and brought a practical end to all political life within the boundaries of the Monarchy. But the international situation developing out of the Crimean War brought a serious setback to Austria. Moreover, its own clumsy diplomacy greatly contributed to this situation. Also, a prolonged economic crisis and the general dissatisfaction of the nationalities aggravated it.

When Sardinia, under the skillful leadership of Cavour, provoked Austria to declare war, Austria was far from ready. The situation became desperate when Napoleon III joined the war. The war started badly for Austria, and abruptly ended after a confusing battle at Solferino which left the French forces dominating the field. From the outset, some of the Austrian troops proved unreliable. This was especially the case with the Hungarian regiments. Furthermore, confusion was created in the ranks when the soldiers found themselves faced with Hungarian, Polish and parts of Croatian legions fighting on the side of the enemy. After the dubious performance of his army, Francis Joseph lost heart and signed the armistice at Villafranca. The war was ended by the Peace of Zurich in which Austria ceded Lombardy to France (1859).

The humiliation resulting from the Italian campaign spelled the end of the absolutistic regime. Francis Joseph then entered a period of constitutional experimentation, vacillating between the federalistic ideas, which were supported by the conservative aristocracy, and centralistic liberalism, which had its support

153

in the German middle class of Austria. Because he was either unwilling or unable to make up his mind, the experimentation proved to be the political tactics of delay rather than a straightforward policy. The Hungarian aristocrats were the most experienced and politically astute and therefore did not take long to seize the opportunity to assert themselves. They presented the Emperor a petition in which they advocated the restoration of the historico-political units that had originally composed the monarchy.

A special Imperial council, the reinforced *Reichsrath*, was called into session as a consultative body in Vienna in March 1860. All of the former political units were represented by a few selected representatives. The following were the representatives of the Kingdom of Croatia: Bishop Josip Juraj Strossmayer represented Slavonia, Baron Ambroz Vraniczanyi, Croatia, and Count Manfred Borelli, Dalmatia. As a result of Vienna's deliberation, the Diploma of October was promulgated as a basic law of the country (October 20, 1860). The Diploma was a kind of compromise between the federalistically minded aristocratic conservatives and the centralistically oriented German liberal bureaucracy. It aimed at the establishment of an historical federalism in which each unit had a local diet which dealt with matters not reserved for the central *Reichsrath*.

* * *

In order to win over the recalcitrant Croats, the most striking features of defunct Bach absolutism were abolished. General Baron Josip Sokcevic, the former Jelacic adjutant, was appointed to replace the outgoing *ban,* Count Ivan Coronini, who had been an outspoken supporter of absolutism. The press was given a certain degree of freedom. This enabled the opposition to launch a new paper, *Pozor* (Attention), which joined the existing papers, i.e. *Narodne Novine,* in the Croatian language, and *Die Agramer Zeitung,* printed in German. The Croatian language was reintroduced as the only official language of the administration, as well as of the judicial and educational systems.

A new period of political development began in Croatia with the events of 1860. *Ban* Sokcevic was sent to Zagreb to win the Croats over to the October Diploma, i.e. to establish closer ties between Vienna and Zagreb by getting the Croats to recognize the central government in Vienna at the price of local autonomy. This policy received the full support of the official bureaucracy and was generally accepted in the Croatian and Slavonian Military Border. But it was rejected by the followers of the former political parties, viz. both the National and the Magyar parties. But the National Party entered the new period badly split over who its leaders were to be and what goals it would pursue.

Following his instructions, Sokcevic called fifty-five outstanding public personalities to a special conference. At the first session, the conference decided to send a delegation to the Emperor to let him know the country's wishes. They were: the reintroduction of Croatian as the official language; the formation of a royal chancellery for Croatia; the appointment of a new *veliki zupan* (chief administrator of the *commitat*); and the reunification with Croatia of the Military Border, Dalmatia, the Adriatic islands and the three districts of Istria (Volosko, Labin and Novigrad), which were historically and ethnically Croatian. Francis Joseph agreed to only a few of these wishes: The Court Chancellery for Croatia was formed and Ivan Mazuranic was made chairman. The reunification of Dalmatia was approved in principle, but nothing was done to make it a reality. In fact, General Mamula, the Governor of Dalmatia, received instructions telling him to discourage any efforts toward reunification occurring among the people of Dalmatia.

At the same time, Francis Joseph attempted to win the support of the Magyars who wanted to return to the status prior to 1848 by abolishing Serbian Vojvodina and detaching Medjumurje from Croatia and incorporating it into Hungary. Furthermore, the question of Rijeka was reopened: Due to Magyar propaganda and promises of economic advantages, the local Italian and italianized population clamored for the town's incorporation into Hungary as a special unit separated from Croatia.

*   *   *

Vienna's experimentation did not stop there. The newly appointed head of the government, Anton Schmerling, issued the *February Patent* (February 25, 1861), which was to be the interpretive instructions for the application of the *October Diploma.* In accordance with this *patent,* both the Hungarian Diet and the Croatian *Sabor* were called into session. The Hungarian Diet immediately voted an address to the Emperor which demanded the return to the status prior to 1848 and then adjourned, without even beginning to discuss Vienna's proposals.

A special *Sabor* for Dalmatia met at Zadar. It consisted of thirty-one Italians, nine Croats and two Serbs. By a majority vote, it decided to join the *Reichsrath* in Vienna rather than the Croatian *Sabor* in Zagreb, thereby preventing the reunification of Dalmatia with Croatia.

The Croatian *Sabor,* which also included representatives of the Military Border, but not of Rijeka, was elected on the basis of the same electoral law used for the election of the Jelacic *Sabor* in 1848. It met on April 15, installed *Ban* Sokcevic and voted an address to the Emperor which demanded the unification of all Croatian lands into a single political entity. Answering the Imperial rescript to open negotiations with the Hungarian Diet regarding future relations between the two countries, the *Sabor* expressed the opinion that the events of 1848 had ended all ancient relations between Hungary and Croatia. But Croatia was willing to open negotiations with Hungary to establish a real union. However, the *Sabor* insisted on Hungarian recognition of Croatian independence and territorial integrity. This insistence was a result of the attitude of the National Party which represented the majority in the *Sabor.*

A second motion was introduced by Count Julije Jankovic

and it aimed to establish a real union with Hungary without any preconditions. And a third motion by Eugen Kvaternik in the name of the Party of Rights insisted on the complete independence of Croatia from both Austria and Hungary, retaining only a common sovereign and a common policy in some foreign affairs. Since this last motion based its contents on existing historical and political constitutional rights of Croatia, it became the political program for the Party of Right's *Pravasi*.

The *Sabor* unanimously rejected the Imperial rescript to join the deliberations of the *Reichsrath*, declaring that Croatia did not have any affairs in common with Austria. This decision brought about the dissolution of the *Sabor*.

The Schmerling government gave way to a new cabinet under Count Belcredi which was favorably disposed to a federalistic solution to the problems of the Monarchy. Some Croatian leaders had second thoughts as to the position of Croatia in this new situation. Ivan Mazuranic advocated agreeing with Vienna before Hungary made the same move. His followers formed the Independent Party and received Belcredi's support. But, Strossmayer's National Party joined with the Magyars and the *Pravasi* to attempt to defeat this new trend.

The election of the new *Sabor* in 1865 went in favor of the National Party. Following the instructions of the Imperial rescript, the *Sabor* elected a delegation of twelve members who met with an equivalent Hungarian delegation to negotiate future relations between the two countries. Bishop Strossmayer headed the Croatian delegation and Count Anton Majlath presided over the Hungarian delegation. The Hungarians rejected all Croatian demands and offered to recognize Croatian autonomy in internal administration, justice, religion and education instead. After two months of fruitless negotiations, the delegations separated.

The Hungarians were better informed on current events than were the Croats and they were just biding their time. Strossmayer had greatly misjudged the situation and Croatia's strength when he refused to follow Mazuranic's advice and negotiate with Vienna before the Hungarians did. Subsequent events favored Hungary. Thus, Croatian politics were facing an unpleasant dilemma: Negotiate with Vienna on Vienna's conditions, or Budapest on Budapest's conditions. In any case, Croatia was not in the position to impose its own conditions.

CHAPTER XII

THE NAGODBA

Between Vienna and Budapest — Cleavage of Croatian politics — Strossmayer — Starcevic — Austro-Prussian war — Ausgleich — Unionists and the Nagodba — Dual system at work — Its impact on Croatia — Mazuranic — Occupation of Bosnia and Hercegovina.

Mazuranic and Kukuljevic seconded Sokcevic in advocating the orientation of Croatian policy toward Austria, i.e. they urged reconciliation with the central government regarding the future status of Croatia in the Empire. On behalf of the Independent National Party (Sokcevic's faction), Mazuranic prepared an address to the Emperor which stressed this Croatian demand: The unification of Croatia, Slavonia, the Croatian and Slavonian Military Border, the city of Rijeka, Dalmatia and the three Croatian districts of Istria.

Opposition to Sokcevic's Vienna oriented policy was raised by the nobility under the leadership of Baron Levin Rauch. Rauch insisted upon the traditional constitutional rights of the nobility which he and his peers thought could be best safeguarded through close ties with Hungary. The majority opinion in Croatia, however, supported Strossmayer in his belief that as of 1848 all existing ties between Hungary and Croatia had been severed and that the primary condition for future relations between the two countries would be Hungary's recognition of Croatia as an equal. The real choice for Croatia narrowed down to whether it should deal with Austria or Hungary.

*   *   *

Croatian public life would be dominated by two personalities in the coming decades, viz. Strossmayer and Starcevic.

Josip Juraj Strossmayer (1815-1905), of croatized German origin on his father's side, was known for his brilliant sermons when he was still a young clergyman. As a result of this early fame, he was called to the Imperial Court where he became confessor to Archduchess Sophia, mother of the future emperor, Francis Joseph. Upon the proposal of Jelacic, and fully supported by the Imperial Court, he was appointed Bishop of Djakovo in 1851. The Bishopric of Djakovo was one of the richest in the whole Empire and assured Strossmayer not only material independence, but also left at his disposal considerable wealth which he was free to use for the advancement of his national and political ideas.

Strossmayer was a highly cultured man with a striking personality. He was full of ambitions and enjoyed an evergrowing reputation as an outstanding orator. In 1870 he achieved world-wide fame at the Vatican Council as a promoter of the unification of the Catholic and Orthodox Churches. As the spokesman for the Austrian bishops, he opposed the dogma of Papal infalibility with great oratorical skill. Aside from representing the official position of his colleagues in this oppostion, he had reasons of his own to take such a controversial stand: Papal infalibility presented an insurmountable obstacle to his lifelong dream for the reconciliation of the Churches.

Strossmayer was heir to the Illyrian succession in politics. But to him the word "Illyrian" was artificial and foreign; he used the geographical term "Yugoslav" instead. The term "Yugoslav" was simply derived from Vienna's administrative language which drew a geographic distinction between the Northern Slavs of the Monarchy (the Czechs, Poles, Slovaks and Ukrainians) and the Southern Slavs (Croats, Slovenes and Serbs). Southern

160

Slav in German (*die Sudslaven*) translated into the Croatian *Juzni Slaveni, Jugosiaveni.*

The "Illyrian" dream of the unification of the Southern Slavs in a common homeland which would extend from Villach in Carinthia to Varna on the Black Sea exactly corresponded to Strossmayer's concept of the Yugoslav state. First of all, Strossmayer aimed at giving the new nation its own intellectual life and developing it to its fullest. Toward this end, he acted on the advice of his friend, Canon Franjo Racki, who was a reputed historian, as well as on the approval of Vienna, in providing the financial means for the foundation of the Yugoslav Academy of Arts and Sciences in Zagreb (1866). But his attempt to bring about the unification of the Catholic and Orthodox Churches, which he thought was indispensible to the attainment of his goal, proved to be an impossible task.

The political structure of the future Yugoslav state, as it was conceived by Strossmayer, was based on the constitutional rights of Croatia as the nucleus of the Southern Slav union within the more general framework of the Habsburg Monarchy.

Besides dominating the political and religious stages, Stross-mayer also asserted his authority in a decisive manner on the country's intellectual life. He was able to exert an unlimited influence on Croatia's intellectual development by means of large financial gifts to the University of Zagreb, and more especially to the Yugoslav Academy of Arts and Sciences. Artists, writers and scientists who wished to enjoy the advantages offered by the Academy, or in some cases, simply to survive, dutifully adopted the Bishop's lofty ideas of a unique Yugoslav nation. Notwithstanding that the Academy was still an institution of almost exclusive Croatian learning and achievement, it was designated by the significant adjective "Yugoslav." Thus, for instance, the historical documents pertaining to Croatia's past were published under the designation "Yugoslav." This term was also used for the ethnographic studies of Croatian villages.

Strossmayer's national and political ideas found their most bitter antagonist in Ante Starcevic (1823-1896) who became the

161

"Father of the Fatherland" to his followers, or the only true prophet of Croatian nationalism. He, too, had been predestined to a spiritual profession. But in his second year of theological studies at Budapest he absorbed so much free thinking that he became a convinced atheist. He left the seminary and thereby disappointed his protector, Ozegovic, Bishop of Senj. At any rate, his rebelliousness and extremely stubborn and uncouth character, as well as his misanthropic tendencies, hardly made him a good candidate for the priesthood.

Starcevic, like Strossmayer, had joined the Illyrian movement in his youth. Later, when the government of Vienna thwarted his hopes of obtaining a professorship at the Zagreb Academy of Philosophy, due, he believed, to Ozegovic's antagonistic intervention, he nurtured an evergrowing hatred for the Catholic clergy as such, and for Strossmayer in particular. In the heat of similar feelings for Vienna, he devised his theories of pure Croatian nationalism: "God and the Croats," "Croatia for the Croats," "Neither Vienna nor Budapest." These nationalistic sentiments were tied down to historical documents: To develop his personal doctrine, Starcevic unearthed historical evidence which endowed the Croatian state with rights to a definite political and national system of its own. Moreover, these rights claimed that the only thing Croatia had in common with the rest of the Monarchy was the person of the king. Most of the Croats held a relationship to those rights that bordered on religious faith.

While Strossmayer's political philosophy rested on the romantic Panslavist Movement, Starcevic was influenced, on the one hand, by the liberalism of French Jacobinism, and on the other, by the example of the Hungarian politicians who habitually based their claims on historical precedent, i.e. documents. The tendency to buttress an argument for political transactions with historical rights became one of the characteristics of the Danubian Monarchy.

Eugen Kvaternik was Starcevic's intimate friend and collaborator. Within two decades he had been a revolutionary, a republican, a conspirator with the exiled Kossuth and the French prince, Jerome Bonaparte, a Panslavist and Cavour's confidant. He had taken part in the hatching of every conspiracy against the Habsburg Monarchy. Subsequent to the fall of his idol, Napoleon III, he single-handedly raised an armed revolt in the southern part of the Croatian Military Border, proclaiming himself ruler of an independent Croatia. A few days later this revolt was suppressed, resulting in the bloodshed which cost Kvaternik his life (October 1871).

Starcevic's teachings, supported by his reputation for personal integrity, found many followers among the young intellegentsia and especially among the lower bourgeoisie. His stubborn and persistant attitude in refusing to acknowledge any connection between Croatia and either Vienna or Budapest, except in the person of the King, had a strange appeal to the people.

* * *

The final moments of Austria as the leading power of the German Confederacy were rapidly approaching. Austria's eventual fall was prepared by Bismarckian diplomacy. By the summer of 1866 the Austro-Prussian war was inevitable. Neither the Austrian military victory at Custozza on June 24, nor the naval triumph at Vis against the Prussian ally, Italy, on July 20, could eradicate the military disaster at Koniggraetz on July 3. At that time Bismark imposed an armistice on his reluctant King which was soon followed by the Peace Treaty of Prague on August 30.

Even before the peace treaty was signed, Francis Deak, leader of the Hungarian Liberals, paid a discrete visit to Vienna and told the Emperor that ". . . Hungary's demands after Koniggraetz remained the same as they were before. . ." Time was running out for Count Richard Belcredi's government and for its experimentation in federalism. On October 30, Frederick Beust, former head of the government of Saxony, took the reins in Vienna and vowed to prepare for revenge against Prussia.

But his primary task was to satisfy Hungary. The Hungarian cause also enjoyed the wholehearted support of Empress Elizabeth and her son and heir to the throne, Prince Rudolph.

Francis Joseph decided to come to an agreement with the Hungarian nobility. By this agreement (the *Ausgleich*) the Habsburg Monarchy was divided into two parts: One part consisted of the kingdoms and lands represented at the *Reichsrath*, commonly known as Austria and dominated by the German bureaucracy and the liberal middle-class; while the other part consisted of the St. Stephen crown lands and included Hungary, Croatia, Slavonia, Dalmatia and Transylvania, each with an independent government for all matters that were not strictly reserved as common.

Those affairs agreed on to be common and therefore reserved for the deliberation of the government at Vienna were matters of foreign policy, war and the financing of the two branches of the service. Legislation regarding these common affairs was reserved for the regular meeting of two delegations of equal number from the *Reichsrath* and the Hungarian parliament. The economic relations and the customs union between the two parts of the Monarchy were negotiated for ten year periods with arrangements for renegotiation at the end of each period. A special provision for negotiating its relations with Croatia was imposed on Hungary. The Compromise or the *Ausgleich* in the form of Article XII was then put into force. Beust was appointed Prime Minister of Austria and Count Julius Andrassy, former officer of the rebellious Hungarian army of 1848, was made Prime Minister of Hungary (February 20, 1876).

While the negotiations between Vienna and Budapest were under-way the Croats grew alarmed and attempted to make themselves a factor in the settlement. On October 19, 1866, the *Sabor* paid belated attention to Sokcevic's advice by voting in favor of opening direct negotiations with Vienna. It was too late. The *Ausgleich* had become a reality. As a consequence of the *Ausgleich*, Francis Joseph was to be crowned King of Hungary, Croatia, Slavonia and Dalmatia and the *Sabor* was invited to send a delegation to the event. The *Sabor* demurred, declaring that relations between Hungary and Croatia were not yet settled. Thus, the coronation took place on June 8, 1867, without Croatian representation. At that time Francis Joseph gave the Hungarian government *carte blanche* for settling its relationship to the recalcitrant Croats. Budapest thereby became a decisive factor in Croatian affairs.

Ban Sokcevic resigned and Baron Rauch, the leader of the Unionist Party, became acting *Ban* for the end of paving the way to a Hungaro-Croatian understanding. The partisans of both the National and Independent Parties were his first victims. Persecution of political opponents became the order of the day. A new electoral law which greatly reduced the number of electors was enacted, and an increased number of virilists were invited to the *Sabor*. The virilists were made automatic members of the *Sabor* by virtue of their origin (e.g. princes, counts and barons) or by their official positions (e.g. archbishop, bishops and *zupans*).

Thus securing victory, Rauch called for elections. The Unionist Party elected fifty-two members while the combined opposition elected only fourteen. The opposition at once protested against the inequity of the electoral law as well as against electoral abuses and then refused to take their seats in the *Sabor*. The rump *Sabor* reinforced by the numerous aristocrat-virilists elected a royal delegation of twelve members to begin negotiations with a similar delegation from the Hungarian Parliament (January 30, 1868). Although they had been carefully selected, the members of the Croatian delegation were nevertheless divided. A minority group headed by Count Julije Jankovic opposed the proposed compromise and voted against it.

The compromise became known in the Croatian language as the *Nagodba*, or Article of Law IXXX, and was a compound of seventy articles sanctioned by the Emperor-King on November 18, 1868. It became the basic or constitutional law for the Kingdom of Dalmatia, Croatia and Slavonia, as the country was officially called. The triune kingdom was to retain complete independence concerning internal administration as well as concerning the police, judicial affairs, public instruction and religion. Croatia was recognized as the political nation and the official language for all autonomous and common affairs on Croatian territory was Croatian. The Croatian language was also to be used by the Croatian members of the joint sessions of the Hungaro-Croatian Parliament in Budapest when common affairs were under discussion.

Although the *Nagodba* had formally recognized Dalmatia as an integral part of Croatia, this province, as well as the Military Border, was left outside of the jurisdiction of Croatia. The Military Border was finally incorporated into the mother country in 1881. The question of the city and port of Rijeka, the only Croatian sea port connected to the interior by railway, was suspended pending future Hungaro-Croatian negotiations. Since these negotiations never took place, the Hungarian government, with the consent of the King, imposed the regime of *corpus separatum* on Rijeka, or, in other words, it simply imposed Hungarian administration.

The Hungarian government, acting as the common government, decided all important state questions relating to Croatia's development. The financial system, coinage, weights and measures, commercial treaties, banking, exchange, patents, copyrights, maritime commerce, mining, customs, trades, mail and telegraph, railways, harbors and shipping were controlled by Budapest.

Political autonomy was further jeopardized by the fact that the *Ban*, who was head of the autonomous government, was appointed by the King on the proposal of the Hungarian Premier. Hence, the *Ban* was almost always a representative of an intrusive Hungarian power instead of an independent head of an autonomous Croatian government.

Croatian hopes for achieving union of all national lands within the framework of the Monarchy had been thwarted by the *Ausgleich* and its Croatian corollary, the *Nagodba*. Dalmatia was represented at the *Reichsrath* and therefore remained under

Vienna's administration. The same was true for the Croatian districts of Istria. Moreover the local administration was entrusted to the privileged Italian minority. The much disputed district of Medjumurje, despite its Croatian character, was simply annexed by Hungary on the sanction of the King. Furthermore, in disregard for Croatian claims to Bosnia and Hercegovina, these Ottoman provinces, which had been under Austro-Hungarian military occupation and civil administration since the Congress of Berlin (1878), were placed under the administration of the Austro-Hungarian common Minister of Finance as a Vienna-Budapest condominium.

After royal sanction, the *Nagodba* became the basic law of the country. Consequently Rauch was appointed *Ban*. Koloman Bedekovic joined the Andrassy Cabinet as Minister for Croatia. The Croatian Royal Chancellery in Vienna was abolished and its competency passed on to the Hungarian government.

The *Nagodba* was greeted in Croatia with general dissatisfaction and bitter opposition. Almost immediately, Rauch became involved in shady land speculations, resulting in accusations from the press. Unable to attain favorable court action against the press, Rauch was compelled to resign. Bedekovic replaced him. He called for the election of a new *Sabor*. In this election, his Unionist Party was routed, electing only thirteen members to the National Party's fifty-one and the Party of Right's one, viz. Starcevic.

Vienna began to have second thoughts about the dual organization. Beust lost his post and was replaced by Count Karl Hohenwarth, who revived federalist hopes. These hopes were short-lived, however. The unexpected Kvaternik revolt on the Military Border contributed to their demise. Because Bedekovic was suspected of closing his eyes to Kvaternik's preliminary activities, he was forced out of office. Antun Vakanovic replaced him as acting *Ban*.

Vakanovic dissolved the *Sabor*. But the election did not bring much of a change in its composition. Forty-seven Nationals and twenty-eight Unionists were elected, to which Vakanovic added forty-seven virilists who were all sympathizers of the Unionist cause. Since the Unionist regime was highly unpopular in the country, and furthermore, since it was compromised by the policies of both Rauch and Bedekovic, Budapest was willing, on the insistence of Vienna, to re-negotiate certain minor aspects of the *Nagodba*, without, however, changing its substance.

On the express wish of the Court, Mazuranic became *Ban* (1873-1880). He was the first *Ban* who did not belong to the nobility and thus became known as the "plebean *Ban*." Under his rule the country underwent a general administrative modernization. The Zagreb Academy was finally chartered as a university (1874), a modern system of education according to the German pattern was introduced by the *Sabor*, and the *Tabula Septemvirii* (Court of Seven) was instituted as the supreme court of justice. A similar reorganization of the system of justice was implemented on the lower levels.

During Mazuranic's administration the Ottoman Empire became the theater for ominous developments. The Christian population of the European sector revolted against its masters Bosnia was one of the centers of revolt. The barbaric suppression by the Turks of the rebelling Christians (of which the Bulgarian massacre was the most notable instance) provoked a general reaction in Europe. Serbia and Montenegro became involved in a war against their sovereign, the Sultan. In order to prevent their defeat, Russia declared war on Turkey and invaded the Balkans. Turkey was defeated and compelled by the victorious Russians to sign the Peace Treaty of San Stefano (March 3, 1878).

The Russian triumph, however, was jeopardized by the joint diplomatic intervention of Great Britain and Austria-Hungary which referred an ultimate settlement to the Congress of Berlin. As a consequence of a British proposal, Austria-Hungary received from this Congress a mandate for military occupation and civil administration of the Ottoman provinces of Bosnia, Hercegovina and the Novi Pazar Sandjak. Under General Josip Filipovic, the Austro-Hungarian army proceeded to occupy these lands, but not without military resistance on the part of the local Moslem populations. Following the successful occupation, the *Sabor* voted an address to the king which demanded the incorporation of the liberated provinces, Bosnia and Hercegovina, as well as the Military Border and Dalmatia, into the mother country. The address was greeted with the royal admonition that the *Sabor* had overstepped its bounds. Mazuranic thereupon offered his resignation in protest and it was accepted. Since Mazuranic represented the views of Vienna rather than Budapest in Croatian affairs, the loss of his leadership was considered a victory for Hungary. Dating from the time of his dismissal, the policies of Budapest dominated in Croatia.

Upon a recommendation from Budapest, Count Ladislav Pejacevic (1880-1883), a member of the Unionist Party, was appointed *Ban*. Magyar influence in Croatia increased under his administration. In open violation of the *Nagodba*, the Hungarian government promoted the opening of Magyar schools in Croatia. Moreover, it instigated the use of the Magyar language and Magyar symbols, such as the flag and coat-of-arms, in common affairs on Croatian territory. The Croats resisted. The conflict broke into the open when all inscriptions on a new building for the Direction of the Railway System in Zagreb were made in the Magyar language. The population of Zagreb reacted violently in the form of a popular demonstration that required the restraining forces of the army. Even *Ban* Pejacevic resisted the Hungarian violation of the *Nagodba*, and, as a consequence, resigned. Because the disorder spread throughout the whole of Croatia, Hermann Ramberg, the commanding general of Croatia, was appointed military commissioner with orders to pacify the country. Eventually, Count Dragutin Khuen-Hedervary, a Magyar aristocrat and native of Croatia where he received part of his education, was appointed *Ban* (1883-1903).

CHAPTER XIII

BOSNIA UNDER TURKISH RULE

Conversion of the Patarens *to Islam — Bosnia's Moslem nobility — Bosnian* Pashalik *— Christian* rajas *— Decline of the Ottoman Empire — Bosnian dissatisfaction — Hussein Beg Gradascevic — Ali Pasha Rizvanbegovic and the Hercegovina* Pashalik *— Insurrection of the Christian population — Congress of Berlin — Austro-Hungarian occupation and Moslem resistance under Hadzi Lojo.*

Bosnia, or more exactly, Bosnia and Hercegovina, in the contemporary geographical concept, came into being during the Ottoman rule (1463-1878). It formerly included both in the north and south considerable parts of present-day Croatia. The final boundaries were established by the decision of the Congress of Berlin.

Subsequent to the Ottoman conquest of Bosnia, and large parts of Croatia, the new rulers introduced their own political and social system. The new system consisted of a peculiar mixture of social equality and the lawlessness of oriental despotism. In the beginning the Turks did not persecute the Christian population, although all political rights and resulting privileges were strictly reserved for the Moslem population regardless of its national or social origin. Thus, there occurred a massive conversion of the Bosnian *Patarens,* most of whom belonged to the nobility, since they wished to preserve their political, social and economic status. In granting this group political recognition, the Ottoman established the only nobility with rights of succession in the Empire. However, by the eighteenth century, due to the decline of Ottoman rule, similar systems of established nobility found their way into other parts of the Empire as well.

As soon as they had made themselves masters of Bosnia, the Ottomans organized the country as a *Beglerbegluk* ruled by a *Pasha* (vice-roy) who was appointed by the Sultan. The *Pasha* of Bosnia assumed the title of *Vizier*. During the period of active aggression against Croatia, the *Vizier* resided at Banja Luka; later Travnik became the *Vizier*-town. His rule was limited only by the Sublime Porte, upon whom he was entirely dependent for the promotion of his aims, and from whom he risked execution. The *Pasha* was assisted by the heads of the departments of government: the *Reis Efendi* (chancellor), *Mufti* (supreme justice) and *Tefterdar* (treasurer).

For administrative and military purposes the *Pashalik* was divided into eight territorial circles or *Sandjaks*: Hercegovina, Klis (for Dalmatia), Bihac (for Turkish Croatia), Cernik (for western Slavonia), Pozega (for eastern Slavonia), and Bosnia. At the head of the administration for each *Sandjak* was the *Sandjak beg* who was assisted by a *Divan* (council) which consisted of an *Alaj beg, Janissary aga, Dizdar,* and *Khadi* (judge). The application of justice was entrusted to the *Khadi* who used the *Koran* for his legal guide, thus always favoring the loyal Moslem to the detriment of the Christian. The *Khadi* acted simultaneously as prosecutor and judge.

*   *   *

The *Pataren* population collectively accepted the Moslem religion, thus bringing to an end the Church of the Bosnian Christians. The Catholic population became practically extinct since those who did not retreat to the west or north either accepted Islam or were sold into slavery or massacred. The Catholic remnant in the heart of Bosnia was entrusted to the spiritual care of the Order of St. Francis which had monasteries at Sutjeska, Kresevo, Fojnica, etc. The Bishop of Bosnia was appointed from among them.

The members of both the Catholic and Orthodox Christian population were reduced to the status of *rajas* which is an equivalent to the western serf. Besides the usual tax of compulsory labor, the *raja* was compelled to pay the *spahi* (landlord) a tenth of his income. He was also forced to pay an Imperial tax (*harach*) which was levied against each head, and a special blood tax collected every four years. A special Imperial commission was sent from Istanbul to collect the blood tax of all able bodied children of both sexes for the army's *Janissaries* or for the *harem* or simply to be sold on the slave market.

The Orthodox population was able to secure more or less favorable treatment by the Ottoman authorities due to the influence of the Phanoriot Greeks in the Empire and especially due to the establishment of the Serbian Orthodox Patriarch at Pec (1557). But the Catholic population was nevertheless exposed to the heavy hand of Ottoman persecution.

* * *

The seventeenth and eighteenth centuries witnessed the steady decline of Ottoman authority. This enabled the local Bosnian nobility to grow in importance. The lesser administrative posts in the *Sandjak, Kadiluk* and *Nahija* fell to the local nobility by the right of succession to the post of *muselin* (captain). However, the old institution called the *beglerbegluk,* which was ruled by the *Sandjak beg* or the *Pasha,* was discontinued. From the seventeenth century it was ruled by the Imperial governor (*Vizier*) who resided at Travnik. But the *ajan* (Bosnian nobility) continued to enjoy a special position.

The foregoing situation existed at the time Sultan Mahmud II (1808-1839) began his reforms of the Empire. These reforms cut deeply into the privileges of the nobility, and the Bosnians revolted. The newly appointed *Vizier,* Ali Pasha Djeladudin, a capable and ruthless man, re-established order, but not without bloodshed and the usual oriental cruelty. Upon the *Vizier's* premature death (apparently by poisoning), disorder prevailed again.

When Mahmud decided to suppress the *Janissaries* and establish a regular army, the *Janissaries*, headed by Kara-aga Ruscuklija, revolted. The new *Vizier*, Abdurahman-pasha, brought in the regular army, defeating the rebels and executing their leaders. His pacification of Bosnia was abruptly ended when he and his army were called to face the Russian invasion of Turkey in 1828.

The Bosnian *begs* expected nothing good for themselves from the modern reforms, thus they at first gave their help to the revolting *Janissaries*. After the defeat of the *Janissaries* the *begs* decided to act for themselves as a way of protecting their special status and privileges. They gathered at Tuzla where they elected Hussein-beg Gradscevic as their leader. Ali-aga Rizvanbegovic and Smail-aga Cengic, leaders of the Hercegovinan nobility refused to participate, thus separating Hercegovina from Bosnia. The Bosnian army under Hussein defeated the *Vizier*, Namil-pasha, and compelled him to transmit an address prepared by the Bosnian nobility to the Porte requesting autonomous status for the country.

At the same time, Hussein decided to join forces with Scutary-pasha who was the head of the Albanian rebellion. Thus Hussein marched on Skopje with an army of 25,000 men. But he was too late to prevent the Albanian defeat although he did register some military successes.

The Grand *Vizier* was playing for time, instead of trying to subdue the Bosnians. He proposed to Hussein that he assume the post of *Vizier* at Travnik, pending the appointment from Istanbul. Hussein attempted to impose his rule over Hercegovina, but his military expedition was thwarted by the spirited resistance of Ali-pasha. Furthermore, the Porte had no intention of keeping his promise to Hussein who fruitlessly awaited the promised *Firman*. Instead the Turk, Hamdi Mahomed-pasha, was appointed *Vizier* of Bosnia and at the head of the regular army and supported by Ali-pasha and his Hercegovinans came to claim his post. Many of the members of the Bosnian nobility, for one reason or another, deserted Hussein and his highhanded policy. Hussein was thus left with a severely depleted army and was defeated. He fled across the Sava River to Croatian territory and was interned at Osijek by the Austrian military authorities. Ultimately he was handed over to the Turkish authorities and taken to Istanbul. He died there after a short period of time (1832). Ali-pasha Rizvanbegovic was rewarded with the post of *Vizier* of Hercegovina for his contribution to the suppression of the Bosnian insurrection.

The intention of the Ottoman government to proceed with reforms met the stubborn resistance of the Bosnian nobility. The existing feudal system was nevertheless undermined. Due to political developments around Bosnia in the Austrian Empire and in the autonomous Turkish provinces of Serbia and Montenegro, new hopes were placed in the *raja,* provoking a social unrest which brought the Moslem nobility into conflict with its Christian subjects. The powerful Hercegovinian lord, Smail-aga Cengic, was defeated and killed by the Montenegrin insurgents. This event made an impression on the young Croatian poet, Ivan Mazuranic, who described it in his epic, *Smrt Smail-aga Cengica* which became a classic in Croatian literature.

The resistance of the Bosnian nobility was put to an end by the energetic Omer-pasha Latas, the newly appointed *Vizier* of Bosnia. He was a former Austrian officer by the name of Mihajlo Latas who had escaped from his native Croatia, became a Moslem and made a career for himself in the Ottoman service. In 1851 he transferred his seat from Travnik to Sarajevo and thereby made it the capital of Bosnia. At this time, Austria opened a Consulate at Sarajevo in order to have Austrian interests represented there as well as to give protection to the Christian population.

The decline in influence on domestic policy by the Bosnian

nobility gave the serfs new hope in their growing attempt to assert themselves. Their agitations provoked the Imperial government to send several commissions to Bosnia to deal with the problems of agrarian policy. These agitations also gave the European powers an opportunity to dispatch a special commission, representing Austria, Russia, France, Great Britain and Prussia, to study the situation. The Serbian prince, Mihajlo Obrenovic, attempted to turn the occasion to his own profit by interfering in Bosnian affairs. Nikola Petrovic, Prince cf Montenegro, did the same regarding Hercegovina.

It became obvious that the contemporary Turkish government was unable to cope with the rapidly developing situation in the country. Vienna began active preparations to replace the Ottomans at the first sign of collapse. It paved the way by establishing a diplomatic understanding with Russia regarding respective spheres of influence. This premeditated action could be postponed no longer when, in 1875, the Christian population revolted against the tax system as well as the brutal collection of taxes. Many insurgents found support in the Croatian parts of Austrian territory, as well as refuge there when badly pressured by the victorious Moslem masters. Serbia and Montenegro declared war on Turkey in 1875 but were defeated when, in order to prevent their extinction, Russia joined in the fray (1877).

Following the Turkish defeat, Russia dictated the Peace Treaty of San Stefano, but its execution was prevented by Anglo-Austrian intervention. The subsequent Congress of Berlin redrew the political map of the Balkans and gave Austria a mandate for the occupation and administration of Bosnia and Hercegovina, as well as the Sandjak of Novi Pazar. In the face of Austrian occupation, the Moslem population under Hadzi-Lojo organized military resistance. After a few local clashes, General Josip Filipovic entered Sarajevo on August 19, 1878. His arrival opened a new chapter in the history of Bosnia.

CHAPTER XIV

THE ANNEXATION OF BOSNIA
AND HERCEGOVINA

Historical background — Population of Bosnia and Herce-govina — Eastern Question — Development of Croatian and Serbian nationalisms in Bosnia and Hercegovina — Occupation — Annexation — Serbian crisis.

For better insight into the question of Bosnia's and Hercegovina's annexation and the ensuing Serbian crisis (1908-1909) several historical, national and, above all, religious facts should be discussed. Since the fourteenth century, Bosnia's population had adhered to various religious creeds. The majority of the earliest inhabitants belonged to the Church of the Bosnian Christians (known either as the *Patarens* or the *Bogumils*) with a minority following the Roman Catholic faith. During the Turkish rule, the Orthodox Serbs, as well as other Orthodox populations, were added to the two initial groups. At the time of the annexation the population of Bosnia and Hercegovina was composed of 815,000 Orthodox Christians, 612,000 Moslems (who were more or less the former *Patarens*) and 453,000 Catholics. Dating from the middle of the fourteenth century the Orthodox population was identified as Serbian, the Catholic as Croatian, and the Moslem population held a middle position, allying itself with neither side. This potentially turbulent religious, rather than ethnical, situation prevailed at the time of the crisis provoked by the annexation.

In the course of the eighteenth century, Austria had already waged several wars to liberate Bosnia and Hercegovina since, on the basis of Austria's jurisdiction in Croatia, these countries were considered part of the Habsburg inheritance. The issue finally became the chief topic of diplomatic negotiations between Catherine II of Russia and Joseph II of Austria. In September 1782 they reached a secret agreement on the partition of the European portion of the Ottoman Empire. This agreement brought what was termed the Eastern Question into the international arena. It allotted the whole western part of the Balkan Peninsula, viz. Bosnia and Hercegovina, as well as Serbia, to Austria, with Russia taking the remainder.

Austria remained loyal to the commitments of the secret agreement and in 1788 joined Russia in a war against the Turks. However, Austria was experimenting with the major reforms imposed by Joseph and therefore had an unfavorable domestic climate for successful warfare. Moreover, after Joseph's death his brother and successor, Leopold II, was threatened by the revolutionary storm in France and was compelled to sign a Peace Treaty with the Porte at Svistov on August 21, 1791. The treaty affirmed the *status quo ante bellum*. Thus, Austria's attempt to liberate Bosnia and Hercegovina failed.

Russia once again raised the Eastern Question, this time in the thick of the Napoleonic wars. Tsar Alexander I had Prince Adam Czartoriski prepare a plan for the partitioning of the European portions of the Ottoman Empire. This plan was submitted to the Austrian government, and, similar to the former secret agreement between the two powers, it offered Austria a share of the Turkish spoils. But, due to the French wars, the Russian proposal remained a dead letter.

Following Napoleon's fall, Metternich's Austria became the pivot for the prevailing European order, i.e. the Holy Alliance, and, as a consequence, stringently supported the *status quo*. When the widespread changes of 1848 occurred, the foreign and domestic conditions of the Habsburg Empire became so problematic that Vienna could not afford to revive the Bosnian question either then, or for several decades to come.

*   *   *

During the national re-awakening in Croatia, Janko Draskovic outlined a national program (1832) which demanded the unification of Croatia, Slavonia, the Military Border, Dalmatia, and Bosnia and Hercegovina into the single nation-state of Croatia. Even *Ban* Levin Rauch, although a partisan who was for the union with Hungary and who accepted the famous Hungaro-Croatian *Nagodba* in 1868, agreed to this program with reservations: He thought it should be a temporary solution until Turkish Croatia, i.e. Bosnia and Hercegovina, could be liberated and incorporated into the motherland.

Serbia's successful revolt against the Ottomans at the beginning of the nineteenth century had awakened and inspired Serbian national consciousness. Under the Sultan's suzerainty, the new Serbian state began at once to work toward the realization of its national aspirations. This meant no less than the liberation of all the territories of the Ottoman and Habsburg Empires that were populated by Orthodox faithfuls of the Slavic language. Moreover, it meant their ultimate incorporation into the Serbian state.

In 1832 Vuk Stefanovic Karadzic, a linguist and a zealot of the Serbian language, published the pamphlet *Kovcezic* (the Case), in which he propounded the idea of "Serbs all and all over." The text of the pamphlet clamored for the inclusion into the Serbian state all lands speaking the Slavic language. This claim embraced among other lands, Croatia, Bosnia and Hercegovina and Dalmatia. It and other similar ideas of Karadzic became the political *credo* for several generations of Serbian politicians.

Upon the demand of Prince Czartoriski, then leader of the Polish emigrees in Paris, Ilija Garasanin, Secretary for Political Affairs in the autonomous Serbian government, wrote a memor-

179

andum which set up a program for a future Serbian national policy. This memorandum was entitled the *Nacertanje* (Outline) (1844) and included Serbia's claim on Bosnia and Hercegovina. The Garasanin memorandum was paramount to a birth certificate for the Greater Serbian idea. Moreover, this "idea" corresponded to the narrowed Russian idea of Panslavism based on Greek Orthodoxy.

*   *   *

Ever since the Congress of Vienna the Austrian military circles wished to round off the Empire's possessions by acquiring Bosnia and Hercegovina since these countries formed a wedge splitting Austrian possessions in Croatia from those in Dalmatia. The military leaders welcomed Croatian nationalistic claims on Turkish Croatia (Bosnia and Hercegovina) as an historico-juridical pretext to seize the provinces. But they were unable to do so, due to Austrian military defeats elsewhere (Solferino in 1859 and Koeniggraetz in 1866), as well as because of the strong Magyar opposition that developed subsequent to the Austro-Hungarian *Ausgleich* in 1867. Furthermore, the general situation on the Balkan diplomatic and political chessboard changed with the Congress of Paris (1856): During the Crimean war, Russia had intervened in the Magyar Revolution (1849) on behalf of the Habsburgs and had been repaid with ingratitude. St. Petersburg could not forgive Vienna for this rebuff.

In 1858, the Panslav organization was set up in Moscow under the auspices of the Russian Ministry of Foreign Affairs. This new movement had nothing in common with the revolutionary and romantic first Panslavistic Congress which had assembled in Prague in 1848. The new organization, which held its first congress in Moscow in 1867, was closely connected with the Russian Orthodox Church whose chief concern was the liberation of the Orthodox Slavs in the Balkans, viz. the Serbs and the Bulgarians.

Two years later, the Russian chancellor, Prince Gorchakov,

financed a Panserb propaganda center in Belgrade headed by Matija Ban, an official of the Serbian government. Even as early as 1863 a similar center financed by the Russian Consulate in Sarajevo cropped up in Bosnia. This center produced a cover society by the name of *Omladina* (The Youth). Thus the foundations were laid for the later and better known Greater Serbian Movement.

*   *   *

Prior to the Russo-Turkish War in 1877, there had been several meetings between Gorchakov and his Austro-Hungarian counterpart, Andrassy. Although Magyar politicians were in principle most vehemently against an increase in the Slavic population within the Habsburg Monarchy, Andrassy, a Magyar himself, reluctantly came to an agreement with Gorchakov at Reichstadt on July 8, 1876, in which he consented to Austro-Hungarian occupation of Bosnia and Hercegovina should the Ottoman Empire in Europe dissolve. The document was finally signed at Budapest on January 15, 1877. But the exact boundaries of the intended territorial partition had not been clearly defined doubtlessly due to the ignorance of both foreign ministers regarding the geographical situation.

In 1878 Turkey suffered a decisive defeat at the hands of the Russians and, in accordance with the Peace Treaty of San Stefano (March 3), was expelled from the Balkan Peninsula. Thus the fate of the last western provinces of the Ottoman Empire, Bosnia and Hercegovina, was sealed: Their annexation either by Austria-Hungary or Serbia and Montenegro was imminent.

At this time Vienna was prompted to action. Austro-Hungarian diplomacy joined in the maneuver of the British Foreign Office challenging Russian intentions and imposing the dictates of the Congress of Berlin on them. Consequently, the Peace Treaty of San Stefano was declared nul and void. Upon the proposal of Lord Salisbury, the British Foreign Secretary, Austria received a formal mandate for the military occupation and administration of Bosnia and Hercegovina. This proposal became Article 25 of the Treaty of Berlin. Although for all appearances, the text of this article recommended temporary occupation, its most far-reaching implications favored permanence. Andrassy himself, as head of the Magyar resistance to the Slavic addition, settled for "occupation," notwithstanding that he could easily have obtained approval for formal annexation.

In accordance with the mandate, the Austro-Hungarian military forces proceded to effect the occupation within a month's time. The task was intrusted to General Josip Filipovic, a Croat, who at the head of the Croatian XIIIth Army Corps, marched into Bosnia, fighting against the insurgent Moslems all the way. Once established in Bosnia, Filipovic attempted to carry out his orders to set up a provisional civil authority. Since only the Croats could handle the problem because of the common language between themselves and the Bosnians, Croatian civil service and laws were introduced.

The *Sabor*, inspired by the Croatian role in the occupation, voted an address to the Emperor-King requesting incorporation of Bosnia and Hercegovina into the mother country (September 28). This address provoked a furious outcry from Hungary. *Ban* Mazuranic, who had made it an issue, tendered his resignation. It was duly accepted, and, moreover, the *Sabor* was dismissed for transgressing its prerogatives.

By 1883, the Hungarian government had won the issue and Bosnia and Hercegovina were placed under the administrative authority of the common Austro-Hungarian Minister of Finance, the Magyar, Benjamin Kallay. Kallay would be responsible for the destiny of Bosnia and Hercegovina for the next twenty years. The Croatian legal system and civil service were replaced by a new administration and policy.

* * *

During the attempted revival of the Three Emperors's League in 1881, a new statement once again specified that Austria-Hungary was free to annex Bosnia and Hercegovina at whatever moment seemed opportune. This statement was supported by a top secret accord which was signed by Bismarck, Sobourov and Sechenyi on June 18 in Budapest.

In 1906, the change of the heads of the foreign service in St. Petersburg and Vienna also introduced a change in European diplomacy. The former Austro-Hungarian Ambassador to St. Petersburg, Baron Lexa von Aehrenthal, took the post at the Ballhausplatz from the quiet and peace-loving Goluchowsky and Alexander Izvolski succeeded the indolent Count Lamsdorf in St. Petersburg.

Aehrenthal, called the "last great Austrian," was struggling with the idea of how to regain independence from the Berlin tutelage for Austria-Hungary and establish her as a great power in her own right. Well acquainted with the situation in Russia, which had been seriously altered by the disaster in the Far East, he believed that he would be permitted a free hand in whatever course of action he chose. He therefore contrived an ambitious Balkan policy.

Aehrenthal's Russian counterpart, Izvolski, was a fervent Slavophile whose political maneuvers had begun to shift the interests of Russian policy from the Pacific to the Balkans. Thus he began to intensively pursue a policy of Panslavism in relation to the Ottoman Empire: The first step in this direction was to work toward changing the *status quo* at the Straits of Bosporus and Dardanelles in Russia's favor.

Aehrenthal was an open but cautious partisan of the Austrian internal policy of Trialism. To keep this policy alive and make it feasible he was determined to solve the longstanding problem of Bosnia and Hercegovina through annexation. He held to this policy despite strong Hungarian opposition.

On the other hand, Izvolski thought he was a man called by destiny to achieve the ultimate aims of Russian external policy, a task in which his predecessors had failed. Bolstered by excessive self-confidence and a good deal of personal vanity, he ventured from purely diplomatic ground onto the tortuous and dangerous path of politics. He frankly admitted his ambition to personally accomplish Russia's mission in the Balkans.

On June 9, 1908, a meeting between King Edward and Tsar Nicholas took place at Reval. Izvolski participated in the meeting and returned home positively convinced of Great Britain's encouragement and support in the question of the Straits.

Meanwhile, Aehrenthal was sounding out the attitude of the great powers regarding the annexation and thus met Izvolski halfway. The latter was eager to please Austria-Hungary and approved the annexation of Bosnia and Hercegovina in advance, provided that Aehrenthal did likewise with respect to Russian efforts to open the Straits. After some preliminary talks in Buchlau (September 15 and 16), the country seat of Aehrenthal, mutual consent was reached.

It is noteworthy to add that Izvolski was not fully acquainted with the previous agreements of Tsar Alexander and Gorchakov (i.e. the Convention of Budapest in 1877, the Secret Protocol in 1878 and the treaties of 1881 and 1884) in which the question of annexation had already been settled in accord with Austro-Hungarian views.

* * *

The internal situation in Bosnia and Hercegovina had fermented, forcing Vienna to act one way or another. In May 1906 the Catholic and Moslem intellectuals met at Travnik and voted and address to Vienna in which they demanded the incorporation of Bosnia and Hercegovina into the Croatian sector of the Habsburg lands. A year later (November 9 through 13), the members of the Bosnian and Hercegovinian Orthodoxy held an assembly in Sarajevo and resolved for the self-determination of Bosnia and Hercegovina within the context of the Ottoman Empire to which they were already jurisdictionally bound. This last evocation was simply a pretext aimed at bringing about ultimate unification with Serbia.

In July 1908 the Young Turks toppled the old regime in Istanbul and general elections of the National Assembly were called for the whole Empire. Serbian propaganda in Bosnia stirred up the populace to send representatives, not doubting that Bosnia's Moslems would join the Serbs despite their loyalty to Austria.

The situation ripened while Aehrenthal was pursuing his talks with Izvolski. The pressure that was put on the reluctant Hungarian Premier, Alexander Wekerle, by the military was so considerable that he finally consented to the annexation providing that Trialism would be excluded and that Bosnia and Hercegovina would never be united with Croatia. But Izvolski, upon visiting various European capitals, did not obtain the expected consent for the proposal from Great Britain and France. Consequently his project for opening the Straits fell through.

Aehrenthal, paying no mind to his less fortunate partner, precipitated an international crisis by proclaiming the annexation of Bosnia and Hercegovina on October 6, 1908, one day after Prince Ferdinand of Bulgaria, in agreement with Austria-Hungary, had announced the independence of his country. This crisis turned Aehrenthal and Izvolski into antagonists and, above all, seriously complicated matters between the Dual Monarchy and Serbia.

Serbia, harboring the Serbian Panslavist movement or the Greater Serbian idea within her boundaries, was deeply offended. Moreover she was frustrated in her ambitions and yet without a legitimate case for claiming compensation. Prime Minister Milovanovic attacked the Austro-Hungarian action in the National Assembly and sent the whole country into turmoil. His inflamatory words were immediately echoed all over Serbia. The Serbs accused Austria-Hungary of violating the Treaty of Berlin. Moreover, the Serbian press joined the chorus with violent anti-Austrian propaganda which threatened the liberation of the Slavic brothers who were struggling under the Austro-Hungarian yoke. The revolutionary and patriotic organization called the *Slovenski Jug* (The Slavic South), which had branched out into Austro-Hungarian territory, was the direct agent behind such propaganda.

During the month of October, another secret society called the *Narodna Odbrana* (The National Defense) was formed under the patronage of the military conspirators of 1903. Armed volunteer bands of *komitadjis* (later known as the *Cetnici*) began activities along the Austro-Hungarian borders. Furthermore, on the basis of Izvolski's hasty promise of forthcoming help from Russia, Serbia was partially mobilizing for a hoped for war with Austria-Hungary. This promise was magnified by the press in Belgrade and provoked expectations that Russia was in no position to fulfill. To further complicate things, Izvolski feigned to both the Serbian and Russian public that he had never consented to the annexation of Bosnia and Hercegovina. This was apparently a kind of revenge for the way circumstances had favored Aehrenthal. However, Europe seemed disinterested in the Serbian question, seeking above all to avoid these dangerous complications.

In order to be assured of Russian aid, the Serbian Crown Prince George was sent to St. Petersburg and was soon joined by Nicholas Pasic, the chief architect of the Greater Serbian policy and the leader of the governing Radical Party. During these febrile diplomatic activities, the former Prime Minister Stojanovic left for Istanbul to seek a Turkish alliance against Austria-Hungary and Bulgaria. Milovanovic himself toured the European capitals, trying to gain sympathy and support for the Serbian cause. But Europe was disinclined to enter a war over the Serbian issue and Russia was unable to do so on her own. On Izvolski's advice, Milovanovic resorted to a modification of the Serbian stand which he made public in a speech delivered to the National Assembly on January 2, 1909. At this time he asked only for the autonomy of Bosnia and Hercegovina and for the incorporation of the Sandjak of Novi Pazar into Serbia and Montenegro as compensation.

Backed by Germany, which was a partner in the Triple Alliance, the Austro-Hungarian military leaders worked out a plan for the clarification of their country's relations with Serbia in the event that the Serbian government should refuse to recognize the annexation.

On the suggestion of the British and the French, St. Petersburg was to pressure Belgrade to use moderation. However, the subsequent notes exchanged between Vienna and Belgrade still proved to be unsatisfactory to Aehrenthal. He wanted recognition, pure and simple. Consequently, on March 13 Izvolski put the question before the Russian Imperial Council of War which was being held at Tsarskoje Selo. This council decided against open hostilities on the grounds that Russia felt herself too weak. Moreover, this reluctance of the Russians was significantly influenced by the German demand of March 21 in which Russia was to bring pressure to bear on the Serbian government. But the Russian government capitulated not, as Izvolski interpreted it, because of the German "ultimatum," but out of sheer lack of military strength relative to that of Austria-Hungary. Thus Russia withdrew her forces from the border.

At this juncture, the diplomatic initiative was taken by Sir Edward Grey, the British Secretary of Foreign Affairs. After prolonged pourparlers between Vienna and London, the Serbian government was compelled to sign a prepared statement in which she unconditionally recognized the Austro-Hungarian annexation of Bosnia and Hercegovina.

This statement was subsequently read by Milovanovic on March 6 at the National Assembly:

Serbia recognizes that her rights have not been affected by the *fait accompli* brought about in Bosnia and Hercegovina and that she will consequently comply with such decision as the Powers shall take in respect of Article 25 of the Treaty of Berlin. Yielding to the counsels of the Great Powers, Serbia undertakes from this time to abandon the attitude of protest and opposition which she had maintained towards the annexation since last autumn, and in addition

187

undertakes to change the direction of her present policy towards Austria-Hungary in order to the henceforward on terms of good neighborliness with the latter.

In conformity with these declarations and relying on the pacific intentions of Austria-Hungary, Serbia will reduce her army to its strength in the Spring of 1908 in respect of its organization, distribution and effectiveness. She will disarm and dismiss volunteers and the bands and will prevent the formation of new irregular units on her territory.

Since Austria-Hungary had come to a final agreement with the Turkish government on February 26, the diplomatic crisis relative to the annexation of Bosnia and Hercegovina was over with the Serbian declaration of March 6.

CHAPTER XV

MAGYAR ASCENDANCY AND NEW POLITICAL FORMATIONS

Ban Khuen-Hedervary and magyarization — Transformation of old political parties — Formation of new political parties — Croatian Peasant Party — Peasantry.

Ban Count Dragutin Khuen-Hedervary ruled Croatia for twenty years (1883-1903). In that time he left a deep mark upon the public life of the country. Magyar ascendancy, or magyarization, became increasingly more obvious. The long duration of his rule could not be solely ascribed to his enjoyment of the full confidence of the Emperor-King, Francis Joseph. nor to the special favors he received from the mighty Hungarian Premier, Count Kalman Tisza. At the time that he assumed the post of *Ban*, Khuen was young, energetic and intelligent. He was endowed with a fine memory and an understanding of human weaknesses, as well as with a conciliatory attitude toward the people. Applying the tactics of "oats and whip," he pacified turbulent Croatia in the spirit of the slogan, "Work, Order and Law." During his long regime, he perfected the art of politics.

Khuen's rule proved to be a crucial test to Croatian political life and by the end of it the different parties had been completely remodelled. It was with Khuen alone that the *Nagodba* found its full application in accordance with the preconceived Magyar ideas. Even though he showed great respect for constitutional formalism, he divested the basic laws of all practical content. He shortly introduced an electoral law which secured him a permanently obedient *Sabor*. In accordance with this law, the Kingdom of Croatia and Slavonia had a total of 45,381 electors out of a population of 2,500,000. About two-fifths of these electors were in the service, or were officials, of the autonomous Croatian government or of the common Hungaro-Croatian government. Due to the open ballot, the administration exercised absolute control over these electors. Approximately six thousand of the remaining electors were Serbs whose interest always lay with the regime in power. Beyond this, the *Sabor* was packed with numerous magnates or virilists.

The virilists were members of the Croatian *Sabor* by the mere fact of being the Archbishop of Zagreb, Bishops, the Prior of Vrana, the Othodox Metropolitain of Karlovci, *Veliki zupans* (sixteen in all), princes, counts and barons. The princes were Batthyany-Strattmann and Odeschalchi, while the counts consisted of Bombelles, Chotek, Draskovic, Eltz-Kempenich, Erdody, Jankovic, Korocsany, Keglevic, Khuen-Belasi, Nugent, Orsic, Palffy and Pejacevic. The barons were Edelsheim-Gyulai, Inkey, Jelacic, Kavanagh-Balane, Kulmer, Ottenfels-Geschwind and Rauch.

Thus, having a *carte blanche* in his pocket by virtue of royal approval and the support of Budapest, Khuen masterfully applied the famous Habsburg tactics of *divide et impera*.

Before the Khuen era the problem of Serbian nationalism in Croatia was practically non-existent except in the eastern part of the country close to the Serbian border. The Greco-Orthodox population made up about one-fourth of the country's population. Khuen started nascent Serbian nationalism into play among the Orthodox inhabitants, fostered its development and directed it against the Croats. On his insistance, the name of the official language was changed from simply "Croatian" to "'Croatian or Serbian." In return for special favors, the Orthodox population enthusiastically supported Khuen's regime thereby

190

insuring that the conflict between the Croatian and Serbian nationalisms would become a dominant factor in the country's public life.

Furthermore, Khuen used a special "electoral geometry" in favoring the Serbian minority at the expense of the Croats. He dissolved thirteen notoriously oppositional Croatian electoral districts, viz. Krasica, Cabar, Ozalj, Svarca, Sveta Nedelja, Popovaca, Krapina Vanjska, Sveti Kriz, Peteranec, Veliki Raven, Ivanicgrad, Oriovec and Sotin. Through this maneuver, the Serbian electoral districts of Korenica (population 15,941) and Mitrovica (18,822), which invariably elected the government candidates, were each alloted a deputy like the Croatian districts, e.g. Zlatar (48,130) or Bjelovar (56,417), both of which usually sent opposition members to the *Sabor*.

* * *

The former denominations and programatic tenets of the traditional Croatian political parties underwent radical changes. There is some question whether or not a clear-cut political party really existed in Croatia at the time. In Hungary the aristocracy played a dominant role, but in Croatia this group was alien in speech, thought and habits. The comparatively small number of intellectuals manifested patriotism verbally rather than with deeds, out of kindness more than conviction, and out of personal pride and noble distinction instead of genuine national consciousness. The huge majority of the people remained completely uninformed about public affairs and were only then getting a first glance at their country's public life.

But in the formal sense, three parties were represented in the *Sabor*: the pro-government National Party, the opposing Independent National Party (*Obzorasi*), and the Croatian Party of Right (*Pravasi*). The original National Party had accepted the revised *Nagodba* and supported the Mazuranic administration. Subsequently it merged with the former Unionist Party to become a single political body officially called the National Party although it was popularly known as the *Magyaroni* (supporters of the Magyars). Throughout Khuen's twenty year administration, this party did not have a single active political member who was an independent or a non-official party worker. It had no political club, never held a political meeting or electoral rally, and never published a newspaper or any other political literature in the Croatian language. Yet, under Khuen's leadership, this party held about nine-tenths of the votes in the *Sabor*.

In the elections of 1884, 1887 and 1892, Khuen won sweeping victories and reduced both opposition parties to a hopeless state of defeat and impotence. Less than two percent of the people were entitled to vote and Khuen obviously believed that his electoral maneuvers were the ideal solution to the Croatian question. In truth, however, Croatian public affairs were so undermined that some kind of reaction was inevitable.

The tide began to turn in 1893 with the reconciliation of Strossmayer and Starcevic, the symbols, if not the leaders, of the two opposition parties. This reconciliation was followed by an attempt by the followers of these two men to organize a united Croatian opposition. After a laborious meeting of delegates from both parties a common program was approved (1894). The fundamental ideas of the program were consistent with Croatian national aspirations in that they were a logical development of ideas expressed at the time of the Illyrian Movement by Draskovic in his *Dizertacija*.

The text of the opposition program stated:

(1) The Croatian Opposition, on the basis of Croatian State Rights and the principles of nationalities, will use all the legal means at its disposal to achieve the unification of all the Croatian people living in Croatia, Slavonia and Dalmatia, Rijeka (including its district), Medjumurje, Bosnia and Hercegovina and Istria into a single independent state within the framework of the Habsburg Monarchy. Moreover, it will support with all its energies the efforts of its Slovenian brothers to incorporate all Slovenian lands into this state.

192

(2) Furthermore, the united opposition will endeavor to organize the Kingdom of Croatia into a juridical, constitutional, and free state in which its people, through freely elected representatives to the Croatian *Sabor,* will exercise legislative prerogatives in full agreement with the Crown. The Opposition will also work to introduce parliamentarian principles which cover all aspects of national life and which, as is traditional in Croatian parliamentarian government, are incorporated under the leadership of the *Ban.*

(3) In the administration of common affairs the Kingdom of Croatia intends to participate in complete equality with the Kingdom of Hungary, as well as with the other lands of His Majesty. This intention is in complete accord with the *Pragmatic Sanction.*

(4) In the main, the united opposition will concentrate its energies on obtaining a constitution and achieving free and legal independence for the Kingdom of Croatia. This autonomy will be guaranteed by such means as laws permitting liberal elections, the freedom for reunification, the freedom of conscience and speech and the freedom of the press.

(5) A special executive committee will be assigned the task of implementing this program and will welcome the collaboration of all patriots regardless of party affiliation.

The unity of the opposition groups was short-lived. The common program, despite its unanimous acceptance, did not progress beyond the planning stages. Thus, it was not long before Khuen was convinced that he need not pay it undue attention.

On January 15, 1902, the Croatian Party of Right and the Independent National Party merged once more, temporarily assuming the name of the Croatian Opposition and adopting the program of 1894. The final choice for the party name was reserved for the impending gathering in which the deputies representing the Dalmatian and Istrian provincial diets were to

193

take part as well as the members of the Vienna *Reichsrath*. Sandor Bresztyenszky, Professor at the University of Zagreb and president of the former Independent National Party, was elected president of the new political body and Stjepan Radic became executive secretary.

The Croatian Opposition held a general meeting in Zagreb on January 29, 1903. Special delegations from Dalmatia, headed by Ante Trumbic, and Istria, headed by Dinko Trinajstic, attended. The Croatian Party of Right became the name of the new formation and this name was also adopted by the hitherto isolated political parties of Dalmatia and Istria. Additional resolutions were added to the already accepted program of 1894. These aimed at complete financial independence from Hungary, the safeguarding of peasant possessions, the protection of tradesmen and workers and the insurance of personal freedom.

* * *

At the beginning of the twentieth century the political affairs of the Habsburg monarchy had reached an acute crisis. When the Austro-Hungarian economic agreement (a product of the *Ausgleich*) expired in 1903, the Magyar politicians tried to modify the terms of renewal to their advantage. It was a propitious moment to claim complete independence for Hungary: National feeling was aroused against the use of the German language in the command of the common army with the aim of replacing it with the Magyar. Moreover, the discontinuance of Hungary's custom union with Austria was demanded. In the thick of the ensuing crisis in the Hungarian Parliament, Francis Joseph recalled Khuen from Croatia hoping that he could quell the Magyar opposition in the same way he had dissolved Croatian resistance.

Khuen's departure from Zagreb took place in the midst of general unrest and marked the last year of his rule in Croatia. Twenty years of his regime had succeeded in corrupting and destroying all pretense of normal political life. With the passing of the old leaders (Racki died in 1894, Starcevic in 1896 and Bishop Strossmayer, after a steady decline, in 1903), Croatia lost its political personalities and no new ones emerged to take their place. The vacumn created by their demise and Khuen's departure was strongly felt among the younger politicians who thought it was high time for the younger generation to take over.

After taking office as the Hungarian Premier (July 27, 1903), Khuen chose Count Theodore Pejacevic as *Ban* of Croatia and he was duly appointed by the Emperor-King on August 24th. Pejacevic's regime proved to be more or less a continuance of Khuen's except for a general relaxation of the political reigns which, to a certain extent, permitted a revival of the country's political life. One of Pejacevic's first acts was to release several political offenders who were serving sentences received during Khuen's rule.

The country itself plunged into a period of introspection which resulted in a general re-evaluation and reorganization of the political scene. From 1904 to 1905, nine new political parties emerged: The Croatian People's Party (clerical), the Croatian People's Peasant Party, the Croatian People's Progressive Party, the Social-Democrats, the Christian Socialists, the Croatian Labor Party, the Serbian Governmental Party, the Serbian Radical Party, and the Serbian Independent Party. Some of these parties never developed beyond the formative stages and some were actually only ephemeral offshoots of more important parties. Thus, for all practical purposes, the dominant parties were the National Party, the Croato-Serbian Coalition (organized in 1905 by Folnegovic's faction of the Croatian Party of Right, the Croatian People's Progressive Party, the Serbian Independent Party and some independent individuals), the Croatian Party of Right (or the *Frankovci* after its leader, Josip Frank), and the Croatian People's Peasant Party.

The foundation of the Peasant Party was, for the most part,

the work of the brothers Antun and Stjepan Radic. In announcing its formation they stressed its principal aims:

> Having assessed the Croatian past and present it becomes imperative that we pursue a policy that will not only lead to a united Croatia and its complete independence, but also provide a better education and general social progress for its people. For this worthy cause the Party has been founded and we are confident that it will fulfill its calling as a party of the people.

Thus a new term, the "people," emerged in the political vocabulary and it was intended to refer to the largest class of the nation, i.e. the peasantry. Thus, the Peasant Party aspired to function as the vocal organ for the "people."

* * *

The seed of national consciousness planted in Croatia by Napoleonic warfare grew quickly into a much stronger demand for democratic equality and social justice for all. In 1848, when revolutions began to follow one another in rapid succession, the revolutionary spirit became irresistible. In keeping with the general trend, *Ban* Jelacic ordered the abolition of serfdom in the entire territory of Croatia (April 25, 1848). This ordinance was more conservative than the Kossuth Law in Hungary, but at least it was discussed in the *Sabor* and subsequently approved. The Hungarian law did not get into the ideological arena at that time, and after the Hungarian Revolution was crushed, it became a hot potato for generations of Hungarian legislators.

The first elected *Sabor* spent most of its time discussing peasant problems. The National Party of 1848 (the only one represented in the *Sabor*) was split into two factions: The conservatives of Jelacic tried to protect the landlord's interests as much as possible, and the radicals, who were nicknamed the *Jacobins* and led by Baron Dragojlo Kuslan, struggled for the

196

rights and interests of the peasantry. The only genuine peasant representatives were sent from the territory of the Military Border, viz. from the regiments of Djurdjevac, Krizevci and Nova Gradiska.

Jelacic's administration was pressured into solving the peasant problem one way or another, first because of the existing conflict with Hungary and second, but not least, because of the many peasant mutinies throughout Croatia. It was forced to introduce martial law in several *commitats* which resulted in the hanging or jailing of many peasant rebels before order could be restored. Once more, stress should be placed on the historical fact that the Habsburgs again proved to be more favorably disposed to the peasantry and their grievances than did the local magnates or even the lesser nobility.

Bach Absolutism, which followed the 1848-49 revolution, produced a more liberal solution to the peasant issue by segregating the land of the landlords from that of the peasants, thus bringing a definite end to serfdom. But in 1853, almost simultaneously with the end of serfdom, the *General Civil Code,* promulgated by Francis I in 1812, was introduced into Croatia. Due to the extravagant stress placed on individual ownership, it created new problems for the peasantry such as the practice of individual partition of peasant family property.

Abolition of serfdom did not solve the peasant's economic problems. With almost no land to cultivate, he ceased to be a peasant and was compelled to search elsewhere for the work that would provide for his immediate needs. Continuous peasant conflicts and disturbances arose over the common use of pasture and forest. Although these problems had been apt to lead to disorders before, it was only at the turn of the century that they erupted in general unrest with national and political significance.

With the liberation from the yoke of the aristocratic landlord, the peasant found that he had merely changed masters. The civil servant, the gentleman from the city, slipped into the old master's place. Henceforth all dues were paid in money instead of goods. This introduced the problem of capital to the peasant since he was not able to raise the sums required for his taxes.

On the Croatian and Slavonian Military Border serfdom remained unknown. The famous bordermen, the *Granicari*, paid direct tribute to the Emperor by spilling their own blood for him on the many European battle-fields. This old military order was replaced by civil law in 1881 when the Military Border was incorporated into the rest of Croatia. The *General Civil Code* superseded the old system of natural laws and customs but was introduced without adequate preparation. Thus, in many ways, its application proved disastrous. It induced the dissolution of the old institution of the common household known as the *kucna zadruga*.

The legal procedure involved in withdrawing an individual share from the common household cost the peasant so much money that it nearly ruined him. He had to negotiate short term loans at excessive interest rates which grew larger and larger until many peasants went bankrupt. The *Narodne Novine* (the official paper of the government) daily published a long list of peasant property put up for public auction because of bankruptcy and overdue taxes. The government did not stand passively by watching this sad drama, but conspired in an outrageous way with the private banks and speculators to strip the peasants of their last holdings. This state of affairs was openly abetted by the Hungarian government which pursued a policy of systematic depopulation in Croatia by forcing hard-pressed Croatian peasants out of the country and filling the vacancy with foreign immigrants.

The peasant was left alone and helpless in his struggle against this exploitation. According to official records, between 1880 and 1913, 529,025 Croats left their country and only a quarter of these would come back. During the same period the Magyar population increased in Croatia from 5,050 to 105,948, and the

198

German from 13,226 to 136,221. With this expulsion of the Croatian peasant population from its ancestral lands by a policy of ruthless financial exploitation on the part of Vienna and Budapest, the country was rapidly losing its Croatian national character.

Serfdom continued to exist in Dalmatia under somewhat better conditions, despite the fact that it had been legally abolished. This was because the peasants did not own their land but existed until the end of World War I as something like tenant-farmers working for Italian landlords under a system known as the *colonate*.

With the Austro-Hungarian occupation of Bosnia and Hercegovina, serfdom had been abolished as a legal institution, but it remained an economic force until some time after World War I ended.

The alarming proportions of the peasant emigration were shrugged off by the government in apparent disregard or disbelief. Moreover, the attitude of the Croatian patriotic opposition toward this mass exodus was not much better. No one seemed to want to admit the existence of this national tragedy. Only when it took on the proportions of a massive flight of peasants from their centuries old homes did Croatian public opinion begin to feel the impact of the impending economic disaster. But the peasantry itself was being confronted by a far more serious situation than an economic crisis.

*   *   *

The peasantry enjoyed the right to vote, at least in the election of the first Croatian *Sabor* in 1848. In the elections of 1861 this right was again affirmed but not the pretense that the peasants were able to use their franchise properly, since the majority of them were illiterate and politically naive. Only an insignificant part of the population retained its franchise when the electoral law which preceded the *Nagodba* took effect but it was strongly influenced by the fact that electoral votes were sold for cheap favors or, even worse, for the famous electoral "goulash" served on election day. The regime had various means at its disposal to influence the peasant voters, such as the pressure of administrative organs, taxation, and the assistance of the clergy, the majority of which supported the regime. Khuen's regime, especially, brought this system to perfection.

Nevertheless, the peasants managed to put up considerable resistance to pro-regime vote-seekers who were overeager, but only until the regime made use of heavily armed gendarmes. During the elections of 1897, the gendarmes opened fire on the peasant voters at Bosnjaci, killing twenty-eight. Similar incidents occurred in various elections throughout the country.

Eventually the peasants everywhere in the country began to organize for self-preservation. Supported by several progressively minded priests and by the younger members of the intelligentsia, at the beginning of the twentieth century, the peasants founded numerous self-saving cooperatives and peasant public libraries. This trend was soon followed by a more general political movement which protested the financial agreement with Hungary. Toward this end public meetings of protest were organized all over Croatia. It was not long before they assumed the aspect of widespread activity against Khuen's regime. Thus several clashes with armed police occurred and the peasants found themselves in the first ranks of the opposition. Martial law was proclaimed in Podravina and Hrvatsko Zagorje where several peasants were killed in conflicts with the police.

The already widespread restlessness of the peasants was steadily growing and had to be channelled in some way. The question of who would transform it into an organized political movement arose. Out of this newly emerging awareness of political need the parties began to adorn themselves with the adjective "popular." The Croatian Peasant Party eventually came closest to satisfying peasant needs.

CHAPTER XVI

THE GREAT DILEMMA OF
CROATIAN POLICY

Croato-Serbian conflict — Post-Khuen period — Bloody Putsch of Belgrade and its impact on Croatian politics — Monarchy in crisis — Rijeka Resolution and its consequences.

While the Croatian Opposition was looking for ways and means to improve its prospects in the unrelenting struggle with the regime, Khuen did not remain idle. At his instigation, or at least under his approving eye, the conflict between the Croatian and Serbian nationalisms reached its peak. A pretext for open conflict was furnished by Nikola Stojanovic, Serbian politican and journalist, in his article, *Rat to istrage: Srbi i Hrvati* (War to extermination: Serbs and Croats), which was published in Belgrade in the August 1903 issue of the *Srpski Knjizevni Glasnik* (Serbian Literary Gazette).

At the time it was not clear whether Stojanovic had chosen this particular moment by chance or whether he was commanded by Khuen to write this highly inflammatory article which was enthusiastically received by Serbian public opinion. Its basic argument was that the Croats had no language of their own but were using the Serbian, and that they had no traditional customs and no national unity. In fact, it suggested that they had no national life at all, and no clear consciousness of how to form an entity which would have the characteristics of a

201

separate nation. Thus the existing Serbo-Croatian conflict had to be fought out to the bitter end, or, in other words, until one party capitulated. Stojanovic had no doubt that the capitulating party would be the Croats, since they were in the minority and, moreover, were particularly doomed because their geographical position had to a large extent permitted the infiltration of Serbs into their territory. Furthermore, he was positive that in the general process of evolution, the idea of Serbian supremacy was the only one that spelled progress and was therefore destined to triumph.

The *Srbobran* (Serbian Guardian), which was the Serbian newspaper in Zagreb, reprinted Stojanovic's article in full, but without comment, thereby giving evidence of its agreement. The Croatian press protested in chorus and the public reacted immediately with violence. Wild demonstrations against the local Serbs, and the government as well, spread across the country like wild-fire. Whether Khuen's absence from Zagreb was a coincidence or a clever foresight cannot be ascertained. At any rate the army was in the countryside engaged in fall maneuvers and the police force, at least in the beginning, adopted the attitude of a passive and powerless spectator. Later, when the gendarmes entered the picture, they were met with hostile resistance from demonstrating crowds who gave no signs of retreating. In Zagreb, Serbian houses and stores were attacked. Barricades had been erected everywhere behind which enraged anti-Serb mobs entrenched themselves and fought battles.

Another incident, which occurred at the University of Zagreb, prompted students to rush out into the street to protest Magyar policy in Croatia: By curious coincidence, a new inscription in the Magyar language appeared on the Zagreb railway station announcing, in huge gold letters, *Magyar Kiralyi Allan Vasutak* (Royal Magyar State Railway). This was a new breach of the *Nagodba* which had affirmed the use of the Croatian language on Croatian territory. Khuen himself was forced to admit this to be an unlawful act and declared to Vienna's press that the inscription would be replaced by a new one in both Magyar and Croatian. Croatian public opinion resented this statement so much that the *Obzor,* a leading paper of the Opposition, declared in one of its editorials that the crime could not be exonerated by an additional crime. Using both languages only added insult to injury since only the Croatian language was lawful on Croatian territory.

This incident provoked a new outbreak of violence which did not subside until Khuen's departure from the post of *Ban.* The climax was reached on April 11 (the anniversary of the Magyar Revolution of 1848) when Magyar flags were hoisted on most of the Croatian railway stations. This, quite naturally, provoked the wrath of the local populations. At Zapresic, near Zagreb, a group of peasants pulled a flag down and set it ablaze. In an ensuing conflict with the gendarmes, a peasant was killed, several others wounded and a large number arrested. The news of this incident poured fresh oil on the fire, setting the mood of the whole country ablaze. Martial law was proclaimed in several *commitats* and thereby initiated a series of bloody events at Kunovec and Veliki Bukovec — villages of the district of Ludbreg in the Varazdin *commitat.* Several peasants were killed.

Khuen's departure from Zagreb occurred in the midst of the general unrest that had marked the last year of his rule in Croatia. The air on Corpus Christi Day on June 11, 1903, was sultry in Zagreb and the spectre of a storm weighed heavily on the city, strangely altering its face. All of Croatia had been under martial law for several days and army units had been brought in from other parts of the Monarchy to restore order. Powerful cavalry detachments filled the back streets and squares of the city and were poised for intervention should the need arise. The traditional religious procession, with the *Ban* himself participating, was viewed with mounting excitement. Rumors of an attempt on Khuen's life suddenly surfaced, provoking the already excited state of the overworked police. A muffled detonation had actually been heard as the procession moved along the street.

The procession had not yet reached the cathedral when Khuen, without waiting for the solemn *Te deum* to begin, rushed off in his carriage to the palace. The cause of his sudden departure was not fear for his life, but a telegram which had just been handed to him. It contained news of the assassination of Alexander and Draga Obrenovic, Serbia's King and Queen, on the previous night. This, then, constituted the last public appearance of Khuen in Zagreb. A few days later he left to submit his resignation as *Ban*. On the 27th of the same month he was appointed Premier of Hungary.

But Khuen's departure, regardless of appearances, was at bottom, not the consequence of Croatian unrest or the Serbian bloodbath. It was essentially due to Francis Joseph's belief that only he could cope with the serious crisis in Hungary. Nevertheless, after a few days of silence, the Croatian opposition jubilantly affirmed that the rebellion had driven Khuen from Zagreb. Others more soberly made the assessment that the entire Croatian political upheaval had actually been an insignificant gesture so far as Khuen was concerned.

* * *

Although Khuen probably played no direct role in the preparations for the military *Putsch* which brought a change of dynasty in Belgrade, he most likely had full knowledge of the plot by virtue of his position as expert in the Monarchy's Balkan policy, and praticularly regarding Serbia. His personal friend, Benjamin von Kallay, who, as common Minister of Finance and general administrator of Bosnia, was fully aware of Serbian political undercurrents, knew more about the conspiracy than he was willing to disclose. Besides, near the Palace of the Ministry of Finance in Vienna stood the *Hotel Biegler,* which, since 1901 and with full knowledge of the Vienna police, had been the headquarters of the Serbian conspirators and the agents of Karadjordjevic's faction.

Petar Karadjordjevic was a pretender to the Serbian throne who was living in exile in Geneva. Between 1901 and 1903 he met several times, either at Linz or at the *Hotel Biegler* in Vienna, with the leaders of the conspiracy. These meetings and the members of the conspiracy, enjoyed the benevolent tolerance of the Austro-Hungarian authorities. Moreover, it was from these activities in the *Hotel Biegler* that the initiative for action originated when Alexander Obrenovic made it clear that he would intensify his pro-Russian policy.

Since Kallay and Khuen had worked hand-in-hand for the past twenty years in Croatia and Bosnia and Hercegovina in order to widen the Croato-Serbian gap, it can be safely assumed that Khuen was not left in the dark about the plot. According to Kallay, the conspirators had no intention of murdering the royal couple, but only planned to dethrone the last Obrenovic and exile him to Austria-Hungary. However, once the affair had begun it quickly got out of their control. Carried away by personal and political passions, their agents did more than was assigned to them. Nevertheless, the Habsburgs showed satisfaction in the change on the Serbian throne and Francis Joseph hastened to be first among the crowned heads of Europe to recognize Petar Karadjordjevic as King of Serbia. On his way from Geneva to Belgrade after having been elected king, Petar passed through Vienna, provoking wild outbreaks from students. The Vienna police averted their eyes.

*   *   *

The political affairs of the Monarchy had reached an acute crisis. Failing to obtain a working majority in the *Reichsrath*, the Austrian Koerber Cabinet, in order to provide a temporary budget, ruled by decree by virtue of a liberal interpretation of the famous Paragraph XIV.

The *Reichsrath* had been unwilling to vote for the budget. Moreover, the Cabinet was incessantly exposed to the violent attacks of the German Nationalists (i.e. the Pangermans) who were clamoring for union with Germany. The Czechs also assailed the purposes of the Cabinet by making obstruction the principle of their parliamentary practice. And the Italians, Slovenes, Rumanians and other such members stirred up trouble during the sessions. Notwithstanding all these difficulties, Koerber maintained his Cabinet for four full years on the basis of the certainty of the Emperor's support and the efficiency of Paragraph XIV.

After the fall of Koerber in December 1904, the Social Democrats insisted on the introduction of general suffrage. The Young Czechs and the newly formed Christian Socialists of Dr. Karl Lueger joined in. Archduke Francis Ferdinand, the heir to the throne, gave his support. In 1906 general suffrage was granted. As a result of its application, the elections of 1907 produced a new profile in the *Reichsrath*: Out of a total of 516 members, the Germans elected 233, the Czechs 108, the Poles 80, the Ukrainians 34, the Slovenes 32, the Croats 14, the Serbs 2, the Italians 19 and the Rumanians 5. Thus the German majority dwindled to a minority.

When the economic and financial Austro-Hungarian agreement, an offshoot of the *Ausgleich,* expired in 1909, the Magyar politicians saw the opportunity to modify the terms of renewal to Hungary's advantage. It was a propitious moment to claim complete independence. Toward this end the politicians roused nationalistic feeling against the use of the German language in the command of the army, aiming to replace it in Hungary with the Magyar language. At the same time, a demand for the discontinuance of Hungary's customs union with Austria was orchestrated.

The all powerful Magyar oligarchy, which had been forced into narrow straits by various political schemes and intrigues, was exposed to reciprocal accusations that it had abused its privileges, showed widespread family favoritism and abetted unlawful profits by conspiring with Jewish financiers. The existing Hungarian Parliament for example, was elected by only five percent of the total population. More than one fourth of that five percent consisted of civil servants under the absolute control of the government. Of 413 members of the Parliament, only eight were Rumanian, one was Slovak and one was Serb. The balance was made up of Magyars whose excessive number in the Parliament contrasted sharply with their proportion in the country itself: There were 8,700,000 Magyars to a total population of 19,240,000.

In the thick of the crisis the Magyar opposition, which consisted of the Democratic Party of Independence (headed by Francis Kossuth, son of the old revolutionary leader, Louis Kossuth), the Catholic Party (led by Count Zichy), and the Aristocratic Conservative Party (under the leadership of Count Apponyi), formed a coalition aimed at paralyzing the governing machinery. A series of governments were formed and dissolved, but none was strong enough to last. It was at this juncture that the Emperor recalled Khuen from Croatia in the belief that he had found the man who could quell any opposition, be it Croat or Magyar.

The Habsburg Monarchy carried all the latent problems that had been developing since 1848 into the twentieth century. The dual system, which was a product of the year 1867, was unsatisfactory to everyone except the Magyar and German ruling classes who found it satisfactory so long as they were able to hold sway over their respective territories. Among the other nationalities all kinds of internal political turmoil was fermenting, prefiguring either the complete reorganizaton of the Monarchy or its destruction.

One of the forces contributing to the turmoil was the Magyar nationalistic movement which was striving for complete independence. Another was the Pangerman Program which was demanding the incorporation of Austria into the German *Reich*. The Italian *irredenta* was using all its energies to pave the way to the annexation of South Tyrol, Trieste, Gorizia, Gradisca, Istria and Dalmatia to Italy. The Serbian nationalistic movement, following the Magyar example, aimed at the formation of a "Greater Serbia" which would include all Habsburg territories where an Orthodox population could be found, viz. Bosnia and Hercegovina, Dalmatia, part of Croatia and southern Hungary. A similar movement was alive within the Rumanian population and was working toward the incorporation of Transylvania into Rumania. The Russian Neo-Panslavists were also a threat to the Monarchy: Not only had they instilled in the Russians the desire to protect their weaker brethren of the Orthodox faith in the Balkans, but they also advocated annexation of Galicia and Bukovina.

Within this general crisis, the Croatian issue was bound to take on revolutionary proportions. However, its nationalistic political aims, insofar as they were outlined in the program of the Croatian Opposition in 1894, could not be associated with any of the forces bent on the dissolution of the Monarchy. If the Pangerman program should become reality, the German *Reich* would include all the Slovenian lands which had formed a part of the Holy Roman Empire, as well as Istria, thus moving its boundaries as close as some ten miles from Zagreb. The Italian *irredenta* wanted Istria and Dalmatia, and the Magyars were determined to swallow up Croatia in the process of forming an independent national state stretching from the Carpathian Mountains to the Adriatic Sea. "Greater Serbia" was also reaching for vital portions of the Croatian territory.

Unlike their neighbors, be they friends or enemies, the Croats could not count on allies to support them. The Magyars had the Germans, and the Italians and Serbs had the Russians, but the Croats were forced to seek among the dissatisfied nationalities of the Monarchy that happened to have similar interests.

*   *   *

The new generation of politicians in Croatia was slow to produce new leaders because, under the changed circumstances, they had to be sought in different geographical centers. In an effort to lift Croatian affairs (in the midst of new unrest) out of a deplorable state of inertia, the Croatian members of the *Reichsrath* and the provincial legislators of Dalmatia and Istria sent a deputation to the Emperor in the spring of 1903. Their assumption was that the Emperor's information on Croatian affairs was unilateral and needed a corrective balance. The mission of the deputation was to explain the fact that Dalmatia wished to be unified with the mother country.

The Austrian Premier, Koerber, prevented the deputies from being received at the Imperial Court. Thus they were forced to return with their mission unaccomplished. This incident created a disturbing impression in all Croatian lands. The deputation contented itself with issuing a public manifesto stating that Dalmatia, which had vainly been seeking reunion with Croatia since the end of the French occupation, was upset and indignant over the deplorable way Croatian affairs were handled by the responsible authorities. The failure of this manifesto was even more dismaying inasmuch as a previous resolution of March 30, 1897, on the same subject had been brought before the *Reichsrath* but ignored.

From the economic point of view Dalmatia was the most neglected province of Austria. She was above all a maritime province, but the approaching twentieth century found her harbors neglected or abandoned. A few small fishing crafts and some unimportant sailing ships lent the only life to an otherwise bleak picture. Moreover, at that time phylloxera, a vine blight, ravaged Dalmatia's vineyards, destroying its only other major source of income. The government in Vienna made no move to help the distressed population. Everywhere the young and vigorous citizens departed from Dalmatia, leaving behind only the aged and the children.

At the beginning of the twentieth century the situation in Dalmatia was hopeless. More than six hundred villages had no drinking water; but worse still, stagnant and contaminated water covered the rich valleys of Neretva, Sinj, Imotski and Vrana. But while the economic situation in Dalmatia deteriorated, the Austrian government spent large sums modernizing the city and harbor of Trieste. By 1857, the new harbor was already completed and the city was connected with Vienna by railroad. In

1907, a new and improved double-track line across the Alps from Trieste to Vienna was inaugurated. But neither the Austrian nor the Hungarian governments found the necessary means to build the ten or so miles of rail that separated the end of the railroad in Croatia from its Dalmatian connection. This project was neglected despite the fact that Dalmatia was the natural outlet for the Croatian and Bosnian hinterland.

Speaking before the Dalmatian *Sabor* (the Provincial *Landtag*), Trumbic, the leader of the Croatian Party of Right in Dalmatia, challenged the Monarchy: ". . . In the Monarchy there is no justice for the Croatian people, but I must add that this Croatian nation existed before the Monarchy and it will exist after it. . ." Trumbic was one of the new political personalities who would steer Croatian politics into new waters. The new issue that was emerging and which men like him were bringing to public awareness was no longer confined to problems in the relations between Budapest and Zagreb, but moved out into the realm of the Croatian problem as such, with all its accompanying complexities.

Alongside Trumbic emerged another Dalmatian, a selfmade man and an able journalist by the name of Frano Supilo. Supilo had also been a follower of the Starcevic idea. Living in Rijeka since 1900, he was the publisher of an independent paper called the *Novi List* (New Journal). (The role of this paper in Croatian politics before World War I will become evident in the course of events.)

Both Trumbic and Supilo had been exposed to the Italian influence which prevailed in the schools and public life of the province. Italy and its language were their means of contact with Western Europe. They had easily accepted the spirit of the Italian *risorgimento* and tried to apply it to their own nation. For the last few decades the Italian *irredenta* had flourished under the liberal Italian regime, aiming arrows of hatred in the direction of Austria. Thus the Croats from Dalmatia, angered by the repeated frustrations of the past, were only too willing to join the ranks of Austria's arch-enemies.

With the situation daily aggravated within the Monarchy and with the prolonged internal crisis in Hungary, the expectation of political profit grew within the circle of Croatian Opposition leaders and they developed new confidence. In their opinion the propitious moment to advance the Croatian cause had arrived. But first of all a number of difficulties which stood in the way of reunion with Dalmatia and made political conditions unbearable in Croatia had to be cleared away. Toward this end the Serbian factor had to be taken into account since the Croatian and Dalmatian authorities used the Serbian minorities to complicate Croatia's legitimate claim for reunion. This fact is more readily understood when it is realized that both regimes (i.e. the Croatian and the Dalmatian) enjoyed the support of the Serbs who were ubiquitous among the civil servants and the police force and who carefully watched out for their own interests. Therefore, Supilo spent all his time on and spared no effort in smoothing over Croato-Serbian differences and in finding a common cause for fighting the Austro-Hungarian oppression. With this purpose in mind, he even went so far as to declare the Croats and Serbs a single nation under two different names.

The next step for the Croatian leaders was to work out a *modus vivendi* with the Magyar opposition whose extremist attitude toward Vienna was showing signs of success and had the Croats believing that they might share in the success if they joined the game. But the prolonged Austro-Hungarian crisis forced them to take a definite stand in the conflict: Twenty-four members of legislative bodies from Croatia, Dalmatia and Istria met on August 24, 1905, at Dubrovnik on the invitation of the Party of Right. The meeting was characterized by two opposing views: Speaking for Starcevic's Party of Right in Croatia, Josip Frank proposed a resolution stipulating that Croatia should pursue its own political goals independent of Austria and Hungary. The majority maintained the opposite view, namely that a unification of Croatian lands (i.e. the incorporation of

211

Dalmatia) could not be achieved without the support, or at least the consent, of Hungary. A final session took place in Rijeka on October 2 and 3. All Croatian political parties from Croatia. Dalmatia and Istria, except the Magyaron National Party, were invited to participate. However, neither the Starcevic Party of Right nor the newly founded Radic Croatian Popular Peasant Party attended. At the end of two days deliberation, the "Rijeka Resolution," drafted by Trumbic, was accepted.

The "Rijeka Resolution" assessed the Croatian political situation and outlined its aims:

In view of the delicate political situation which developed in the Monarchy as a result of the Hungarian crisis, the Croatian deputies have decided to meet to resolve their own attitudes toward the issue and to direct their political activities accordingly, insofar as a question of undisputed, common interest is involved. These activities, be they in the parliament, the political club or the military, must be pursued without detriment to the fundamental principles to which every Croatian politician adheres.

The Croatian deputies consider the actual situation in Hungary as evidence of that nation's determined struggle toward complete national independence.

The Croatian deputies find this aspiration justified by the assumption that every nation has the inborn right to decide its destiny freely and independently.

The Croatian deputies are convinced that both the Croatian and the Hungarian nations are bound to each other not only because of historical ties but also because they are close neighbors and therefore are dependent on each other for actual survival, international trade and mutual defense. They conclude from these facts that all causes for discord between the two nations must be eliminated and a harmonious relationship fostered.

With due respect for the above established premises, the

212

Croatian deputies consider it their duty to collaborate with the Hungarian nation for the attainment of full state rights and liberties in the good faith that these rights and liberties will ultimately benefit the Croatian nation as well. May this resolution, therefore, be the cornerstone for a lasting agreement between Croatia and Hungary. The first condition for success is the incorporation of Dalmatia into the triune Kingdom of Croatia, Slavonia and Dalmatia of which it is already, virtually and juridically, a part.

To effect this incorporation it is above all necessary to get rid of the unbearable parliamentarian and administrative procedures hampering all proper political progress in Croatia and Slavonia and to create a relationship that will take care of the country's cultural needs and guarantee its rights to freedom. Toward this end the following liberal constitutional ordinances are suggested: (a) An electoral law that will assure such a measure of national representation at elections that they could truly be called the expression of the will of a free nation; (b) Complete freedom of the press which would include the elimination of the so-called objective procedure and the establishment of jury trials for all press and political offenses; (c) Freedom for reunification and the free expression of thought; (d) Realization of juridical independence by securing permanent status for judges as well as by releasing them from responsibility for juridical acts; (e) Formation of an administration court to safeguard the interests and political rights of the citizens from administrative arbitrariness; (f) Formation of a special court to try the legal transgressions of public servants.

The Croatian deputies have no doubt that a permanent understanding between Croatia and Hungary can be reached immediately by strictly exercising the rights guaranteed to the Croatian nation by the Croato-Hungarian *Nagodba* and by a revision of common affairs relations between Croatia, Hungary and the western part of the Monarchy (Austria) to the extent of allowing the Croatian nation an independent political existence which in time will mark a cultural, financial and economic progress.

This evolutionary progress in Croatia, Slavonia and Dalmatia will have a beneficial influence on her brethren in other lands, such as Istria.

In order to effectively carry through the above mentioned program, a committee of five members will be elected to study and work out the way the more detailed aspects affect our lands, always keeping the national welfare in mind.

* * *

Although the members of the Serbian Club of Deputies at the Dalmatian *Sabor* had received an invitation to participate in the deliberations at Rijeka, they did not attend. Since all the Serbian members of the Croatian *Sabor* were part of the Magyaron regime's majority, none of them had received an invitation from the camp of the opposition. Thus, the Serbian deputies from Dalmatia and some of the political personalities from Croatia gathered in Zadar on October 17 to pass their own "Serbian Zadar Resolution." This resolution aired the Serbian views regarding the Rijeka Resolution:

The desire of each nation for self-determination deserves the wholehearted sympathy of everyone who is engaged in the same struggle for freedom.

We welcome the present struggle of the Magyar people because the state against which this struggle is directed has done everything in its power to block the development of our fatherland, i.e. of the Croatian and Serbian nation.

The independence of Hungary as a state with a life of its own and as the master of its own forces will lead to conditions that must induce the Magyars to come to adequate terms with the non-Magyar population in Hungary. The Magyars will appreciate the strength of this population and also would depend on the support of the triune Kingdom of Dalmatia, Croatia and Slavonia for their national future and security.

Consequently, the Serbian deputies and the delegates of the Serbian political parties, having taken stock of the actual political situation in the Monarchy and having taken into consideration the views expressed by the Croatian deputies at the Rijeka deliberation, are ready, together with the Croats, to support the Magyar cause in an effective manner provided that the Magyar Coalition gives proof of its sincere intention to realize not only its own claims but also to help Croatia and Slavonia toward the same goal of increased political, cultural, economic and financial independence.

In keeping with the above, the undersigned have an interest in helping to establish new democratic institutions in Croatia which will replace the inequitable system existing at present and guarantee free constitutional development.

Having thus clarified their views, they naturally expect that the Magyar Coalition will not hesitate to set right its relations with the non-Magyars in Hungary by respecting the latter's own national and cultural expression.

As regards the demand of our Croatian brethren for the incorporation of Dalmatia into Croatia and Slavonia (which has already been granted by a definite law), the Serbian parties are willing to contribute their share towards the realization of this legitimate objective provided the Croats perform their part in helping the Serbs of the Littoral (Dalmatia) keep their promise by treating them as their equal.

* * *

After the Serbian demands were examined point by point at the session of the Dalmatian *Sabor*, the Croatian members accepted them by voting for the *Sabor* resolution which declared that the Croats and Serbs were of a single nation and that hitherto the "Croatian language" would be officially called the "Croatian and Serbian language."

* * *

215

At the meeting in Rijeka, five committee members were appointed: Trumbic, Melko Cingrija and Vice Milic of Dalmatia; Stjepan Zagorac and August Harambasic from the Party of Right of Croatia. Two days after their appointment, the committee met with Stjepan Radic, president of the Peasant Party, hoping to win his support. At their last meeting, Radic read them an answer that he and his brother Antun had prepared in the name of the party:

For us the Rijeka Resolution of October 3 marks a very unfortunate beginning since the Croatian national deputies had no reason at all to take such steps regarding the Hungarian crisis and its impact on the rest of the Monarchy. They should have borne in mind on the basis of cruel past experiences that every conflict between Vienna and Budapest is settled to the detriment of the Slavs, particularly those of Croatia, since under the dualistic system they have been divided into four parts. The text of the Resolution is, therefore, the antithesis to our true political aims, despite the fact that it claims to be the initial step toward their achievement.

(1) The present happenings in Hungary do not express a struggle for gradual independence, but rather the belief, dating from 1876, of all its governments, including the Magyar oppositional parties, that education and the state administrations are inadequate for the successful magyarization of most of the non-Magyar populations in Hungary. At all times the leading Magyar factions have tried to use the common army of the Monarchy to speed-up magyarization. This army, however, can only maintain its international importance so long as it does not lend itself to systematic exploitation.

(2) Hence this tendency in Hungary, or more precisely, in the actual representatives of the Magyar nation, can hardly be identified with the words ". . . Every nation has the right to freely decide upon its existence and destiny. . .", but must be considered the most unscrupulous kind of violence with no

previous example in contemporary European history except that of the Prussian policy toward the Poles.

(3) The Croatian deputies can no more admit to the existence of the "Hungarian nation" than to that of the "Austrian nation". The "Hungarian nation" can never be anything else but the Magyar nation in Hungary and therefore must gain absolute control over all other factions. Therefore the Croatian deputies should consider such an admission disastrous to their politics since it implies the renunciation of all hopes of Slavic resurrection, especially their own. Close neighborhood is the worst possible reason to hope for favoritism. It has, on the contrary, almost always been a point of friction even between such nations as Sweden and Norway. To speak in terms of the Resolution, longstanding historical relations are outweighed by the more pressing needs of actual life as well as by a common defense system in which only one of the concerned parties is required to eliminate all causes of disagreement. In 1903, the Croatian deputies fought one of these causes, i.e. Magyar oppression, with courage; and now they want to deny their own convictions in order to avoid discord with the Magyars.

(4) Under the circumstances, it appears impossible that the Croatian deputies could regard it as their duty to collaborate with the Hungarian nation for the latter's full state rights and liberties. They are neither Hungarians nor Magyar patriots and would have to be in order to be willing to embrace the political cause of Count Khuen whose regime has been based on exactly that peculiarly Hungarian cause.

(5) The Croatian deputies cannot honestly believe that those state rights and liberties will ultimately benefit the Croatian nation as well since past experience ought to have taught them better. Never had the Croats and all the other Slavs in the Monarchy been more strangled than during the period from 1893 to 1900 when Magyar ascendency reached its heights.

(6) It is an incomprehensible and fatal error to see in this

217

Resolution a guarantee for liberal constitutional legislation and to expect such a guarantee to be offered from the very same Magyar politicians who through their stooges in Croatia, from Baron Rauch to Count Pejacevic, kept all the Bach *Patents* in force and even unanimously maintained that the former Austrian absolutism had been too lenient in dealing with the rebellious Croats.

(7) The fact that the Croatian deputies imagine a lasting agreement between the Croatian and Hungarian nations to be immediately within reach once the Croatian rights guaranteed by the *Nagodba* are strictly respected is no less incredible when it is remembered that up until October 3rd the same deputies singled out the *Nagodba* as the principal cause of dissatisfaction in Croatia. At any rate, the Croatian deputies had to admit that Croatia's rights remained an illusion, whereas the Budapest appointed *Ban* was a hard fact.

(8) It is hardly to the credit of the Croatian deputies to have contented themselves with such a vague declaration of Croatian national unity. Not a single positive demand justified their action. Instead, they expressed the timid hope for some favorable progress of their own in the wake of a Hungarian triumph, adding a touch of bitter irony by mentioning defenseless Istria, but not daring to claim it rightfully theirs.

The Resolution is obviously the result of the misused cabinet politics of Italo-Magyar diplomacy to which our politicians subscribed without the support of the people and, therefore, without any political responsibility. The whole affair has begun under an ill-omened star and must end in disaster.

* * *

After the foregoing positions were taken, the parties from Croatia, which had participated in the Rijeka and Zadar deliberations and had adopted both resolutions, formed the Croato-Serbian Coalition on December 12, 1905, and published their program in the form of a public manifesto. These parties were the Party of Right (Folnegovic's faction), the Progressive Party (still in the process of formation and basing its tenets on the teachings of the Czech leader, Thomas Masaryk), the Social-Democrats and the newly formed Serbian Independent Party. Some independent politicians such as Supilo, Franko Potocnjak, Count Miroslav Kulmer, *Ban* Pejacevic, Baron Vladimir Nikolic, Milan Rojc, and Alexander Badaj joined the Coalition, and Supilo assumed the leadership.

For the Croatian Serbs, the acceptance of the resolutions was nothing but a tactical move. Their ultimate goal was the formation of "Greater Serbia" to be erected at the expense of the Monarchy.

*   *   *

The domestic troubles of the Dual Monarchy reflected, on a smaller scale, the general European crisis. The very survival of the Monarchy was at issue and its heterogenous subjects were compelled to make a choice. The Croatian issue, which had narrowed down since 1868 to the simple question of "for or against the *Nagodba*," suddenly took on a different and more ominous character.

The new political attitude of Croatia which issued from the Rijeka Resolution was an attempt to improve the Croatian position in the Monarchy through the reinforcement of the points of the *Nagodba* which were in Croatia's favor. With the help of the victorious Magyar Coalition, this was to ultimately lead to the incorporation of Dalmatia. As a counterpart to the Magyar Coalition, the signatories of the Rijeka Resolution joined the signatories of the Zadar Resolution to form the Croato-Serbian Coalition in Croatia. This Coalition vehemently opposed the dualistic system of the Monarchy and also, by hotly attacking clericalism, opposed the influence of the Roman Catholic Church.

The motives for such a radical attack on clericalism were for the most part unfounded and seemed to be a mere aping of Czech modernism. Above all the clerical influence on the exist-

219

ing Magyaron regime was non-existent since this regime was essentially liberal. The new Croatian Popular Party (clerical) was a body devoid of any political significance, thus the majority of the Catholic clergy adhered either to the Coalition itself or to Starcevic's Party of Right. Apparently Supilo, in his zeal to equal Masaryk, had overreached his mark.

The idea of Serbo-Croatian or Yugoslav national unity had for the first time been converted into a practical political plan which had sinister implications of conspiracy for the Habsburg Monarchy. Moreover, the promoters of the Rijeka Resolution hoped to make the Croatian Question the issue of the entire Monarchy and therefore the issue which would threaten the Monarchy's very existence. In spite of the careful wording of the resolution and the elaborate structure of the Croato-Serbian Coalition both of these factors were apt to produce dire consequences. Their dominant themes were the hatred of Austria and retaliation for the repeated Habsburgian betrayal of Croatia.

The Coalitionists completely ignored Croatia's political program of 1894 by omitting Istria from their demand for a unified Croatia and by passing over Bosnia and Hercegovina in silence. With the emphasis on a purely Croato-Serbian national unity the Slovenes were also left out. Obviously the authors of the Rijeka Resolution had been forced to respect Serbia's primary interest in Bosnia and Hercegovina in order to gain Serbian support for the Croatian demand for the incorporation of Dalmatia.

As a tactical move to pressure Budapest into supporting Croatia's solution for her national problems, the stratagem of the Croato-Serbian Coalition was doomed from the outset: The Rijeka Resolution marked the initial step in a policy which sought to settle the Croatian Question by achieving Croato-Serbian national unity; thus it prepared for the downfall of the Monarchy. Croatia's own national dilemma was now formally converted into the much larger "Southern Slav Question," a term first used at Masaryk's instigation by the two prominent English journalists and historians, Henry Wickham Steed and

Robert William Seton-Watson (alias Scotus Viator). These men gave this Question universal publicity.

The Croats nevertheless were still faced with the more urgent task of finding a satisfactory way to unite their lands into a single body within the Habsburg Monarchy. Starcevic's Party of Right, known as the *Frankovci* (after their leader Frank), and the Clericals, openly opted for a trialistic solution. The Peasant Party, on the other hand, followed a traditional course by seeking a solution in the translation of the Habsburg Monarchy into the context of the Danubian Federation.

CHAPTER XVII

A TIME OF CRISIS AND VIOLENCE

Croato-Serbian Coalition at work — Annexation of Bosnia and Hercegovina and the ensuing crisis — Zagreb Treason Trial — Capitulation of the Coalition — Period of violence — Assassination of Archduke Francis Ferdinand in Sarajevo.

Ban Pejacevic, together with the *Sabor* elected in 1901 under Khuen's regime, ruled Croatia for nearly two years. The governmental crisis in Hungary dragged on despite many efforts to reach a compromise and was only resolved by the Emperor-King's threat to introduce universal suffrage in Hungary. Because the implementation of this threat would break the preponderance of the Magyars it was resisted by all Magyar parties. Thus when the Universal Suffrage Bill was actually brought before the Parliament the Magyar Coalition decided to abandon its military demands.

A parliamentary government was formed on April 8, 1906, by Alexander Wekerle. Francis Kossuth, the leader of the Independence Party, held the post of Minister of Commerce. It was not until the formation of this government that Pejacevic called for the election of the new *Sabor*. The elections gave the governmental National Party thirty-five members, while the Croato-Serbian Coalition won thirty-four and the Starcevic Party of Right nineteen. The Coalition received substantial help from the new government in Budapest which instructed all its employees in Croatia to vote for Coalition candidates.

With most of the former Magyarons joining the ranks of the Coalition it soon began to assume the character of a governmental party. Nevertheless the Coalition had to swallow a bitter pill: It was barred from assuming the leadership of the government. Instead, Pejacevic retained his position and, for the sake of convenience, joined the Coalition ranks, while Baron Vladimir Nikolic, Serb and former Magyaron, was appointed Vice-*Ban*. No leading member of the Coalition qualified for a governmental position.

The happily anticipated collaboration between Budapest and Zagreb in the spirit conjured up by the Rijeka Resolution did not materialize. After only a few months, it received a death blow from the common Minister of Commerce, Kossuth, who allegedly was one of its promoters: Kossuth managed to get the Pragmatic Law submitted to the common Hungaro-Croatian Parliament. This law provided for the enforced use of the Magyar language on the state railways in Croatia, thereby violating Article 57 of the *Nagodba*. In spite of the Croatian Delegation's vehement protest and noisy activities of parliamentarian obstruction, the government secured the passage of the law.

To effectively meet Croatian obstruction, the Wekerle government had contrived to reduce the entire law to a single article. *Ban* Pejacevic, who gave his support to the Croatian Delegation and refused to comply with Budapest's order, was forced to resign on June 26, 1907. On the same day, Aleksandar Rakodczay, President of the Zagreb Court of Justice, was nominated to fill his vacancy.

Due to the Magyar betrayal of Hungaro-Croatian collaboration, the influence of the Rijeka Resolution came to an end, leaving a series of fundamental changes in the political orientation of the Croats in its wake. With all hope for a peaceful transformation of the Monarchy frustrated, a surge of rebellious feelings flooded the ranks of the Coalition. Conspiritorial designs for the overthrow of the Habsburg Monarchy came more and more into evidence. By 1906, Croatia, Bosnia and especially Dalmatia, had fallen to a great extent under the spell of Greater Serbian propaganda.

* * *

Austro-Hungarian hopes for recovering the ground lost in 1903 when Serbia changed dynasties were quickly snuffed out. The new king, Petar I Karadjorjevic, was little more than a figurehead and was forced to leave all important decisions to the country's real rulers, viz. the military conspirators and the powerful Radical Party. On its own initiative, the new regime, oriented toward Russia, engaged in an energetic anti-Turkish and anti-Austrian campaign. Its objective was the formation of a Greater Serbia which would unite all Serbs who were re- siding either in the Ottoman or Habsburg Empires with their mother country. In its logical extremities, the idea urged the unification of all Southern Slavs under Serbian leadership.

The Belgrade High School (equivalent to a contemporary col- lege) became the center for a political and literary movement formed in 1904 and called the *Slavenski Jug* (Slavic South). A paper of the same name served to disseminate propaganda championing the union of all Southern Slaves. Although harm- less on the surface the *Slavenski Jug's* hidden activities caused the Austro-Hungarian authorities severe headaches. The society's secret statutes were written by Milan Pribicevic, an Austrian officer who had fled to Serbia and brother to Svetozar Pribicevic, a leader of the Coalition. The nefarious results of *Slavenski Jug's* propaganda prompted the Croatian government to send a warn- ing on February 24, 1906, in the form of a circular letter which listed several leading personalities of the Coalition (e.g. Pribi- cevic, Bogdan Medakovic, Supilo, and Potocnjak) as being un- der suspicion of conspiracy.

The confidantes of the Belgrade government, Potocnjak in Croatia and Josip Smodlaka in Dalmatia, played an important part in influencing Croatian public opinion. But the case of conspiracy was dropped and the interest of the Croatian author- ities diminished after the electoral victory of the Coalition in

April. The subsequent truce was short-lived and Rakodczay was replaced by Baron Pavao Rauch on January 8, 1908.

The new *Ban* was the son of the former *Ban* Levin Rauch under whose administration the *Nagodba* was institued. The new *Ban* was Vienna's confidant and was the personal as well as political foe of Khuen and his Magyaron policy. In authoritative circles, he was considered an exponent of Vienna's policy regarding the Monarchy's Southern Slav problem.

This problem was an aspect of a vast political set-up which was conceived in the circles of the heir presumptive, Archduke Francis Ferdinand, and engineered by both the new Minister of Foreign Affairs, Baron Alois Lexa von Aehrenthal, and the Chief of the General Staff, Conrad von Hoetzendorff. These people aimed at rendering Austria-Hungary independent of Berlin and establishing it as a great power in its own right. In 1907 Baron Leopold Chlumetzky published a *ballon d'essai* in the April issue of the *Oesterreichische Rundschau* (Austrian Review) in which he advocated reforming the Habsburg Monarchy on the basis of Trialism, i.e. he proposed the unfication of the Southern Slavs into a third single state with an equality of rights with Austria and Hungary. (The idea of Trialism found staunch support in military circles where many personalities were of Croatian and Serbian origin.)

Conrad believed that the only way to safeguard the Monarchy was to change the dualistic constitution by providing for an adjustment of Hungaro-Croatian relations on a new basis of equality. One manifestation of this adjustment would be the enforced introduction of universal suffrage throughout the entire Monarchy.

Aehrenthal, too, was a partisan of Trialism and although he was cautious, he had decided as early as 1906, when he had taken over the post of Minister of Foreign Affairs, to remove in one move the Monarchy's external difficulties and at the same time initiate the first step towards internal reorganization. He intended to do this by solving the longstanding problem of the annexation of Bosnia and Hercegovina in spite of strong Hungarian opposition. During the consequential crisis of annexation, Aehrenthal declared to the German Ambassador: "It is altogether a matter of indifference to me as to who rules in Serbia, for I hope that in the future the King of Croatia will replace the ruler of Belgrade."

Ban Rauch was entrusted the task of preparing the ground for the new policy in Croatia. As soon as he took office he dissolved the *Sabor* and called new elections for February 27 and 28. On this occasion he revived the old Unionist Party under the new name of the Constitutionalist Party and thereby achieved a unique result. Wishing to prove his intention to rule constitutionally, Rauch did not employ the usual pressure on the electors and thus created a case without precedent in Croatia's electoral history: His party did not obtain a single mandate. The Coalition registered its greatest success with fifty-six, the Party of Right twenty-four, and the Peasant Party three. Five were listed as Independent. Nevertheless, the electoral defeat did not prohibit Rauch from staying in power.

To pave the way for annexation and to fight the agitations of Serbian propaganda, Rauch staged a monster trial in which fifty-three members of the Serbian minority were charged with high treason. The principal persons accused were the Pribicevic brothers — Valerian, an Orthodox priest, and Adam, a journalist. Most of the material upon which the case was built was furnished by Gjorgje Nastic, a Serb from Bosnia who had emigrated to Serbia and won the confidence of the members of Serbian nationalistic circles. After a few years he left Serbia and published a pamphlet called *Finale.* It appeared in Budapest on August 5, 1908, in the thick of the annexation crisis, and was a kind of intimate report on the *Slavenski Jug's* activities. The information it provided the Croatian authorities made possible the arrest of the suspects on August 18 on charges of conspiring with the *Slavenski Jug,* as well as on the related charges of espionage and high treason.

On Januray 19, 1909, the government demanded suspension of immunity and extradition for Svetozar Pribicevic, Jovan Banjanin and Srdjan Budisavljevic, all of whom were members of the Coalition faction in the *Sabor* and who, in this capacity, had been members of the Croatian Delegation to the common Hungaro-Croatian Parliament. They had taken refuge in Budapest where they procured a sympathetic reaction from the Parliament. It refused the demands of the Croatian government.

The Zagreb High Treason Trial lasted seven months. A poorly-conducted prosecution, together with a clever defense, won the sympathy of the press of the Western World for the accused. This press was especially vulnerable to the cause of the defendants since it had alreday demonstrated indignation over Vienna's annexation procedure. It now followed a line of investigation that was orchestrated by Masaryk, who was a member of the *Reichsrath*. After considerable investigative efforts and much communication with Vienna, Budapest, Zagreb and Belgrade, Masaryk was able to prove that Nastic, the author of *Finale*, was simply an *agent-provocateur*. The Court thereupon reached a verdict of guilty on October 6, 1909; but as soon as the Coalition came to terms with the government and received governmental support, the condemned were granted a special amnesty.

The Friedjung Trial in Vienna was a corollary to the Zagreb High Treason Trial. On March 25, 1909, the famous Austrian historian, Friedjung, published an article in one of the leading papers of Vienna (the *Reichpost*) in which he accused the members of the Croato-Serbian Coalition of conspiracy and high treason against the Monarchy. This accusation left the Coalition no alternative but to sue Friedjung and the *Reichpost* for defamation. At the trial in Vienna in December 1909, it was clearly established that Friedjung's sources for his article were doubtful and, in fact, that he had been intentionally supplied with forged documents by the propaganda office of the Ministry of Foreign Affairs. In the face of convincing evidence from Masaryk and Professor Boza Markovic, President of the *Slavenski Jug* in Belgrade, Friedjung was forced to publicly retract his statements.

Although the plaintiffs withdrew the charges, Vienna was damaged by this public exposure. However, in the course of the trial the witness for the defense, Baron Chlumetzky, had made a seriously damaging statement against the Coalition chief, Supilo. Chlumetzky alleged that Supilo had once been in his pay as a secret agent for the government. This charge compelled Supilo to offer his resignation from the leading position in the Coalition, and soon after he left its ranks entirely. Henceforth, the Coalition was controlled by its Serbian partner with Pribicevic as its foremost figure. Under Pribicevic's guidance, it underwent a gradual change. It renounced its former principles and developed into an opportunistic political body that remained servile to the government of Budapest until the end of the Monarchy.

The crisis concerning the annexation of Bosnia and Hercegovina thrust Croatia into political discord. As its major and semi-government party, the Coalition disapproved of the annexation because, on the one hand, of a previous Croato-Serbian understanding among the members and because, on the other hand, of its compliance with the dictates of the Budapest government. (The Magyars were opposed to bringing an additional Slavic element into the Monarchy.) Moreover, the Coalition proved susceptible to the Serbian demands concerning Bosnia and Hercegovina. Its press accepted at face-value the Russian and Entente press propaganda which presented the annexation as the first step in the German *Drang nach dem Osten* policy. In truth it was both the first move of Austro-Hungarian diplomacy to recover independence from Berlin and a much needed attempt to reorganize the Monarchy internally.

In the midst of these conflicting attitudes, Supilo asserted his own opinion in a lengthy speech during a session of the *Sabor*. Frequently interrupted by violent outbursts from members of the Party of Right, he declared: ". . . In the desirable event that Bosnia and Hercegovina should have the opportunity to separate themselves from the Monarchy, it would be natural for all Croats to rejoice in seeing Bosnia and Hercegovina join

Serbia rather than foreigners if, in the first instance, it could not join Croatia. . ."

Both factions of the Party of Right, i.e. the *Starcevicanci* and the *Frankovci*, as well as Radic's Peasant Party, wholeheartedly welcomed the annexation in the hopes that it would be a mere prelude to an eventual reunion of Bosnia and Hercegovina with Croatia.

* * *

As the annexation crisis began to subside, the Hungarian government shifted ground once more. Wekerle was forced to resign after a bitter struggle in which he had at last yielded to Vienna's demand for annexation on the condition that Bosnia and Hercegovina could not be united with Croatia under any circumstances. Khuen succeeded him (his second time as Premier) on January 11, 1910, and his old foe, *Ban* Rauch, resigned immediately. Khuen and Nikola Tomasic, actual leader of the Magyarons and the newly appointed *Ban* (February 5), met with the new and much subdued Coalition in order to conclude a formal pact for mutual collaboration and support.

In regard to this pact, Khuen saw to it that any persecution of the Serbs still in effect from the policy of Rauch's regime was checked and that the *status quo ante* Rauch's government in regard to Serbian affairs in Croatia was fully reinstated. This latter took form in the renewal of the official name for the language, viz. "Croatian or Serbian," in the use of the Serbian Cyrillic alphabet and in the distribution of the electoral seats.

To assure the stability of his government, Tomasic made the gaining of the support in the *Sabor* his chief concern. Besides the support of his own party he enjoyed the support of the Coalition.

Tomasic's contemporaries thought his personality was difficult to understand in spite of the fact that they could not deny him certain outstanding qualities. He was proud of his ancestry, cherishing the fact that he was the last descendant of the Mogorovici family, the old nobility whose representative helped conclude the *Pacta conventa* in 1102. Tomasic was also an ardent

Croatian patriot who took pride in the past glory of his country and who was fully aware of Croatian state rights. But he proved as well to be a realistic politician who could not afford to ignore Croatia's present union with Hungary and who therefore had to deal with the situation accordingly. In his position as outstanding historian and Professor of Constitutional Law at the University of Zagreb, he wrote the brilliant treatise *Fundamenta juris publici regni Croatiae: Pacta conventa.*

Honoring his agreement with the Coalition, on May 28 he bypassed the Hungarian Premier and submitted a new electoral law for Croatia to the Emperor-King himself. Although the electoral geometry remained the same according to the new electoral law, the number of electors jumped from 45,000 to 190,000.

The new elections were held on October 28. This time the Coalition obtained thirty-seven mandates, the National Party of Tomasic sixteen, the *Frankovci* fourteen, the *Starcevicanci* ten, and the Peasant Party nine. Two mandates were listed as Independents. The *Sabor* received five members directly from "plough and hoe" thanks to the Peasant Party. They were received with derision by the middle-class majority. The peasant leader, Radic, answered the sneer in a speech delivered on April 13, 1911: ". . . I am not founding a Jesuit army, nor am I founding a party which would accept men as they should be, but I am taking the people as they are. . . ."

Cooperation between Tomasic and the Coalition could not possibly last long since it was based upon Tomasic's misconception that the Coalition, in the true neo-Magyaron spirit, would make it a point to always support his government unconditionally. Moreover, the already troublesome Radic proved even more trying to Tomasic, until finally the *Ban's* attitude of tolerance changed into outright animosity. To press the issue, Tomasic called for new elections. But the elections went against his expectations. The Coalition received twenty-four mandates, the National Party twenty-one, the Party of Right twenty-seven and the Peasant Party eight. There were a handful of Independents.

Tomasic was not only dissatisfied with the electoral outcome but also disgusted with politics in general. In this mood he had no desire to confront the new *Sabor*, so he tendered his resignation on January 19, 1912. On his suggestion, Slavko Cuvaj, Head of the Department of Interior, was appointed *Ban* the next day. Cuvaj's first act in office was to dissolve the *Sabor* on the grounds that ". . . its present composition does not guarantee constructive work . . ."

The subsequent unconstitutional regime of Cuvaj stirred oppositional forces throughout the Croatian lands. On February 3, delegates of the Party of Right from Croatia, Dalmatia, Istria and Bosnia and Hercegovina gathered in Zagreb to draft a resolution of protest against Croatia's unconstitutional administration. They submitted it in the form of a memorandum to the Imperial Chancellery in Vienna and to the Military Cabinet of Archduke Francis Ferdinand. There was no sympathetic reply. On the contrary, tightening measures such as the suspension of the Constitution on April 5 were applied. Moreover, Cuvaj was appointed Royal Commissary of Croatia and ruled the country in this capacity for two years.

The *Sabor* was dissolved without provision for new elections. Thus the last sparks of political life, save a few sporadic demonstrations by youthful enthusiasts, were extinguished. It is ironical that, although the *Sabor* ceased to exist, the Croatian Delegation representing it continued its functions as the common Hungary-Croatian Parliament in Budapest.

*   *   *

After the annexation of Bosnia and Hercegovina, the legacy of the Greater Serbian conspiracy passed from the *Slavenski Jug* to the more spirited *Narodna Odbrana*. The *Narodna Odbrana* was a revolutionary organization formed in Belgrade during the annexation crisis by military and civilian conspirators who worked under the leadership of Colonel Dragutin Dimitrijevic-Apis. This organization grew in intensity until it finally spilled over into Croatia, Dalmatia and Bosnia and Hercegovina.

Youth organizations, whose members attempted to assassinate various public servants, were cropping up everywhere. A number of Croatian and Serbian students from the Monarchy were baited into the conspiracy by generous scholarships from the Serbian government. Several received training for direct action: On June 15, 1910, in Sarajevo, Bodgan Zerajic, a young Serb from Hercegovina, attempted the assassination of the Military Governor of Bosnia and Hercegovina, General Bogdan Veresanin. Two years later, on June 8, 1912, Luka Jukic, a Croat student from Bosnia, made an attempt on the life of Cuvaj in Zagreb. He missed Cuvaj but killed Councilor Hrvojic and a police agent who tried to arrest him. Both these young men had been trained by and received their weapons and minute instructions from the Cetnik Commander in Serbia, Milan Ciganovic.

To the disturbances created by the *Slavenski Jug* and the *Narodna Odbrana* were added others of a similar nature but originating in the United States of America. On September 15, 1912, the *Hrvatski Savez* (Croatian Alliance) was formed in Kansas City, Missouri, under the leadership of Rev. Niko Grskovic, a parish priest from Cleveland, Ohio. He was editor-in-chief of the *Hrvatski Svijet* (Croatian World), a paper for Croatian emigres in the United States. The statutes and program of this organization revealed only its cultural and national purposes but concealed more alarming underlying activities: During the summer of 1913, the *Hrvatski Savez* dispatched Stjepan Dojcic, a young worker, to Croatia under orders to kill Commissary Cuvaj. Cuvaj, however, had left Croatia for an indefinite time after the previous attempt on his life. A new Commissary was appointed on July 21. The new Commissary, Baron Ivo Skrlec, became the target of Dojcic's mission, but the assassination attempt failed.

* * *

Serbian successes during the two Balkan Wars (1912-1913) compelled the Hungarian government to seek an understanding with the Coalition. The first steps had been made by Khuen, but the constitutional government was not reinstated until Count

Stephen Tisza became Premier. Baron Skrlec, the Royal Commissary, was appointed *Ban* on November 29, 1913. He immediately announced that elections for the *Sabor* would be held on December 16. The Coalition, which was virtually the government party and which thereby received the support of the entire state apparatus, triumphed with forty-seven mandates. The National Party received thirteen, the *Starcevicanci* twelve, the *Frankovci* eight, the Peasant Party three and the Independents one. Of 208,411 voters, only slightly more than half used their rights. The Coalition obtained 43,645 votes, the National Party 15,716, the Party of Right (i.e. the *Starcevicanci* and *Frankovci* together) 33,356 and the Peasant Party 12,917. These elections were actually the last held for the Croatian *Sabor*.

After accepting the *Ban* chosen by the Hungarian Premier, the Coalition was called to form the government. The new regime at once faced a serious crisis: Early in 1914 the Hungarian government presented Parliament with a Bill of Expropriation regarding the major part of the Croatian Littoral. This act provoked massive resistance in Croatia. Radic immediately launched fierce attacks on the Magyars and their accomplice, the Coalition. To please Budapest, the majority of the Coalition countered by invalidating Radic's mandate with a flimsy pretext provided by obscure legal phrasing that supposedly proved his ineligibility at the time of the elections.

In the by-election in April, Radic was elected again without an opponent only to find his mandate once more invalidated a few days later. Another by-election on June 28, 1914, gave Radic a unanimous victory for the third time. The result of this election was proclaimed simultaneously with the world-shaking news of the assassination in Sarajevo of Archduke Francis Ferdinand and his wife, Sophia of Hohenberg.

CHAPTER XVIII

WAR ANXIETY

Reaction to the assassination in Sarajevo — Sabor's *war* sessions — *Croatian Constitutional Bloc* — *Emperor-King Charles's vacillation* — *Yugoslav Committee* — *Serbian policy* — *Secret Treaty of London* — *Supilo's activities* — *Supilo's Memorandum to Sir Edward Grey* — *Corfu Declaration* — *Corfu Declaration's background and consequences.*

The Yugoslav concept of Croato-Serbian national unity was for the most part an ideal held by some of the intellegentsia without the support of the larger populace. Even for most of its proponents the idea served only as a means for intellectual peroration. The Croats felt little love for Serbia when Austria-Hungary declared war on July 28, 1914, and even the Serbs from the Monarchy responded dutifully, it not enthusiastically, to the mobilization. Radic, who was always keenly aware of public sentiment, was simply expressing general opinion when he asserted that the Serbs (or Serbia) were "the unscrupulous enemy of the August Dynasty, of our Monarchy and especially of the Croatian way of life". Furthermore, rightly or wrongly, the assassinated Archduke had been considered a friend of the Croats and a welcome ally against the intolerable Magyar domination.

On the other side of the fence, in Serbia, the Archduke had

been considered a mortal enemy of the entire Serbian nation and for years the Serbs had exchanged the challenge: "Whoever dares to kill Francis Ferdinand will become another Milos Obilic". (Obilic was a Serbian national hero who had killed the Turkish Sultan, Murad I, in the battle of Kosovo on June 28, 1389, — the St. Vitus Day, *Vidovdan*, which marked the end of Serbian independence.)

Austria-Hungary's three unsuccessful offensives against Serbia in 1914 could not be attributed to a lack of military valor among the Monarchy's Croats and Serbs, who carried the principal burden of the military operations. Rather the lack of success should be imputed to the command's blunders, Serbia's military superiority in its high command, the number of men in the field, arms and better preparedness.

The instant war was declared the entire Monarchy was put under a military regime. Constitutional and political affairs of the country were suspended. In Croatia the *Sabor* closed its doors. The press, quite understandably, adopted the official viewpoint of the War Ministry in Vienna. The most intimate Croatian hopes were best expressed in the words of Radic to his friend Macek: ". . . The only chance for the Croats lies in the total defeat of Austria-Hungary without, however, causing its dissolution. A victory for the Dual Monarchy allied with *Kaiser* William's Germany would have catastrophic results for all peoples within the framework of the Monarchy except for the Germans and Magyars. On the other hand, the dissolution of the Habsburg Empire would spell disaster for all of them, Germans and Magyars included . . ."

In fact Radic hoped that Koeniggraetz would be repeated and the Monarchy subject to another internal reorganization. For the Slavs of the Monarchy this would entail a concession to their national rights, a concession long overdue and one that would make Radic's cherished dream of a Danubian Federation a reality.

The realities of the war were quite different from Vienna's arrogantly contemplated "military parade" into Serbia with the whole country serving as "breakfast" for Potiorek's army. (General Potiorek, Military Governor of Bosnia and Hercegovina, was in command of the invasion of Serbia.) But instead of a punitive expedition into Serbia the Monarchy found a war with Russia on its hands.

Pressure from the Russian armies (especially from their penetration into Hungarian territory) prompted the Hungarian government to call Parliament into session in April 1915. Most likely, Budapest had seized this pretext to reassert Hungary's independence from Vienna and to put a limit on the latter's irksome military domination. But what was granted to Hungary could not long be denied to closely linked Croatia: The *Sabor* was called into session on June 14. The immediate reason for the opening of the *Sabor* doubtlessly was the entrance of Italy into the war on May 23. Italy had territorial pretensions concerning the eastern shores of the Adriatic and only the *Sabor* was qualified to represent the threatened population.

The first war-session of the *Sabor* was marked by an opening address on Croatian political aims which was read by the chairman, Pero Magdic, in the name of the majority (i.e. the Coalition). This address was a demand for the national unification of all Croatian lands with the Monarchy into a single political body based on Croatian state rights and the principles of nationality. It aimed to guarantee the free development of Croatia's political, cultural and economic life.

In the name of the opposition Radic delivered an answer to the government address. In a lengthy address he stressed the undeniable Croatian character of Dalmatia and the adjacent Adriatic islands. His words made it obvious that by that time the Croats were well aware of the Italian pretensions. While Radic still expressed loyalty to the Habsburg Dynasty, he nevertheless vehemently protested the Monarchy's dualistic organization and the Magyar domination of Croatia. But on the other side, he did not forego the opportunity to direct some strong verbal punches at the hated Coalition. During the session of June 25 he put forward a motion to alleviate the extreme poverty in the villages caused by the war, and in a subsequent debate entered into an acute conflict with the government. The next day the Coalition majority voted for his exclusion from the next fifteen sessions. When he protested by calling this action infamous, the *Sabor* banned him for an additional sixteen sessions. Thus he was barred from attending the *Sabor* until the following year.

* * *

The Peasant Party, the Croatian Party of Right and the National Party formed the Croatian Constitutional Democratic Bloc which opposed the opportunistic policy of the Coalition with its accompanying subservience to the Hungarian government. The Coalition derisively called it the "Holy Alliance". The Bloc looked for support from the military circles which already bore ill feeling toward the Coalition: Their foremost leader, Pribicevic, had seen his two brothers, Valerijan and Adam, accused of high treason. Moreover, a third brother, Milan, was fighting in the ranks of the Serbian Army against the Monarchy.

Presumably, the Bloc's tactics were motivated by hopes placed in the new Emperor, Charles I (or, Charles IV, in his function as King of Hungary and Croatia), successor to his grand-uncle, Francis Joseph, who had died on November 21, 1916. It was believed that he intended to rebuild the entire structure of the Monarchy along the federalistic lines defined by his assassinated uncle, Francis Ferdinand. But, although Charles was full of good intentions, he lacked the courage, intelligence and determination to follow them through. The much stronger-willed Hungarian Premier, Tisza, had no difficulty obtaining the young ruler's consent to be crowned King of Hungary and Croatia at the earliest date which was December 30, 1916. At the ceremony, Charles swore to uphold the Hungarian constitution and the integrity of its territory. Thereafter Charles was committed to respect the *status quo* in regard to relations between the different nationalities in Hungary, i.e. he was committed to Hungarian domination.. Thus, the only possibility for change was a *Putsch*.

In an attempt to start separate peace talks, Charles approved

238

the convocation of the *Reichsrath* on May 30, 1917. Simultaneously he continued to scheme regarding the reorganization of the Monarchy. Although it was incompatible with the oath he had taken at his coronation in Budapest, in order to promote a general reorganization of the Monarchy he advocated the idea of Trialism, calling together various leading personalities in Croatian politics from Dalmatia, Istria, and Bosnia and Hercegovina.

Charles conceived the Trialistic solution as the creation of a single Croatian political unit which included, besides Croatia herself, Dalmatia and Bosnia and Hercegovina. But, in view of the fact that the Slovenian provinces (viz. Carniola, Styria, Carinthia, Gorizia and Gradisca), as well as Istria, were left out of this project, the Yugoslav Club at the *Reichsrath*, entirely composed of Croats and Slovenes, voted a resolution which was read on May 30 at the first session of the newly convened *Reichsrath*. Anton Korosec, president of the Club and a leader of the Slovene Populist Party, read the statement: "With respect for the principles of nationality and Croatian state rights, the deputies and members of the Yugoslav Club demand the unification of all the Monarchy's territories inhabited by the Slovenes. Croats and Serbs into a single independent state free from any foreign domination and founded on a democratic basis under the scepter of the Habsburg Dynasty. The members will spare no effort to achieve this goal."

At the same time, the *Sabor* in Zagreb discussed an answer to the Royal Message. On behalf of the opposition, Radic stressed the necessity of the Monarchy's reorganization. According to his views, Austria was nothing but a reflection of a Europe which needed to undergo fundamental changes in order to become its essential self which was, in effect, a commonwealth of free and independent nations. If it could transform itself into this commonwealth it would then be in possession of its own ultimate justification or *raison d'être*.

Within the foregoing context, Croatian nationalism demanded unification with Croatia, under the Habsburg scepter, of Dalmatia, Istria and Bosnia and Hercegovina, as well as the Slovenian lands of Carniola, Gorizia, Southern Styria and Southern Carinthia. The initial and indispensable step toward the realization of this program, which was recommended by the Bloc, was a change of government in Croatia, beginning with the resignation of the *Ban*. *Ban* Skrlec was unacceptable due to his past as a high official in the Hungarian government, and the same went for the *Sabor* since it did not represent the true will of the nation. In a final demand, Radic formulated the Bloc policy as a call for (a) complete emancipation from Hungary, (b) the immediate termination of all central agencies, as well as the revocation of all Magyar officials in Croatia, (c) the closing of all Magyar schools set-up in Croatia by the Hungarian government, (d) the unification of Croatian and Slovenian lands into a single body under the Habsburg Dynasty, and (e) the establishment of a true peasant democracy.

The coronation of Charles in Budapest and his oath to observe the Hungarian constitution, as well as the integrity of Hungary's territory, was a sharp blow to the Bloc and could only be countered by the latter's refusal to take part in the ceremony. On the other hand, the Coalition was dutifully present. Thus, instead of the Bloc, it was the Coalition, supported by the Hungarian government, that triumphed. On June 29, 1917, one of its members, Anton Mihalovic, a former Magyaron, succeeded Skrlec as *Ban*. The Coalition thus formally assumed power for the first time.

* * *

While Austria-Hungary's war regime had pretty much reduced Croatian politics to mere declaration which carried no weight or to passive observation, fate put the emphasis on activities related to the Croatian emigration to allied or neutral countries. These activities were centered around the Yugoslav Committee.

One of the principal causes leading to World War I was the general dissatisfaction of the nationalities with the dual organization of the Monarchy. This dissatisfaction was further aggravated by the Monarchy's strained relations with Serbia, which through the assassination of Francis Ferdinand, provoked the actual declaration of war.

The question of Austro-Hungarian relations with Serbia formed only a part of a much larger question, i.e. the question of the Southern Slavs. Its character was twofold: Its first aspect consisted of the fact that the Croats had become increasingly dissatisfied with the duality of the Monarchy. Bishop Strossmayer's original idea of seeking the unification of all Southern Slavs (viz. the Croats, Slovenes, Serbs and Bulgarians) under Habsburg rule, but with Croatia holding the dominating position, had undergone considerable transformation. A group of politicians opposed the idea developed by Starcevic's followers, and allegedly accepted by the late Archduke, Francis Ferdinand, in which Croatia and Slavonia, Dalmatia, and Bosnia and Hercegovina were to be united within a "Greater Croatia" which was to be the third partner of the Monarchy. This group fell under the influence of the propaganda of the strong Serbian *irredenta* and formed the Croato-Serbian Coalition which accepted the idea that Austria had to be destroyed in order to create a common state consisting of all Southern Slavs. This idea of an annihilated Austria was developed further by the Croats who emigrated at the beginning of the war and who formed the Yugoslav Committee.

The second aspect of the Southern Slav question posed the spectre of a successfully liberated Kingdom of Serbia and, to a lesser degree, Montenegro (which had been greatly enlarged after the two Balkan wars). Both countries proved to be fertile ground for the new Serbian ambition to create a "Greater Serbia," i.e. to free and annex all parts of the Habsburg Monarchy which had a Serbian Orthodox population. Such ambitions gave rise to extensive revolutionary propaganda, ceaseless terroristic activities and the determination to take Bosnia and Hercegovina, Dalmatia, and other Slav districts belonging to Austria-Hungary. The restlessness provoked by this activity reached a climax of crisis proportions in the assassination of Francis Ferdinand and his spouse in Sarajevo.

The Serbian ambitions had already been asserted during the annexation crisis (1908-1909) when Nicholas Hartwig, Russian Minister to Serbia, wrote to his chief, Izvolski, that ". . . Serbia must be the advance-post in the Balkans and must annex Bosnia and Hercègovina as well as the Slav districts of Hungary. . ."

The two conflicting aims — the Croatian and Serbian — created many frictions during the changing fortunes of the war and dominated the Yugoslav Committee activities and its relations to the Serbian government.

* * *

Shortly after the assassination at Sarajevo the Serbian government came to the realization that the ensuing crisis would lead to a declaration of war on the part of the Austro-Hungarian government. Therefore, it took the precautionary measures in its foreign policy that led to the unconditional support of Russia. Simultaneously it increased the country's military preparedness step by step. Nikola Pasic, president of the government and Minister of Foreign Affairs, harbored no illusions about the possibilities of a peaceful settlement to the crisis, but he hid his doubts during the electoral campaign which preluded the Austro-Hungarian ultimatum.

Once the war became a reality, the government issued a proclamation to the Serbian population which appealed to them to rise up and defend the country against the aggressor. But for a long period it did not come out into the open with its war aims. Pasic was confident that the "big brother" and protector of the Slavs, Tsar Nicholas II of Russia, would help the Serbs acquire the long-desired parts of the Austro-Hungarian lands. When the real master of Serbian foreign policy, Hartwig, died of a sudden heart attack, his substitute, Nicholas Strandmann, the *chargé d'affaires,* sent a report to Petrograd which reminded the Russian government of its promises to create a "Greater Serbia" through the annexation of Bosnia and Hercegovina to

Serbia after the war. This annexation would give the Serbians free access to the sea.

When the three Austro-Hungarian offensives of August, September and December 1914 ended in failure and were followed by a stalemate in France, the Serbian government, heartened especially by the spectacular Russian success against Austria-Hungary, openly declared its war aims. They were announced by Pasic at the session of the National Assembly convening in Nis. Pasic called for ". . . the liberation and union of all enslaved brethren: Serbs, Croats and Slovenes. . ."

Pasic stuck to this rather ambiguous formula, advancing the right of Serbia to liberate and annex the Southern Slavs of Austria-Hungary at the end of the war. He counted on the wholehearted support of Tsarist Russia. But when the question of liberating the Croats and Slovenes was raised before the Russian authorities, Izvolski vehemently protested. He opposed in a most determined way any proposed unification of Serbia and Croatia because he believed that, under the influence of the Catholic Croats, Serbia would forfeit its Orthodox character and become westernized.

When in 1915 the diplomacies of the British and French were trying to win over reluctant Bulgaria, or at least insure its neutrality, they were prepared to grant it the part of Serbian Macedonia which Bulgaria had lost to Serbia after the second Balkan War. To compensate for the prospective loss in Macedonia, Pasic immediately demanded from the Western Allies the promise of Bosnia and Hercegovina, part of Croatia, and what would be left of Dalmatia after the application of the secret Treaty of London. Thus the lofty aims of liberation and unification of the Southern Slavs had dwindled to the simple question of compensation for lost territory and reward for military efforts.

*   *   *

Following the Serbian success in the Balkan Wars, the inevitability of an armed conflict between Austria-Hungary and Serbia became apparent to many public personalities. Even as early as 1913, the sculptor, Ivan Mestrovic, had reliable information from Pasic that it was believed in St. Petersburg that Germany would not wait for Russian rearmament but would provoke a war before its completion. When he was on his way to Italy from Belgrade in 1914, Mestrovic passed on Pasic's suspicion of imminent war to Trumbic, urging him to emigrate.

The Croatian leaders in Dalmatia, Trumbic and Josip Smodlaka, and the Serbian leaders in Bosnia and Hercegovina, Atanasije Sola and Nikola Stojanovic, met in secret at Split. They agreed that in the event of war they should demand the unification of Croatia and Bosnia with Serbia and that some of the prominent personalities involved would have to go into exile for the duration of the war to work toward these aims. Thus, on the eve of the war, Trumbic left for Italy and Stojanovic went to Serbia. Supilo, who had received the information through his own channels, also took refuge in Italy. The three who found themselves in Italy, viz. Mestrovic, Trumbic and Supilo, formed the nucleus of the organization for Croatian political exiles. They first met in Venice, but on Mestrovic's suggestion chose Rome as the center of their political activities. Supilo received a letter there from Henry Wickham Steed who was then the political editor of the *Times* in London. He invited him to London. At about this time, Hinko Hinkovic, a lawyer from Zagreb and a member of the Coalition, also joined the exiles in Rome

Through the intermediary of Ljuba Mihajlovic, the Serbian *chargé d'affaires*, Trumbic, Supilo and Mestrovic paid visits on September 28 and 29 to the Allied ambassadors, Camille Barrère (France), Sir James Renndell Rodd (Britain) and Anatol Krupenski (Russia). They presented the ambassadors copies of a memorandum on the ethnic character of the Croatian lands that were claimed by the Italian *irredenta* and expressed the wishes of the Southern Slavs of Austria-Hungary to be united with Serbia. Rodd found these wishes not unreasonably intransigent with the Italian claims.

The first opportunity for a public measure was provided by

the speech of the Hungarian Premier, Tisza, in the Budapest Parliament in which he paid tribute to the courage of the Croatian troops in the Austro-Hungarian army. The *Corriere della Sera* of December 14, 1914, published a letter in which these men protested Tisza's assertions and proclamied their belief in Croato-Serbian national unity. They signed the letter the "Croatian Committee."

Supilo, who had enjoyed a certain amount of international fame because of the Friedjung Trial, left for Bordeaux in October (Bordeaux was at this time the seat of the French government.) There Supilo submitted a memorandum to Theophile Delcassé in which Croatian politics were dealt with and the project of the unification of the Southern Slavs was suggested. He presented a similar memorandum to Izvolski who was then the Russian Ambassador to France. Supilo went to London from Bordeaux and found the ground well prepared for his activities thanks to Steed and Robert Seton-Watson, a professor and historian and an old acquaintance. He was received by the British Prime Minister, Herbert Asquith, and the Foreign Secretary, Sir Edward Grey, to whom he submitted a memorandum similar to those submitted in France.

*   *   *

In the meantime the international situation regarding the Italian neutrality had greatly changed. Fierce propaganda from the Italian press calling for joining the war on the side of the Entente and demanding the eastern coast of the Adriatic aroused considerable anxiety among the émigrés. During the winter of 1914-1915, Italy became the scene for intensified propaganda directed at Austria-Hungary. The Italian *irredenta* secured its hold on public opinion which began openly demanding for Italy Dalmatia and Istria (the two Austrian provinces populated by Croats) and other territories.

To forestall Italy, Supilo left for Petrograd in the spring of 1915 seeking Russian support for his cause. Through a conversation with Sazonov, Russian Minister of Foreign Affairs, he became aware of the existence of the secret Treaty of London which was signed on April 26, 1915, by Great Britain, France, Russia and Italy. The main provisions of the treaty can be tabulated as follows: (1) For entrance into the war Italy was promised the annexation of Trent as well as the whole of southern Tyrol as far as Brenner Pass; (2) Italy was further promised territories and islands such as Trieste, Gorizia, Gradisca and portions of Carniola and Carinthia, which would place some 500,000 Slovenes and Croats under its rule; and (3) Northern Dalmatia and most of the Dalmatian islands were promised to Italy, putting 500,000 more Croats under its rule.

These stipulations in themselves practically annihilated Supilo's hopes, but they were followed by Sazonov's open declaration against Serbo-Croatian union and by his insistence on an aggrandizement for Serbia through the incorporation of Bosnia and Hercegovina, Southern Dalmatia and the eastern parts of Croatia (Srijem). Supilo vainly protested. He sent a telegram to Pasic asking him for the support of the Serbian government. Under pressure from the Serbian Opposition, Pasic felt obligated to express a mild protest against Italy's designs on the eastern coast of the Adriatic Sea in a speech to the National Assembly.

The passive attitude of Pasic's government toward the Treaty of London inflicted an unfortunate and painful impression on the members of the Croatian emigration. Supilo rushed from Petrograd to Nis, the temporary seat of the Serbian government, to find out the exact position of the Serbian government regarding the projected national unity of the Southern Slavs. At the same time he hoped to gain the government's support in contesting articles two and three of the Treaty of London. (These articles dealt with the Croatian and Slovenian territories.) But Pasic's attitude remained unaltered, and Supilo became painfully aware of the difference between the hopes of his Croatian émigrés and those of Serbian policy regarding national unity and the destiny of the Southern Slavs. Because the disagreements became particularly obvious in this meeting of Pasic and Supilo it can be said that it marks the moment of the transformation of the "Croatian Question" into its aspect as the Serbo-Croatian conflict, a conflict which would later mar the life of the new common state.

When Italy's intervention in the war became a reality, the members of the Croat group left Rome for Paris, since Italy was becoming less and less propitious toward their political activities. They held a general meeting in Paris at the Hotel Madison on April 30, 1915, where they formed the Yugoslav Committee as the representative body of the Southern Slavs from Austria-Hungary. Trumbic became president.

The members of the Yugoslav Committee were received by Delcassé on May 6 and they presented him a memorandum which listed the national territories of the Southern Slavs in the following order: (a) Serbia and Montenegro, (b) Bosnia and Hercegovina, (c), Dalmatia and all islands, (d) Croatia and Slavonia, including the cities of Rijeka and Medjumurje, (e) the southern part of Hungary along the River Drava and former Serbian Vojvodina, Backa and Banat, (f) Istria, including accompanying islands and Trieste, (g) Carniola and Gorizia, and (h) southern Carinthia and southern Styria with the adjacent southwestern part of Hungary.

In a subsequent interview with Izvolski, Trumbic explained the Committee's program for the unification of the Croats and Slovenes with Serbia. Izvolski outrightly rejected the program, claiming that it was contrary to Russian policy prohibiting the mingling of peoples of the Orthodox faith with adherents of other creeds and that, therefore, a union of Catholic Croats with the Orthodox Serbs could never be allowed. He was even more insistent in his conversation with Steed some days later, claiming that the Croats must keep to themselves.

On May 8 the members of the Committee left for London, making it their official seat. They had barely arrived in the city when, on May 12, they made public the Manifesto of the Yugoslav Committee, addressing it to the British Nation and the Parliament. Its content was similar to that of the memorandum presented to the French and Russian authorities in Paris. The political aims and activities of the Committee can be summarized as follows: (1) The liberation of the Southern Slavs in Austria-Hungary through the dissolution of the Habsburg Monarchy; (2) the prevention of the application of articles two and three of the secret Treaty of London which concede to Italy the Croatian and Slovenian territories of Dalmatia, Istria, Trieste and Gorizia as well as parts of Carniola; and, finally, (3) the accomplishment of the union, on equal footing, of the Austro-Hungarian Slavs with Serbia and Montenegro in a single state.

The Yugoslav Committee and the Serbian government were in agreement on the first point. But regarding the second point there was a difference of opinion: Pasic turned down the Committee's request for support when he made this statement to the *Corriere della Sera* on April 16, 1916: ". . . I declare with the utmost determination that no serious disagreement exists between Serbia and Italy. . . We Serbs are willing to recognize the indisputable right of Italy to hegemony on the Adriatic Sea. . ." Pasic's declaration was further corroborated by an editorial in the paper which states that ". . . Mr. Pasic deserves praise for approving, in the name of his country, the new situation against which the Yugoslav Committee had waged stubborn and defiant propaganda. . ."

Pasic's declaration, as well as the general attitude of the Serbian government, regarding the national unity of the Serbs, Croats and Slovenes touched off a serious crisis within the Committee. Besides the problem of his personal rivalry with Trumbic, Supilo's strained relations with the Serbian members of the Committee provoked open conflict.

While the Committee remained passive in the face of Pasic's declaration, Supilo foresaw the political consequences and expressed his views in a memorandum which he presented to Grey:

The Croats, Serbs and Slovenes are, ethnically, one people. Regarding historical traditions, political constitution, public law, culture and civilization they express their differences un-

248

der three names, but they speak the same language and are of the same race.

The leading role among the Croato-Serbo-Slovenian people in the Habsburg Monarchy belongs to Croatia as a *prima inter pares*. Outside the Monarchy this role has devolved on Serbia. Notwithstanding the question of Serbia or Croatia, the principles of complete equality between the political elements of the two peoples shall be established and so shall complete equality and freedom of religion.

In the eyes of all Croats, wherever they may be, Croatia proper, with its capital at Zagreb, represents the head and heart of the Croatian cause; in like manner, Serbia, with its capital at Belgrade, represents the head and heart of the Serbian cause. For the Croats, Croatia and Zagreb play the vital role in the existence of their political and constitutional individuality. The lands inhabited by the Croats outside Croatia proper consider themselves to be members of the Croatian nation.

The idea of the national unity of the Serbs, Croats and Slovenes, in its political and logical implications, leads to the unification of these peoples in one free national state in which each branch of the Serbo-Croato-Slovenian tree would contribute its particular traditions and its best abilities and energies to the assets of the common nation. This new unitary formation would be the harmonious result of all our energies fusing the various ideas, traditions and hopes into one common effort aimed at the securing of a common future. A state of twelve to thirteen million people would thus be created (seven million Greek Orthodox, five million Roman Catholics and eight-hundred thousand Muslim Slavs) which would be strong enough to bar the natural gate to German imperialistic expansion to the East. This state would be, therefore, a natural ally to all who oppose German hegemony.

This national unification and fusion cannot be properly carried out unless Croatia (with Zagreb) wholeheartedly collaborates in the task as the true representative of the Croatian cause.

Should forces stronger than justice prevent the realization of the national union, that is, if for instance Croatia were to be excluded from the block of Slav lands united with Serbia it would become necessary for Serbia itself to carry out, at a suitable moment, a national, political, constitutional and moral reform which would render the creation of a rival Yugoslav state, or the organization of a movement in favor of such a state impossible. In other words, it would become necessary for Serbia itself to carry out an internal transformation which would enable it to become the standard bearer of the cause of Yugoslav unity.

If it were otherwise, the Croats and Slovenes would no longer have the desire for liberation, nor would they desire union and fusion with Serbia; they would be faced with an exclusively Serbian Orthodox imperialism and the threat of conquest and domination. Serbia would thus demonstrate that it possesses neither will nor power to adopt the idea of Yugoslav unity as the basis for its policy. The accomplishment of that unity would have to be left to a more propitious moment. As long as that moment does not arise it shall be the duty of all Croats to advocate the joining with Croatia of all those Yugoslav lands in which the majority of the population favors such a union by a genuine and freely expressed will.

Supilo's action impelled the Committee to meet in Paris on June 5, 1916. At the plenary session, Supilo read the text of his memorandum to Grey and tried to explain what he thought to be the future for the Croats and Slovenes under Serbian hegemony: ". . . their great majority would unhesitatingly prefer even the present sad Austrian bondage to the new moves made against them. . ." (Supilo was here referring to the application of the secret Treaty of London and the policy of the Serbian government.) After this declaration, Supilo resigned from the Committee.

The Serbian defeat in the fall of 1915, and the disastrous retreat of the remnants of its armies through Albania, imposed a serious crisis between the government and military circles. The officers, who were members of the *Crna ruka* (the Black Hand), held Pasic responsible for the catastrophe. (Officers of the *Narodna Odbrana* had split into two opposing factions by 1911: One faction, the *Crna ruka*, was headed by Colonel Dimitrijevic; and the other, the *Bela ruka* — or the White Hand — followed Prince Aleksander and Premier Pasic's orders.) After the retreat through Albania in the direction of the Adriatic coast, the government established its seat on the Greek island of Corfu.

In 1916 Russia was also facing a grave crisis precipitated by a series of severe defeats: These defeats had accentuated the already existing difficulties in the country. In October the first tentative effort was made to obtain peace with Austria-Hungary. It was renewed in February of the following year, a few days before the outbreak of the revolution.

Meanwhile the aging Emperor, Francis Joseph, died on November 21, bringing about a change on the throne of Austria-Hungary. His successor, Charles I, made immediate peace overtures to the French government through his brother-in-law, Prince Sixte of Bourbon Parma, who was serving in the Belgian army. Prince Sixte began his peace-seeking mission on December 5, 1916. Since the Entente's principal aim was to break up Germany, not the Habsburg Monarchy, it viewed Charles's efforts favorably. In the course of the negotiations, the opinion that Serbia should be restored and, further, should have equitable and natural access to the Adriatic Sea was generally held.

At that moment an exceptional change occurred in Russia due to the Revolution of March 14, 1917. The newly formed government of Prince Lvov was not willing to support the former Tsarist policy toward Serbia. Miliukov, the new Minister of

251

Foreign Affairs, did not see eye-to-eye with the Serbian government. He preferred to lend his support to Bulgaria's claims on Macedonia and he was inclined to take a more understanding attitude toward the claims of the Southern Slavs of Austria-Hungary regarding their liberation.

Supilo's own activities in London had led Grey to a declaration in favor of the union of the Southern Slavs, provided that the Serbian government was willing to agree that after the war Bosnia and Hercegovina, Southern Dalmatia, and Croatia and Slavonia would be given the opportunity to decide their own destinies, as well as the freedom to act on their own decisions.

Pasic's foreign policy had been based on the assumption that Tsarist Russia would unconditionally back all Serbian claims. With its main buttress gone with the collapse of Tsarism, the "Greater Serbia" program lost its former force with the Western Powers. Pasic, confronted by several attempts to gain peace, found himself in a precarious situation since he no longer had Russia's backing. In an endeavor to forestall his internal Serbian opponents and at the same time shed himself of the responsibility for the Sarajevo crime on the *Crna Ruka*, Pasic staged the Salonika Trial of Colonel Dimitrijevic and his followers. Dimitrijevic and his two close collaborators were executed.

Alarmed by the peace talks, Pasic sent Stojan Protic, a member of the government and the second strong man in the Radical Party, to France and Switzerland to attempt to sound out the feelings of the Yugoslav Committee regarding the new situation. Ljuba Davidovic, leader of the Independent Radicals who had left the government in protest of the Salonika Trial, also went to Switzerland since Switzerland was then the center for a variety of discussions aimed at eventual peace. What Davidovic learned in Switzerland prompted him to send a letter to Pasic demanding him to immediately open official negotiations with the Yugoslav Committee. In Davidovic's opinion this was necessary because of the Russian Revolution. The new Russian regime was favorably disposed towards Bulgaria. Moreover, Davidovic considered these negotiations necessary because of the Rumanian catastrophe and Rumania's capitulation. But he thought so especially because of the Croats who, through Supilo's activities, were likely to win the sympathy of the Western Allies and jeopardize Serbia's aggrandizing hopes. After receiving Davidovic's letter, Pasic instructed Protic to open negotiations with Trumbic in Cannes.

Supilo's personal effort in Great Britain, aided by the "Serbian Society of Great Britain" and directed by Steed and Seton-Watson, made headway against Pasic's policy and led to a serious reexamination of the Southern Slav issue. The personal rivalry between Trumbic and Supilo prompted Trumbic to interfere. He asked Seton-Watson to leave the question of Yugoslav unity to him and to Pasic, since they were about to begin negotiations.

The new principles of the self-determination of peoples that were proclaimed by revolutionary Russia as well as by the United States were on the lips of every negotiator. Pasic was fully aware that without Russian support he could not expect to create his "Greater Serbia" even by making use of these very principles. He therefore decided to fortify his own position vis-a-vis the Serbian Opposition and the military conspirators who had been shaken by the Salonika Trial, and to, furthermore, neutralize all possible opposition to the Committee regarding the overbearing role of the Serbian government. He also wanted to secure the position of the Karadjordjevic Dynasty by winning support for it from the Yugoslav Committee.

Trumbic, for his part, sought a compromise in order to gain the Serbian government's official recognition of the Committee, since that government had hitherto refused such recognition. And last, but not least, Trumbic hoped by winning this compromise he could outscore his rival, Supilo.

In April 1917, Pasic officially invited Trumbic to Corfu to discuss the problems of the relationship between the Serbian government and the Yugoslav Committee. He suggested that Trumbic bring a Croat from Croatia (Trumbic being from

Dalmatia), a Serb from Bosnia and a Slovene. The Committee accepted the suggestion, thus Hinko Hinkovic from Croatia, Dusan Vasiljevic from Bosnia and Bogumil Vosnjak from Slovenia joined Trumbic on his journey to Corfu. Dinko Trinajstic, a permanent Committee representative to the Serbian government, and Potocnjak, traveling from Russia, were also present at the talks. Pasic, Protic, Marko Djuricic and Momcilo Nincic represented the Serbian government, while the opposition was represented by Davidovic, Milorad Draskovic and Voja Marinkovic. The conference opened on June 15 and ended with a declaration on July 20. In all, twenty plenary sessions were held.

The attitude of the Serbian government was most simply expressed by the well-known political program that Pasic followed. He insisted on Serbia's right to liberate and annex all branches of the Southern Slav peoples still under Habsburg rule, emphasizing that the Serbian government was the only power that had a mandate for carrying out such a plan. In his view, all Southern Slavs were to be integrated into a "Greater Serbia" which would be organized into a centralistic, democratic and parliamentarian monarchy under the Dynasty of Karadjordjevic. He was vigorously opposed to any idea of a Yugoslavian state and was definitely antagonistic to any sort of federalistic organization of the future state.

Trumbic, representing the views of the Committee, put stress on the liberation of the Southern Slavs from Austro-Hungarian sway in order to form a common state with Serbia and Montenegro on the basis of self-determination. Of course this plan would not permit Serbia's aggrandizement into a "Greater Serbia" at the expense of the Croats, but would mean the emergence of an entirely new state under the name of Yugoslavia and on the foundation of complete equality.

Such divergent viewpoints could hardly be reconciled, but the international situation made some kind of compromise not only desirable, but necessary. Trumbic feared that a negative result from the conference would publicly reveal the difference between the Serbian government and the Yugoslav Committee to the advantage of the Italian claims on the eastern Adriatic shores. With this in mind, he asked the members of the Committee for their consent to sign any possible agreement that could be reached.

On Protic's proposal, it was finally agreed that the new state would be named the Kingdom of the Serbs, Croats and Slovenes. The points upon which no agreement could be reached were omitted and on July 20, 1917, the document, known as the Corfu Declaration, was signed. Its text runs as follows:

The authorized representatives of the Serbs, Croats and Slovenes, recognizing that the desire of their people is to free themselves from any foreign yoke and to constitute themselves an Independent National State, agree in declaring that this state must be founded on the following principles:

(1) The State of the Serbs, Croats and Slovenes, who are also known as the Southern Slavs or Yugoslavs, shall be a free and independent kingdom with an indivisible territory and unity of allegiance. It shall be a constitutional, democratic and parliamentarian monarchy under the Karadjordjevic Dynasty which has always shared the feelings of the nation and has placed the national will above everything else.

(2) This State shall be named the Kingdom of the Serbs, Croats and Slovenes and the title of the sovereign shall be the "King of the Serbs, Croats and Slovenes."

(3) The State shall have a single coat-of-arms, a single flag and a single crown with all emblems composed from those presently existing.

(4) The individual Serb, Croat and Slovene flags and coats-of-arms may be freely hoisted and used.

(5) The three national names shall be equal before the law and may be freely used in public life.

(6) The two alphabets, the Cyrillic and the Latin, shall also rank equally throughout the Kingdom.

(7) All recognized religions shall be exercised freely and publicly. Particularly the Orthodox, Roman Catholic and Mus-

lim creeds, which are chiefly professed by our people, shall be equal and shall have the same rights in relation to the State.

(8) The calendars shall be made uniform as soon as possible.

(9) The territory of the Kingdom shall include all territories compactly inhabited by our people and shall not be mutilated without attaint to the vital interests of the nation. Our nation demands nothing that belongs to others but only that which is its own. It desires freedom and unity. Therefore, it consciously and firmly refuses all partial solutions to the problem of its deliverance from Austro-Hungarian domination as well as to the problem of its unification with Serbia and Montenegro in a state forming an indivisible whole.

(10) In the interest of freedom and of the equal rights of all nations, the Adriatic Sea shall be free and open to all.

(11) All citizens shall be equal and shall enjoy the same rights in relations to the State and before the law.

(12) Members of the National Assembly shall be elected by universal suffrage with equal, direct and secret balloting.

(13) The Constitution to be established by a Constituent Assembly elected by universal suffrage after the conclusion of peace shall be the basis for the life of the nation.

The Constitution shall give the people the opportunity to develop their special energies in autonomous units provided by natural, social and economic conditions.

Only a numerically qualified majority shall be competent to adopt the Constitution at the Constitutional Assembly.

The Constitution shall be effective after receiving the Royal sanction. The nation thus formed shall be a State of some twelve million inhabitants which should be a bulwark against German aggression and an inseparable ally to all civilized nations.

The declaration was signed by Pasic and Trumbic. Its text was immediately communicated to the Allied representative to the Serbian government in Corfu. However, Pasic, despite the previous understanding that he would communicate it, through Serbian legations, to the Allied governments as the official Serbian government war program, refused to do so.

The personal as well as political relationship between Pasic and Trumbic had never been friendly. The Corfu negotiations did nothing to improve it; on the contrary, they rekindled the former animosity. After the signing of the Declaration, Trumbic insisted on its immediate application, but Pasic refused. Shortly thereafter, on September 10 in Rome, Pasic met with Sonnino, the Italian Minister of Foreign Affairs and one of the fathers of the secret Treaty of London. The two came to complete agreement as to the common Italian and Serbian war policies, an agreement which in effect stripped the Declaration of all meaning.

After this blow, Trumbic attempted to utilize Supilo's tactics. (Supilo had meanwhile died.) Yet his diplomatic probings were too little and too late. The Yugoslav Committee ranked with the Czechoslovak and Polish committees which were also trying to gain official recognition by the Allies as representatives of their respective peoples. While the Czechoslovaks and Poles were successful, Pasic, in close cooperation with the Italian government, prevented this in the case of the Yugoslav Committee.

While the Yugoslav Committee expected the Corfu Declaration to be a milestone toward Yugoslav unity and the guarantee for the equality of the Serbs, Croats and Slovenes, Pasic considered it to be merely a piece of propaganda which he had signed in order to "impress European public opinion."

CHAPTER XIX

THE DISSOLUTION OF THE
DUAL MONARCHY

Contacts between Zagreb and the Yugoslav Committee
— Impact of the Peace Treaty of Brest Litovsk — Prague
as a center of conspiracy — Formation of the National
Council of the Slovenes, Croats and Serbs — Pribicevic's
ascendancy — Charles's proclamation of October 16 —
President Wilson's Fourteen Points — Proclamation of
independence by the Croatian Sabor *— Armistice and*
its consequences — Geneva Declaration.

There were no direct connections between Croatia's politicians and the Yugoslav Committee; the latter had no noteworthy personalities from Croatia among its members. Since Trumbic and Supilo were former members of the *Starcevicanci* (a faction of the Party of Right), it was the only political party to sporadically try to establish contact. But the importance of these contacts was later unduly stressed. Some writers who were latecomers tried to prove with them that the Committee was the true representative of the country's wishes.

Msgr. Fran Barac, Rector of the University of Zagreb and member of the *Starcevicanci,* went to Switzerland in August 1915 and met with Hinkovic, a member of the Committee, and Markovic, a member of the Serbian opposition. From these talks Barac received the impression, an impression not at all corresponding to reality, that Serbia was pursuing war aims

259

similar to those of the Committee. This misinformation prompted Barac's political friends and a few members of the Coalition to hold a meeting in Zagreb to prepare instructions for his guidance in the projected meeting with Trumbic in Lausanne. The gist of the instructions given to Barac consisted of the already familiar demand for a Croatia which would be a separate state standing side-by-side with Serbia and Slovenia in the future Yugoslavia. In view of their unwillingness to surrender their national state rights, the Croats considered this proposal as the only one acceptable before a unification could be made. Trumbic and Barac met in September, with Trumbic, fresh from his Corfu negotiations, flatly refusing to share in the Croatian views and insisting that the Corfu Declaration must serve as the cornerstone for the complete merger into a single nation-state.

Having no clear-cut policy of their own to pursue, the *Starcevicanci* yielded to Trumbic's logic. They concentrated, for the time being, only on the dissolution of the Habsburg Monarchy, not worrying too much about the internal organization of the projected common state. In their opinion, that project would somehow resolve itself later.

* * *

At this critical period there was not a single outstanding figure among Croatia's political personalities to take over the leadership. Yet, the lack of a responsible and generally accepted leader was not only cruelly felt in Croatian politics, but also a great confusion reigned among the parties regarding national goals and procedures. The discussions held on behalf of the country's future varied widely in their scope and content and often proved as contradictory as they were futile. Instead of clearing up the chaos of ideas and aims, and ways and means, these discussions only deepened the confusion. Everyone professed his own version of national unity. For some it meant an abstract unit with a dogmatic basis, for others it was no more than a geographical idea.

Lack of political training and experience left people blissfully ignorant of the actual meaning and distinctive sense of such terms as unitarism, self-government, autonomy, federation and confederation. The term "democracy" was to them a *panacea*, that is, some sort of magic formula which would solve all their problems once and for all. They overlooked the fact that the concept of a Yugoslav democracy was nonsensical since the only existing Yugoslavs were a handful of self-styled members of the intelligentsia.

Devoid of adequate leadership and utterly disoriented in their political struggle, Zagreb's politicians looked to outsiders, like the Yugoslav Committee, for guidance. The Committee's program was, in the last analysis, more or less a plagiarism of the program of Masaryk's Czechoslovak Committee whose chief aim was the destruction of the Habsburg Monarchy. The politicians of Zagreb now aligned themselves with those seeking salvation in Prague which was the center of all Slavic policy-making concerning the Monarchy, with the exception of that of the Poles who pursued their own policies and ambitions.

The beginning of the peace talks at Brest Litovsk between the Central Powers and the Soviet Union in December 1917, and, even more than these talks, the content of points nine and ten of President Wilson's message of January 8, 1918, prompted the Prague politicians to act. Point nine specified that Italy's boundaries should be readjusted along clearly recognizable lines of nationality and point ten demanded that the peoples of Austria-Hungary be granted the opportunity for free autonomous development since Austria-Hungary's place among the nations had to be safeguarded and assured.

The Czech political organization, known under its conspiracy name as the "Mafia," was well acquainted with the difficulties facing the Monarchy. It also, through secret channels to Eduard Benes, Masaryk's principal collaborator, knew the Entente aims well. Thus it decided to arrange a secret meeting between Czech and Southern Slav leaders in Prague.

Vienna greatly contributed to the Mafia's plan through the activities of Ottokar Czernin, Minister of Foreign Affairs, who replied to Clemenceau on April 2 regarding Prince Sixte's abortive peace mission: To shield the Emperor, Czernin stoutly denied any weakness in the fabric of the Monarchy or in its war efforts and thereby declared that the Monarchy could not be forced to seek a separate peace settlement. On the contrary, Czernin insisted that the Monarchy's main objective was to uphold its system of dualism through German and Magyar supremacy.

Ante Pavelic, Dragutin Hrvoj, Ivica Kovacevic (of the *Starcevicanci* faction), Radic (of the Peasant Party) and Budisavljevic (a dissident of the Coalition) journeyed to Prague. It was at this time, in a secret meeting, that these men agreed to the further close Czechoslovak and Southern Slav cooperation that would ultimately lead to the dissolution of the Monarchy.

Upon their return to Zagreb, Radic talked about the conditions of peace: ". . . True and lasting peace can be achieved only if all peoples, those from the borders of the former Russian Empire as well as those from the Danubian area and from the Balkans, are allowed to fully exercise their right to self-determination. In this way, later they will be able to enter into a common federation by their own free will and on equal terms in their new quality as popular national states."

Bent on carrying the decision made in Prague through, Radic proposed the formation of a National Council of Croatia composed of the *Starcevicanci*, the Peasant Party, the Social Democrats, dissidents of the Coalition and some independents. But his project was relegated to the background for the time being, while the Czechs transformed the Mafia into the Czechoslovak National Council on July 14 and the Slovenes formed the National Council of Slovenia on August 17. The politicians in Zagreb continued to hesitate until October 4 when Vienna asked for an armistice on the basis of Wilson's Fourteen Points. By that time the imminent defeat of the Monarchy was obvious and made it imperative for Zagreb to take steps.

The politicians called a meeting under Pavelic's chairmanship for October 5 in Zagreb. The Coalition was also invited but refused to attend, except on its own terms, which were to be recognized as absolute master of the council. After two days of deliberations a compromise was finally reached; and on October 8 the National Council of Slovenes, Croats and Serbs was formed. It consisted of a plenum and a smaller executive central committee. Korosec, leader of the Slovenian populists, was elected president, while Pribicevic and Pavelic served as vicepresidents. Mate Drinkovic, Budisavljevic and Ivan Lorkovic were the secretaries. Radic, who was the chief promoter of the council, was pushed aside. Moreover, since the plenum of the National Council never met (apparently a deliberate piece of negligence), the Central Committee was left with a free hand in decision-making.

Pribicevic had succeeded, with well calculated tenacity, in imposing the Coalition and himself as the real masters of the National Council. He carried things further by manipulating events to get president Korosec sent to Geneva and Paris so that during the president's absence he could concentrate all power in his own hands. He also succeeded in gaining complete control over the police, appointing Grgur Andjelinovic, a former *Starcevicanac* from Dalmatia, as its head. (Andjelinovic was a devoted and ambitious young man who organized a permanent street mob of young Serbian officers, students, sailors, and other similar enthusiasts into a terrorist gang.)

Pribicevic was also instrumental in deciding who, from the Coalition as well as from other political parties, would be appointed to serve in the Central Committee, which was the committee that decided all issues without any regard for the plenum. From the outset, the *Frankovci*, the Magyaroni and the Independents were completely eliminated. Taken together they represented more than one-third of the former Croatian electors.

Pribicevic, as chairman of the Central Committee, flatly refused to consider Radic's motion that the *Sabor* proclaim the deposition of the Habsburgs from the Croatian throne and, therewith, the severance of all ties to Austria-Hungary. It was not until the fact that Wilson declined the Austro-Hungarian demand for an armistice on the basis of the Fourteen Points had become known in Zagreb on October 18 that the National Council came alive. In answer to Charles's proclamation of October 16, announcing the federal reorganization of Austria with due recognition of the "integrity and unity of the lands of St. Stephen's Crown (Hungary)", the National Council via the Central Committee came out into the open and demanded the national unity of all Serbs, Croats and Slovenes.

When, on October 21, the news of President Wilson's answer to Austro-Hungary, as well as the Emperor's proclamation of federal reorganization, reached the Croatian units stationed at Rijeka, they mutinied. Other Croatian troops on the Italian front followed suit. Still, there was no revolutionary activity nor any gesture in that direction by the National Council. Only when the Czechoslovak National Council in Prague proclaimed national independence on October 28 did its counterpart in Zagreb decide to act.

On October 29, on the initiative of the National Council, the *Sabor* held its last session, debating and voting on the council's motion. It urgently demanded that: (1) The Kingdom of Croatia, Slavonia and Dalmatia sever all relations with Austria and Hungary and (2) proclaim complete independence in the form of a common sovereign State of the Slovenes, Croats and Serbs based on the principle of national unity and disregarding international boundaries. The *Sabor* voted for the motion without dissent and proceeded to transfer all its prerogatives to the National Council. Thus, the end of the Habsburg Monarchy was sealed.

*　　*　　*

Korosec had been in Vienna since October 21 consulting with

Karl Kramarz, the leader of the Czech Mafia, as well as with Karl Lammasch, who had been entrusted by Charles to prepare a draft for the federal constitution. Upon receiving the news of the *Sabor's* resolution, he left for Geneva and Paris: In the company of Gregor Zerjav and Cingrija, he went to Switzerland to meet with the members of the Yugoslav Committee, and finally to go to Paris to prepare for the Peace Conference.

In the meantime, the Central Committee appointed Trumbic its official representative at the armistice negotiations with Austria. The appointment was sent by a telegram transmitted through the Serbian government and did not reach Trumbic until the armistice had already been signed, thus preventing the participation of a representative from the National Council.

*   *   *

Since the Corfu Declaration remained a dead letter, the Yugoslav Committee had been seeking Allied recognition as the representative of the Croats, Serbs and Slovenes in Austria-Hungary: By June 1918, the Czechoslovaks and Poles were already well on their way toward obtaining recognition, but Sonnino and Pasic most vehemently opposed similar recognition of the Committee. In the name of the Serbian government, Pasic claimed the sole right of Serbia to liberate and represent its Southern Slavic brothers.

In order to secure such a mandate for the Serbian government, Pasic undertook a diplomatic mission to London in the autumn of 1918. But his demand did not find a very warm reception. Because the British were familiar with the Southern Slav problem, they were aware of Pasic's plan to create a "Greater Serbia" which would incorporate all territories of the Habsburg Monarchy that he considered to be Serbian, leaving what remained of Croatia to freely join Serbia as a province. Thus the British outrightly rejected Pasic's most ardent wish (which was also the wish of the Serbian militarist circles), by turning their backs on his desire to annex and "Serbify" the

Southern Slav provinces of Austria-Hungary without any pretense at uniting with them in a manner agreeable to all interested parties.

When the terms of the armistice with Austria-Hungary were discussed in Paris on November 2, the Serbian delegate, Miljenko Vesnic, agreed without reservation to the provision which ordered the former Austro-Hungarian Navy to surrender to Italians, even though the Navy had been in the hands of the National Council since October 30. He also agreed that all officers and sailors of that Navy should be taken prisoners of war despite their Croatian origin. Furthermore, Italy was to occupy all territories assigned it by the secret Treaty of London, as well as all additional strategical centers of communication which were to be determined by the judgment of the Italian military authorities.

In consideration of Pasic's mission and Vesnic's attitude, the British and French friends of the Yugoslav Committee tried once more to secure Allied recognition of the Committee. Great Britain, France and the United States were favorably disposed to the move and pressure was brought to bear on the Italian Premier, Orlando, to agree in the name of the Italian government. On the insistence of Wickham Steed, he finally gave in and sent an invitation to Trumbic, through Benes, to pay him a visit in order to begin the regularization of activities surrounding the pending question.

When Steed called on the French Foreign Minister on November 5, Philippe Berthelot, Permanent Undersecretary, told him: "That is excellent, as far as words go. But do you know what Orlando has done? He called upon Clemenceau at 8 o'clock this morning and begged him, literally with tears in his eyes, on no account to sanction any recognition of the Yugoslav National Committee since Italy was determined not to recognize it; and I have reason to fear that Clemenceau has committed himself."

By peculiar coincidence, Trumbic was at the same time hastily invited by Pasic to meet with him and the delegation of the National Council in Geneva to come to terms regarding the recognition of the National Council as the official representative of the Dual Monarchy's Southern Slavs. The last attempt to obtain diplomatic recognition of the Committee was thereby permanently frustrated.

While the question of recognition was still being debated in London and Paris, the alarmed Pasic informed the Serbian government on November 2 that the western statesmen considered Serbia a nation distinct from Yugoslavia. The Allies pledged, he added, to re-establish pre-war Serbia, but they also insisted on the right of Yugoslavia (the Southern Slav territory of the Habsburg Monarchy) to decide for itself whether it wanted to stay with Austria-Hungary or become a free and independent state.

In connection with the late developments in Paris, Pasic contrived by other means to prevent the recognition of the Committee and to prevent the representative of the National Council to reach Paris. He was in a special hurry to accomplish this because Poincaré pressed for a speedy agreement with the representatives of the Southern Slavs and Clemenceau had brought the matter up at the meeting of the Great Powers, informing them that he intended to give the Yugoslav Committee the same recognition as he had given to the Poles and Czechoslovaks. Thus Pasic refused to give Korosec the Serbian passport which would enable him to go to Paris and thereby stalled him in Geneva. At this time, Pasic invited Trumbic to the conference in Geneva.

On November 5 the armistice with Austria-Hungary became effective and Pasic left Paris for Geneva. On his initiative and invitation, the conference was held at the Hotel *National* on November 7, 8 and 9. Pasic was the official representative of the Serbian government, while Draskovic, Marinkovic and Marko Trifkovic represented the Serbian opposition. Korosec, Cingrija and Zerjav represented the National Council, and the Yugoslav

Committee was represented by Trumbic, Gregorin, Vasiljevic, Stojanovic and Banjanin.

The Serbian government officially acknowledged the National Council as the government of the Southern Slavs from former Austria-Hungary. The Serbian government and the National Council would each rule their respective territories until the constitution for the united country could be prepared. A common ministry was formed for foreign affairs, military affairs, maritime affairs and the supervision of preliminary measures for the election of a constituent assembly. The conference prepared an address to the Peace Conference in order to challenge the Italian claims on the Southern Slav territories. It was finally decided that Montenegro also was an integral part of the common State of the Serbs, Croats and Slovenes. At the close of the conference, on November 9, a joint declaration was signed by all participants:

Through the common efforts of the Allied Nations and the United States of America and by the strong will of the Serbs, Croats and Slovenes, all tyrannical bonds hindering Southern Slav union have been broken in a struggle on land and sea. The representatives of the Royal Government of Serbia and its parliamentarian groups, of the National Council of Zagreb and of the Yugoslav Committee in London, meeting in Geneva, are happy to solemnly announce to the entire world their unification into the State of the Serbs, Croats and Slovenes. There is no doubt that the people of Montenegro, who have always cherished the same ideal, will eagerly join us.

By this day and this act our new State comes into life and presents itself as an indivisible national commonwealth and a member of the community of free nations. The boundaries which hitherto separated us no longer exist.

The common State shall be represented by a common government formed from those of the Serbs, Croats and Slovenes and using their executive and administrative organs.

268

The formation of this government has already been announced. Its jurisdiction shall be announced later when an agreement has been made regarding the recognition of all national factors on the basis of administrative needs as well as on the basis of adopted form of union which shall take over common public affairs.

The Royal Government of Serbia and the National Council in Zagreb shall continue to attend to all public affairs in the respective territories already established until the Constituent Assembly of the Serbs, Croats and Slovenes, elected by a general, equal, direct and secret ballot cast by all citizens, definitely votes the constitution of the State. This constitution shall be the foundation for all public life and for all powers and rights. The entire life of the State shall be regulated in the spirit of democracy.

The boundaries separating the State from its neighboring countries should be determined with respect to the ethnic claims and the right to self-determination of all peoples. Our people are firmly convinced that they are acting according to their rights and on the principles of justice proclaimed by their Allies and endorsed by the conscience of the entire civilized world which stands guarantee for them.

Pasic communicated the declaration to the Prince Regent, Aleksander, and to the Serbian government. After the conference he left for Paris and was followed a few days later by Trumbic, Korosec and other participants. The alleged purpose of the journey was to demand official recognition of the new State from the Peace Conference. Thus it was greatly surprising when, after a delay of a few days, Stephen Pichon, French Minister of Foreign Affairs, informed Trumbic and Korosec that the purpose of their quest had been rejected by the Serbian government and that another solution would have to be sought. This information came to Pichon from Pasic himself.

Actually Pasic staged the whole Geneva affair to keep Trumbic and Korosec away from Paris at a crucial time; thus he had signed a document he had no intention of honoring. Orlando and Pasic were in need of no lessons from one another in duplicity; both were consummate masters of it.

The Serbian government rejected the Geneva agreement and then resigned as a sign of protest against it since, in Protic's words ". . . it presented a disavowal of the Serbian merits for liberation. . ." Protic explained this attitude in a letter to Pasic: ". . . We will not be able to obtain acceptance of our views that Serbia should represent all our peoples until the conclusion of the Peace Conference. Trumbic prevailed because he was supported by illegal opposition. . . It is clear that our brethren from the former Austrian territories have been liberated materially at the price of Allied blood but have not yet been liberated spiritually. They still live in the Austro-Hungarian ideology. . ."

Pasic replied to Protic expressing his reasons for accepting the Geneva agreement: ". . . certain individuals among our own peoples are making propaganda that the regime in Serbia is reactionary, unconstitutional and unparliamentarian; that our political opponents are persecuted and so on; that it would be dangerous for all Serbs, Croats and Slovenes to unite with Serbia; and that it would be much better to unite in a new State which would bear the stamp of more modern ideas and institutions than to unite with Serbia. . ."

Furthermore, Serbia was most strongly opposed to the idea of dualism. And, to make matters worse, all power in the National Council of Zagreb was, in the meantime, concentrated in the hands of the Serbian representatives led by Pribicevic. These men were working toward an immediate and unconditional unification with Serbia.

It was not until November 18 that Pasic consented to a meeting with Korosec, Trumbic and Cingrija and communicated to them that the Prince Regent and the Serbian government had not sanctioned the Geneva agreement and that consequently his Cabinet had resigned. He added that he himself had been entrusted the task of forming the new government. He asked them to accept the representatives of the National Council and the Yugoslav Committee as members of the Serbian government.

He made it clear that, considering the circumstances, they had no choice.

The Geneva Declaration was short-lived: In less than twenty-four hours, it was worthless. Pasic forgot it in the sleeping-car from Geneva to Paris. With his maneuver, Pasic had undeniably scored a decisive victory over Korosec and Trumbic since, at the right moment, he had prevented them from making any serious move to obtain recognition for the National Council as the representative at the Peace Conference of the State of the Slovenes, Croats and Serbs.

Pasic always held onto his initial idea that Serbia should annex the Austro-Hungarian Southern Slavs to form a "Greater Serbia." He simply turned all negotiations into a device to frustrate the possible combined efforts of Trumbic and Korosec. He figured that if he could not immediately realize his dream of a "Greater Serbia" and that if the unity of the Serbs, Croats and Slovenes (i.e. the unification of Serbia with the Southern Slav territories) became inevitable in the meantime, he could at least impose the conditions under which the unification would take place. That, in the end, would amount to virtually the same thing as his concept of a "Greater Serbia."

CHAPTER XX

FORMATION OF THE KINGDOM OF THE SERBS, CROATS AND SLOVENES

National Council and the problem of unification — Pribicevic's action — Radic's resistance — Pasic's dilemma — Prelude to unification — Act of December 1st — Formation of the first government — Croatian opposition.

The proclamation of the Croatian *Sabor* on October 29, 1918, which announced the severance of all ties between Croatia and Austria-Hungary, and the signing of the Geneva Declaration on November 9, which meant the dissolution of the Habsburg Monarchy, were, in a way, consequences of Wilsonian diplomacy. Both acts followed Wilson's refusal to discuss the armistice with Austria-Hungary on the basis of his Fourteen Points, as well as from his subsequent demand for the complete independence of the Czechoslovaks and the Southern Slavs.

The proclamation of the *Sabor* was, in its true form, the legal act of a legislative body which lacked only the sanction of the sovereign. Once the connections with Austria and Hungary were severed and the State of the Slovenes, Croats and Serbs was formed, three ways of resolving the future opened themselves up to the National Council as the governing body of the new state: (1) the formation of an independent state following the pattern established by Czechoslovakia; (2) the continuation of its association with Austria and Hungary in a federalized empire; and (3) unification with Serbia and Montenegro.

Pribicevic, who had emerged as the undisputed master of the National Council, chose to follow the last course. *Ban* Mihalovic immediately responded to the new situation by putting himself at the disposal of the National Council as its executive. Ministries were created for affairs hitherto administered by Budapest and Vienna. Pribicevic had the last word in selecting members of the provisional government, thus preventing the appointment of Radic as Minister of the Economy. The immediate result was a growing conflict between Pribicevic and Radic which began to take on the proportions of a merciless duel between two spirited and stubborn antagonists who were striving for opposite goals. To emphasize the way he differed from the policy pursued by the National Council under Pribicevic's leadership, Radic radicalized his position by declaring himself against the monarchy and for the republic. While Radic's spectrum of activity was limited to merely the profession of principles, Pribicevic had the means at hand to enforce his policy of an unqualified merger of Serbs, Croats and Slovenes into a single unitarian nation.

The National Council had inherited the administrative and police organizations of the defunct government and could still use, as a nucleus for future armed forces, the retreating remnants of the former Austro-Hungarian Army which contained a fairly large officer-cadre whose members were of Croatian and Serbian origin. But Pribicevic would have nothing to do with such a plan. Thus the Council ignored the offer of cooperation from Field Marshal Svetozar Borojevic and his fellow-officers. Instead, Lieutenant Colonel Slavko Kvaternik, former Adjutant of Borojevic, was entrusted with the task of organizing the new army. But the task never got beyond the planning stages.

Pribicevic imposed his views on the Council, which resulted in an invitation to the Serbian army to occupy the country on November 5 even though, as at least Pribicevic well knew, its depleted ranks were no longer suited to the task: According to a report Pribicevic had received from General Misic, Chief of Staff of the Serbian Army, its number was around 28,000 men.

Another 28,000 men of the Yugoslav Legion, which was formed during the war from Austro-Hungarian prisoners-of-war of Southern Slavic origin, could be added to the initial figure.

The role assigned to the Serbian Army as the occupying force in Croatia was, above all, political: Under the pretext of maintaining order, the army was actually to enforce Pribicevic's policy of unconditional union with Serbia. But the task of occupation *per se* fell to the French colonial troops drawn from the ranks of General Franchet d-Esperey's Army of the Orient. For the people who experienced the liberation and occupation of these soldiers, such souvenir expressions as "There came the white Negroes and the black Frenchmen", were left behind in memorium.

Because he had been pushed into the role of the leader of the opposition, Radic began to drift farther and farther from the National Council. Thus he became the only politician to maintain regular contact with the population and to be in close touch with its true feelings. On the whole, the people approved of a clean break with Hungary and Austria, but thought of possible union with Serbia with reservation, if not outright alarm. Although the enthusiasm of October 29 had cooled down, Zagreb still seemed stirred by a current of excitement. But it was, for the most part, artificially maintained by street demonstrations of students who were largely Serbs from Croatia and Croats from Dalmatia supported by sailors from the former Austro-Hungarian Navy. After the surrender of their units to the Italians, these sailors had been brought to Zagreb by the masters of the National Council in order to specifically shore up the student demonstrations. The demonstrations became daily events and would eventually take a menacing and terroristic turn.

The situation was different in the villages. The peasants felt that the Croats were bound to succumb to Serbian hegemony after shedding Magyar domination. They regarded the monarchy as chiefly responsible for the war and their misery and they started talking about republicanism. Moreover, now that they were free of the monarchy they were faced with a new dynasty which was considered even more inferior than the former one. In the course of the war many of them had had the opportunity to acquaint themselves with the conditions in Serbia and they found them to be worse than their own. By tapping the supply of tales that they circulated, Radic was able to publicly vent the general current of dissatisfaction among them, as well as their more specific misgivings of the policy of the National Council.

Heedless of these warnings and in full control of the National Council, Pribicevic was determined to carry out his policy regardless of the cost. His chief support came from the Serbian Military Mission to the National Council and through it he maintained regular communications with Belgrade and Paris. Furthermore, he found a kindred soul in one Lieutenant Colonel Dusan Simovic, head of the Mission. Simovic wished nothing else but to give his wholehearted cooperation to the ruthless policy of the head of the National Council.

* * *

Meanwhile Pasic had failed to obtain the mandate from the Great Powers which would permit Serbia to free and annex the Southern Slavs of Austria-Hungary. Finding his efforts wasted, on November 10 he sent a secret wire to Prince-Regent Aleksandar, urging him to pressure Pribicevic into hastening the actual act of unification with Serbia. When he received Aleksandar's message on November 19, Pribicevic decided to act at once. A provisional government of Dalmatia was formed *ad hoc* and it presented a motion to the National Council which demanded immediate union with Serbia.

Since Korosec was absent, Pribicevic, as first vice-president and acting chairman, called the Central Committee into session on November 20 in order to consider the motion. To subvert the anticipated resistance of Radic, Andjelinovic, Pribicevic's trusted man, mustered a number of his Dalmatians to demonstrate in support of the motion. Aided by police agents, the demonstrators invaded St. Mark Square and, in the vicinity of the *Sabor*, clamored for immediate unification with Serbia and for Radic's

276

head. The mob became violent. It eventually got so far out of hand that it became a menace to the entire National Council. The *Starcevicanci,* the Socialists and some independents refused, under the circumstances, to open the session. Radic publicly accused Pribicevic of instigating the affair. Pribicevic responded by assigning Andjelinovic the task of pacifying the excited crowd, a task which was executed with little difficulty.

The Central Committee was finally able to open its session at 9:00 p.m. It immediately entered into a debate on the motion of the Dalmatian government, i.e. the motion that had been hatched by Pribicevic and put forward by his stooges. This motion was followed by five more motions and counter-motions. One of them was introduced by Radic: It had obviously been conceived on the spur of the moment and bore altered characteristics from the position evidenced in Radic's program of the preceding June.

The basic contents of Radic's motion can be summarized as follows: The ethnically single nation of the Slovenes, Croats and Serbs whose historical, cultural and political backgrounds have formed three distinct entities, has decided to adopt the status of a federation based on national unity and equality. In a temporary arrangement, three regents shall be its supreme rulers: the Serbian Crown Prince, the Croatian *Ban,* and the President of the National Council of Slovenia. They shall appoint a federal government consisting of the ministries of foreign affairs, national food, supply and production, and defense. The federal government shall be responsible to the Supreme National Council of the Slovenes, Croats and Serbs which is to be composed of members appointed by the following organizations: The Serbian National Assembly, the Croatian *Sabor,* and the National Council of Slovenia are each to appoint ten members; and the Bosnian *Sabor,* the Assembly of Montenegro, the Dalmatian *Sabor,* Vojvodina and Istria are each to appoint two. The administration of all public affairs, which is not expressly reserved for the federal government, shall be incumbent on the national autonomous governments of Slovenia, Serbia, Croatia and Montenegro, as well as on the provincial governments of Bosnia and Hercegovina, Dalmatia and Vojvodina. Each of these governments in turn shall be responsible to their respective legislative bodies.

Radic's motion was dropped from discussion as rapidly as the motion of the Dalmatian government was picked up. A special committee of seven was appointed to prepare the final draft of a proposal upon which they would vote. It was to contain (1) a proclamation of an immediate merging of the State of the Slovenes, Croats and Serbs with the Kingdoms of Serbia and Montenegro to form a unitarian State of the Slovenes, Croats and Serbs, and it was to provide for (2) the appointment of a special committee of twenty-eight members to work out the details of this decision with the Serbian government. Instructions on the procedure for the final organization of the new State were elaborated for the committee in eleven points. One of these was that the new constitution must have the vote of at least two-thirds of the Constituent Assembly to become effective; and another gave full recognition to the Karadjordjevic Dynasty.

When the motion of the seven member committee and their instructions were submitted to the Central Committee for final approval, only Radic opposed them. On the night of November 23, in a last effort to upset the whole scheme and its unavoidable consequences, he made a dramatic plea for rejection of the projected union. Once again he insisted that the acceptance of a "common Croato-Serbia language" was correct only insofar as both the Croats and Serbs belonged to the same Slavic linguistic family; but that consequently, not just the Serbs and Croats, but all Slavic peoples ought to form a single nation. He vehemently protested the concessions for a centralistic and unitarian state that were made to Serbia. "If the Serbs want a centralistic state so badly may God grant it to them," he argued, "as for the Croats, they want nothing but a federal republic." Moreover, he underscored the fact that the self-appointed members of the Central Committee had no right at all to represent the Croatian people. He asserted that, on the basis of the existing differences between the Croats and Serbs, the so-called common language could never be a strong enough tie to mould the two peoples into a single nation. He said that "it must be understood once and for all that it takes much more to sustain a nation than the assimilation of tongues." And further, he suggested that the Central Committee had proposed an act that disclaimed the very principles of self-determination that it had claimed when it announced the liberation from Austro-Hungarian domination.

Radic's concluding words were pathetic:

> Gentlemen, the most terrible thing, the greatest sin, and the greatest political mistake is committed in an act such as yours, for you place our people before the *fait accompli* of a policy decided upon by a select few from the upper crust of society without and against the will of the people. If I cannot convince you now of the truth of this statement, then may God grant that you live long enough — and that need not to be too long — to learn from first-hand experience how the Croatian people will buck in rebellion against this disregard for human dignity and its republican principles, throwing you out of the saddle just as you were about to believe that you were sitting firmly in it. Long live the republic; Long live Croatia.

Radic was alone and unsupported in the Council and his talk went unheeded. Despite his single vote against it, the motion passed. Moreover, regardless of his glaring opposition, he was appointed to the twenty-eight member delegation which would go to Belgrade to proclaim the union. Radic turned down the appointment. The Committee responded by excluding him from its membership on November 26, appointing Janko Simrak to fill his spot in the delegation.

The delegation began its journey on the following day, arriving in Belgrade on November 28 where its members were received as the honored guests of the Serbian capital. After three days of negotiations with the Serbian government, which flatly refused to accept the proposal adopted in Zagreb, the delegation capitulated. An agreement was arranged according to the dictates of the Serbs: The address announcing the union of the State of the Slovenes, Croats and Serbs, as it was voted by the Central Committee of the National Council, was completely changed. The delegation was not even granted the courtesy of preparing the new text, but was compelled to endorse the one drafted by Protic. This new draft put the emphasis on a unitarian monarchy under the Karadjordjevic Dynasty and had a special provision which required the King's sanction of the Constitution or the sanction of the Prince-Regent on behalf of the King. In the meantime, the delegation was compelled to permit the existing Serbian Constitution to be introduced until a new one for the entire country could be voted.

The instructions given to the delegates by the Central Committee in Zagreb were totally ignored. Protic even went so far as to prepare the Regent's answer in advance. The only point conceded to the delegates was that Pavelic, a Croat, should read the address at the audience that the Prince-Regent had granted them. On December 1, in the presence of all the Serbian ministers who were in Belgrade at the time, Prince-Regent Aleksandar received the delegation. He heard its address and answered it with a proclamation of the new Kingdom of the Serbs, Croats and Slovenes. On December 3, the office of the National Council in Zagreb made public the new formation, and announced the cessation of its own functions.

Two days later, Zagreb became the scene of a belated military revolt which was staged by two Croatian regiments stationed there: On December 5 they were informed of the union and were called upon to take an oath of allegiance to King Petar I. Their disorganized response produced a confrontation with the superior shock-troops of Andjelinovic. It lasted only a few hours. Although the incident had been clearly a gesture on behalf of a republican and independent Croatia and bore pro-Radic overtones, Radic was not directly involved in it. The only significant result of the revolt was the disbanding of the Army of the National Council on December 6. This move left the Serbian Army as the sole military force in the newly created State. Strangely enough, it retained its name and the Serbian flag, as well as its old organization, complete with officer-corps, until 1929 when, under Royal Dictatorship, it became the Yugoslav Army.

*   *   *

After the official proclamation of the union, Prince-Regent Aleksandar gave Protic the mandate to form the first government of the newly created Kingdom. After long and tedious negotiating, on December 18 Protic was able to announce his Cabinet. He became Premier, Korosec Vice-President, Trumbic Minister of Foreign Affairs and Pribicevic Minister of Interior (Police).

The new government had to immediately cope with the situation in Croatia. General unrest prevailed in the country, especially in the villages. The peasants were calling for a republic. The government attempted to silence them by sending detachments from the Serbian Army to the most recalcitrant villages. The soldiers used their gun butts on suspects and arrested peasants with such curses as, "Here is King Petar's greetings!" The peasantry's reaction was expressed in such spontaneous shouts as "Down with King Petar!" and "Long live the Republic!"

Radic moved with the general trend. At the general convention in Zagreb on February 3, 1919, his party embraced the republican program and changed its name to the Croatian Republican Peasant Party. Moreover, the convention appealed to the Peace Conference in Paris by submitting a memorandum addressed to President Wilson which demanded the establishment of a neutral republic of Croatia. To give substance to the memorandum some two hundred thousands signatures were collected from the Croatian populace.

Such independent and revolutionary expressions went decidedly against the grain of the policy of the new government and especially of its head-policeman, Pribicevic. Considered by the Serbs as an expert in Croatian affairs and holding the appropiate post of Minister of the Interior, Pribicevic was given a free hand in Croatia. Wishing to nip Radic's plans in the bud, he channelled both the police force and units of the Serbian Army into a campaign that systematically persecuted all individuals connected with Radic's party. Scores of inhabitants of the villages were victimized, and terror reigned.

Radic was accused of revolutionary activities on the basis of his speech of February 3 and the subsequent memorandum to President Wilson. He was arrested on March 25 on the charge of high treason. Since his brother, Antun, had died on February 10, the party was now rendered leaderless and Pribicevic was certain that it would thereby also become powerless. But Radic did not remain idle even while imprisoned. He secretly prepared the text of the memorandum and it, together with the list of signatures, was dispatched to Paris via a member of the Italian Military Mission.

The memorandum proved an empty gesture. On the proposal of President Wilson, the newly formed Kingdom of the Serbs, Croats and Slovenes had already been fully recognized by the Council of the Peace Conference on April 23, 1919. With the signing of the Peace Treaty of Versailles on June 28, 1919, the Kingdom of the Serbs, Croats and Slovenes became a fullfledged member of the family of nations and a part of the League of Nations. And Radic, the man who tried to move heaven and hell to prevent the union, was fated to witness this spectacle from a prison cell.

CHAPTER XXI

THE NEW STATE AND THE CROATIAN QUESTION

Temporary National Representation — Treaty of Rapallo — Constituent Assembly — Croatian abstention — Vivdovdanski Ustav — Obznana — Croatian Block and the Geneva Conference — Markov Protokol — Radic's exile: London and Moscow — Radic's acceptance of Pasic's conditions — Crisis of parliamentarianism — Radic's assassination.

When the Kingdom of the Serbs, Croats and Slovenes was formed, the Serbian government and the delegation from the National Council in Zagreb agreed that a Temporary National Representation, composed of representatives from all political parties and groups, should perform the duties of the legislative body until a Constituent Assembly could be elected. Yet, it was not until March 1, 1919, that, by special edict of the Prince-Regent, this assembly was called into session. Radic's party refused to participate. Soon after he was convicted of sedition. This conviction poured fuel on the smoldering fire of general dissatisfaction. Insurrection was in the air in Croatian villages. It was bound to flare up at the smallest provocation.

Serbian military authorities issued orders to draft animals for military emergencies and to brand them. In retaliation, the peasants disarmed police, damaged railroad tracks and killed an overzealous district chief. Instantly the army moved. Local skirmishes were fought in the vicinity of Zagreb and the army soon got the upper hand. While hundreds of peasants were being arrested, the situation in the villages continued to deteriorate. Only when the orders were revoked and elections for the Constituent Assembly were called did the country quiet down. The expectation of, as well as the actual preparation for, the elections had a calming effect on the irritations of the peasantry.

The Temporary National Representation's principal task was to prepare an electoral law whereby the Constituent Assembly could be elected. After a good deal of bickering, a law was agreed upon and the Prince-Regent sanctioned it on September 20, 1920. This law introduced general suffrage to all male citizens over twenty-one years of age. Members of the Assembly were elected from general lists in the proportion of one for every 30,000 inhabitants. Twenty-five percent of the candidates had to have a university education.

* * *

The long-delayed elections for the Constituent Assembly were preceded by three vital decisions regarding a territorial settlement within the new state. The Council of Ambassadors abruptly terminated a longstanding Serbian claim on Skadar (Scutari) by connecting the town with Albania. The plebiscite of October 10 in Carinthia favored Austria. And finally, on November 20, 1920, the Treaty of Rapallo between Italy and the Kingdom of the Serbs, Croats and Slovenes, signed by Count Sforza, the Italian Minister of Foreign Affairs, and Trumbic, but only after a long and bitter dispute, settled the question of the boundaries between the two countries: Istria, Gorizia, and Trieste, as well as the islands of Cres (Cherso), Losinj (Lussino), and Lastovo (Lagosta) and the town of Zadar (Zara), with its adjacent territory, were given to Italy. The sea-port and city of Rijeka (Flume) was declared a free city-republic with Italian consular representation.

* * *

The elections for the Constituent Assembly occurred on November 28. The whole country awaited the electoral returns in the tense anticipation of their first democratic experience. The elections reflected the intricate problems facing the new state in all their crudeness. Although the new state claimed to be based on the principles of self-determination, this first test produced unconvincing evidence for such a claim.

At least nine different denominations asserted themselves from among the twenty-two parties which submitted their lists for the elections. The Serbs, Croats, Slovenes and Bosnian Moslems, who were supposed to be a single nation, were not the only ones to voice their particular grievances; so did the Albanians, Turks, Macedonians, Germans, Magyars and Rumanians. The government did not notably obstruct the electoral campaign except in Vojvodina (the southern part of Hungary alloted to the Kingdom by the Peace Treaty of Trianon on June 4, 1920) and some districts of Macedonia and Serbia.

These were the results of the elections: The Democrats (a new party under Davidovic's leadership comprised of the Serbian Independent Radicals, the Croato-Serbian Coalition and the Slovene Liberals) received 319,448 votes and gained 92 members for the Assembly; the Serbian Radicals led by Pasic received 284,575 votes and 92 members; Radic's party received 230,590 votes and 50 members; the Communists received 198,756 votes and 52 members; the Agrarian Union received 151,603 votes and 39 members; the Slovene Populists led by Korosec received 57,174 votes and fifteen members; Sustersic's faction of the Slovene Populists received 54,000 votes and twelve members; the Yugoslav Moslem Organization led by Spaho received 111,006 votes and twenty-four members; the Socialists received 46,792 votes and ten members; the Croatian Populists received 46,599 votes and nine members; the Croatian Union received 64,267 votes and eleven members; the *Dzemijet*-Turks received 30,029 votes and eight members; the Republicans received 18,136 votes and three members; the Frankovci received 10,880 votes

285

and two members; and the remaining votes and members were divided among other minor groups.

In Croatia and Slavonia the results were: Radic 230,590 (50); the Democrats 78,406 (19); the Radicals 39,050 (9); the Communists 31,281 (7); the Croatian Union 22,950 (3); the Croatian Populists 11,878 (3); the Frankovci 10,880 (2); the Socialists 7,611 (0). Very few members of the former self-styled National Council which had forced Croatia into union with Serbia were elected, fulfilling Radic's prophecy sooner than anticipated.

The sweeping success of Radic came as a disagreeable surprise to his adversaries. Some good reasons could be enumerated to explain his electoral victory in Croatia: (a) the Peasant Party was the only political organization with grassroot support throughout the country, and its program had been updated to adequately respond to the needs of the peasants who were franchised for the first time in their history; (b) a general dissatisfaction with Belgrade's policy, especially that of introducing terroristic methods into Croatia, provoked widespread resistance among the people.

But beyond these two more general reasons was the fact that the Ministry of Finance had issued an order, effective November 1919 to January 1920, to stamp the former Austro-Hungarian currency (the *Kruna*): A total of 5,687,000 *Krunas* circulating in the former Austro-Hungarian territory were stamped. The government taxed citizens holding these *Krunas* twenty-five percent, confiscating 1,137,400 *Krunas* as payment. Moreover, the *Kruna*, which hitherto had been valued at parity with the Serbian *Dinar*, was devalued to 2.50, then 3.00 and finally 4.00 per *Dinar*.

But, ultimately the personal popularity of Radic was due to his stand in the National Council where he unequivocally sided with the people and shared their Croatian national and republican feelings.

The elected members of the Peasant Party gathered in Zagreb on December 7, 1920, and declared themselves the true "Croatian National Representation." They refused to take part in the work of the Constituent Assembly in Belgrade, since, as far as they were concerned, the National Council did not have the people's mandate to carry out the proposed unification. Although, in adopting such an attitude, the Peasant Party lost touch with political reality, it appeared to have perfectly captured the mood of the peasants who almost exclusively filled its ranks.

The Constituent Assembly opened its sessions on December 12. Only 343 of its 419 elected members answered roll call. Two members of the Frankovci abstained along with the members of the Peasant Party.

On January 1, 1921, Pasic formed a coalition government from the ranks of his Radicals and the Davidovic-Pribicevic Democrats. It presented the draft of the Constitution on January 25 which was passed, on examination, to a special committee. This draft was nothing but a copy of the Serbian Constitution of 1903 with slight adjustments so that it would fit the new circumstances. It provided for a Constitutional Monarchy based on the Karadjordjevic Dynasty and a strong central government founded on a parliamentarian system.

The original draft was the work of Protic, who had also written the text of the Corfu Declaration as well as both the address to the Prince-Regent and the reply (December 1, 1918). For Protic, the dynasty, centralism and a unique assembly were undisputable necessities and precluded any discussion. Indeed, the Radicals, which included Pasic as well as Protic were all for a complete integration of the country, or, in other words, they were for the realization of their program of a "Greater Serbia," which would put the Croats in the same category as Macedonia and Montenegro. Thus, in the final draft, the government was even more insistent on the unitarian form of the state and put the strongest possible emphasis on a centralistic and parliamentarian monarchy.

The Croatian Union introduced its own draft, proposing a federal organization for the country and dividing it into the autonomous provinces of Serbia, Croatia, Montenegro, Bosnia and Hercegovina, Vojvodina and Slovenia.

When the government's final draft was brought forward for general discussion on June 11, the fifty-two Communist members left the Assembly in protest of their party's persecution. Four days later the Croatian Union and the Slovenian Populists also walked out, accusing the Serbian majority of attempting to impose a centralistic system on the Croats and Slovenes.

At the reading of the final draft, the government found itself in the predicament of lacking a majority. Thus, bargaining and manipulation behind the scene were resorted to in order to secure the passage of the Constitution. First of all, Bogumil Vosnjak's relatively insignificant group of Slovenian Agrarians (five members) was bought at the price of Vosnjak's appointment to the post of Minister to Prague and some licenses for his friends to export cattle to Austria. Second, the *Dzemijet*, a Turkish minority group representing the Turkish landowners or *begs*, entered into a bargain regarding land reform in Macedonia: The government offered indemnities to the begs for lands subject to the law of Agrarian reform. The same bargain was made with the Bosnian landowners, securing the votes of the Yugoslav Moslem Organization.

The Constitution was finally voted by a simple majority con-sisting of Radicals, Democrats, the Yugoslav Moslem Organization, *Dzemijet*, and the Slovene Agrarians. It managed 233 votes to the opposition 35 cast by the Socialists, Serbian Agrarians and the Republicans. The proportion of voters was 186 Serbs, 18 Moslems, eleven Slovenes, ten Croats and eight Turks. There were 161 members who abstained. These included 83 Croats, 26 Slovenes and 52 Communists who, being internationally minded, did not list their nationality.

The official proclamation of the Constitution fell on June 28, 1921, or *Vidovdan* (St. Vitus Day), which was also the Serbian National holiday; hence the name *Vidovdanski Ustav* (St. Vitus Day Constitution). Following the vote for the Constitution, the Constituent Assembly voted its own continuation as the regular parliament and gave itself the name, *Narodna Skupstina* (the National Assembly).

The promulgation of the Constitution carried Pribicevic to the pinnacle of his career. He let his power be felt especially in Croatia, which was considered his *Pashalik,* and it was there that he continued his persecution of Radic and his followers with even greater zeal than before. He stooped to forming the *Orjuna* (Organization of the Yugoslav Nationalists) out of street gangs that resembled Mussolini's Fascists. The *Orjuna* soon gained a reputation for its use of violence and for its assassinations of political opponents throughout Croatia. It became an example for the formation of other similar organizations, viz. the *Srnao* (Serbian Nationalists) and the *Hanao* (Croatian Nationalists).

Radic countered Pribicevic's terrorism, which made the "Croats smaller than a poppy-seed," by doubling his effort as the tribune of the peasants. His slogans, such as, *Vjera u Boga i seljacka sloga* (Faith in God and peasant concord), *Sav je kulturni svijet za narodni suverenitet* (The entire cultural world is for the national sovereignty) and *Republika svemu svijetu dika* (Glorious republic for everyone), became familiar among the villagers.

The *Vidovdanski Ustav* was the crowning achievement of the Pasic-Pribicevic policy. Although essentially liberal, it was nevertheless designed to impose a centralistic state and Serbian hegemony. Despite its name, the Kingdom of the Serbs, Croats and Slovenes was little more than a "Greater Serbia." Indeed, the majority of the Serbs saw an opportunity at this time to realize their ultimate ambition to make their "Greater Serbia" a reality. By imposing their own Karadjordjevic Dynasty, their army, their diplomacy, and even by giving their Serbian Orthodox Church semi-official status in the Kingdom, the Serbs were able to monopolize all key administrative positions. In imposing their civil service throughout the country, they furthered the life of a whole tradition of bribery and corruption that had been bequeathed to them by the defunct Turkish Empire.

*   *   *

Because they were discontented with the *Vidovdanski Ustav,* the members of the Croatian Union disaffiliated themselves from the work of the National Assembly and joined forces with the Croatian Republican Peasant Party of Radic. An understanding, to which the Frankovci also adhered, was reached on July 26, 1921; and on October 30, the Croatian Bloc was formally established under the leadership of Radic. The chief aim of the Bloc was the invalidation of the Constitution, at least in its relation to the Croats. This aim had the effect of turning the Croatian Question into a kind of chronic antagonism which would gnaw deeper and deeper into the marrow of the new state.

On the day that the Constitution was officially proclaimed, a member of the Communist Party attempted to assassinate Prince Aleksandar. Shortly after, Milorad Draskovic, Minister of the Interior and the man chiefly responsible for the persecution of the Communists, was assassinated by a Communist Party member. In response to these acts, a special law for the protection of the State, the *Obznana,* was promulgated on August 1. It outlawed the Communist Party of Yugoslavia and invalidated the credentials of its members in parliament.

*　　*　　*

The dissolution of the Habsburg Monarchy created a disturbing situation in the Danubian area and attracted the interest of a number of French politicians. One of them, Charles Rivet, traveled to Belgrade and Zagreb in 1919 in order to make a first-hand study of the situation. He discovered fundamental differences between the Croats and the Serbs which, by necessity, effected their relationship. According to him, the Serbs were more docile than the recalcitrant Croats. The Serbs permitted themselves to be dominated by the *comitadjis,* or *cetniks,* as well as by military conspirators in the pay of a powerful military clique. The secret military organization, the *Bela ruka* (White Hand) which had emerged from the splintering of the *Crna ruka* (Black Hand) — led by the famous Colonel Dimitrijevic-Apis, liquidated at the Salonika Trial — was closely linked to the Prince-Regent himself.

After an extensive conversation with Radic, Rivet summed up Croatia's reaction: ". . . If the Croats have not surrendered to Hungary and Austria in eight hundred years, why in the world should they now surrender to Serbia!" The French author drew his own conclusions from his findings: He said that the new state was the embodiment of Serbian military imperialism and would be seriously threatened by the rising tide of Croatian nationalism. Such an overt Serbo-Croatian conflict would inevitably lead to a complete rupture of their relationship.

The Serbs in Belgrade were not, however, spared a certain uneasiness. From the start, Prince-Regent Aleksandar was personally attacked by Radic's republicanism. He showed how deeply he had been wounded by declaring openly to the *Ban* of Croatia, Matko Laginja, that either Radic's head, or his own, must fall.

Divergent tendencies soon became obvious among the parties which formed the government coalition. Some members of Davidovic's entourage, as well as the once powerful Protic, did not see eye-to-eye with Pribicevic regarding his high-handed policy in Croatia. Because Protic had been pushed aside by Pasic and therefore had no official position in the government, he was unable to do more than offer sympathetic words to Radic when they met in Zagreb on August 10. He vainly tried to convince Radic that it was necessary for his party to join the Belgrade parliament.

The man who proved his uncommon dialectical skill when he outwitted Trumbic at Corfu and outmaneuvered the delegation of the National Council utterly failed to bring Radic around. The latter realized only too well that he would be reduced to a mere representative of a minority parliamentarian group in the Belgrade Parliament, and he demanded no less than full recognition as rightful leader of the Croatian nation. Commenting on his talks with Protic, Radic declared: "There is not a single Croat who would not sincerely desire a peaceful settlement with the Serbs regarding the national territory, but there is also not a single Croat who would want to betray his people by capitulating to violence."

*   *   *

Preparation for the Geneva Conference (to be held from April 10 through May 19, 1922) gave Radic's uninformed hopes the prospect of another Peace Conference that would not fail to solve all the European problems that remained. Since the Croatian Question was one of the most acute of these problems, it would doubtless have high priority on the agenda. With this in mind, he planned to send a special Croatian delegation, which would be independent from the Belgrade government, to the Conference. Thus, on January 14, the Croatian Bloc prepared a memorandum which was addressed to the "entire civilized world and especially to the delegates of the Geneva Conference." It outlined the differences between the Serbs and Croats, and it stressed Croatia's western orientation which was determined by the "humanitarian individualism of the universal Roman Catholic Church as well as by her entire social structure which was based on the European literature and system of education." The memorandum offered a new formula for the solution of the Croatian Question: It called for ". . . A sovereign Croatia within the boundaries of the commonwealth of the Serbs, Croats and Slovenes." The draft for this memorandum, however, remained in its early stage and achieved no practical results, except to bring the internal crisis to a head.

In the meantime, on April 26, the government published an ordinance which divided the country into thirty-three departments (*oblasti*). Croatia was thereby divided into four departments. Davidovic, however, was dissatisfied with the general policy of the government and attempted to weaken the Radicals. He attended a Congress of Intellectuals held in Zagreb on September 10. This Congress published a manifesto which protested Belgrade's hegemonistic centralism as it was expressed in the *Vidovdanski Ustav*. Thus the Croats got the impression that they would receive crucial support from a faction of the Serbian Democrats in their demand for a revision of the Constitution. But this attitude of Davidovic and his followers from the Democratic Party which, along with the Radicals formed the governing coalition, was bound to provoke a crisis in the government.

In a message to Belgrade, Radic stressed the fact that the Croatian Question would not be resolved by better administration, nor by a new move on the parliamentarian chessboard, but only by full recognition of Croatia's national individuality and her right to self-determination. To give substance to this message, Radic sent Predavec, Krnjevic and Drinkovic to Belgrade to come to terms with Davidovic and Protic. This precipitated a crisis and Pasic's coalition government resigned.

Pasic was entrusted with the formation of a purely radical government, and therefore prepared for new elections. The latter, held on March 18, 1923, were to a large extent rigged. But, in spite of the fact that he availed himself of all possible means, Pasic fell short of his goal. The election results were: Radicals 562,213 votes and 108 mandates; Radic 437,733 votes, 70 mandates; Democrats 400,342 votes, 51 mandates; Communists 24,321 votes; Serbian Agrarians 153,579 votes, eleven mandates; Korosec 126,378 votes, twenty-four mandates; Moslems 112,228 votes, eighteen mandates; and the remaining votes and mandates went to smaller groups. As a result of the elections, Radic achieved his greatest personal success: From a leader of a political party he was promoted to a leader of national stature in Croatia.

In his vain attempt to gain self-determination for Croatia, Radic adopted a policy of abstention from and passive resistance to the regime in Belgrade. He and his party were persecuted and Serbo-Croatian relations went from bad to worse.

Dating from the elections of 1923, Pasic's Radicals, who were the representatives of Serbia, were pitted against Radic's party, which was now established as the representative of Croatia. Thus Radic engineered direct talks with the Radicals. To prepare ground for these talks, he said that he was ready to accept the existing international boundaries of the State, since they were the best possible under the actual conditions in Europe and seemed most favorable to Croatian interests. Simultaneously, to strengthen his position vis-a-vis Belgrade, he formed a Federalistic Bloc with Korosec and Spaho, thus throwing up a common front for the entire non-Serbian opposition. The chief concern of the Bloc was the revision of the Constitution and the reorganization of the country on a federalistic basis.

The Belgrade press, for the most part inspired by Pribicevic, reacted violently to the mere suggestion of the formation of the Federalistic Bloc. The Belgrade paper, the *Balkan*, threatened Zagreb with bloodshed and promised Radic and all federalists the gallows.

Upon reaching the zenith of his popularity, Radic, to quote his own words, employed tactics that made him the "greatest political acrobat." He attacked his adversaries on all sides at once, piercing his targets with the deadly thrusts of an accomplished and cunning duelist. He overcame all obstacles in his path and contrived ways and means to overcome a moment of danger, either compromising, or, if necessary, capitulating. Inevitably, he emerged as the apparent victor of these contests.

Radic was fully aware of his exceptional position, not only as leader of his party, but, in a way, as leader of his nation as well. He was an accepted authority and although the party's forum deliberated over all problems, the final decisions were left to him. Toward his party he behaved as a patriarch. He promoted his aims by teaching, scolding, threatening, punishing and praising, always ready to forgive the stubborn person that finally surrendered to his will. His attitude and his tactics were saturated with excessive optimism. Indeed, every move he made was guided by an optimistic belief in the goodness of all men.

While Pribicevic's press continued to print threatening articles against Radic and his Federalistic Bloc, Radic surprised Belgrade with a sudden and unexpected move. On April 11, he dispatched Macek and Krnjevic, two of his closest collaborators, to Belgrade to meet with Pasic and negotiate a *modus vivendi* between the Croats and Serbs. Subsequently, Marko Trifkovic, President of the Radical Club, and Voja Janjic, Secretary of the Party, arrived in Zagreb to open formal negotiations with the Croatian Republican Peasant Party. An agreement was reached and a document known as *Markov Protocol* (Mark's Protocol) was signed. Its provisions were: (1) The government must abandon the division of Croatia into the newly announced *oblasti* (districts) in order to preserve its territorial integrity and it must appoint a Royal Governor to administer Croatia; (2) the government must at once stop all political persecution in Croatia, Slovenia and Bosnia and Hercegovina, particularly that directed against the members of the Peasant Party; and (3) the elected members of the Parliament of the Peasant Party, including Radic, promise in return to abstain from their work in the Parliament, thereby assuring Pasic his precarious majority in the rump parliament.

Mark's Protocol was but a tactical move for both parties and it was honored by no one. It furnished the certitude for Pasic that Radic would not come to Belgrade under any circumstances. But having gotten what he wanted, he found it unnecessary to keep his part of the bargain. A month had hardly passed before all of the remaining agencies of the autonomous government of Croatia were abolished and Croatia itself was divided into four districts.

In a speech in Zagreb on June 24, Radic's reaction to the duplicity of the Radicals was sharp. He announced a definitive break with Belgrade. Earlier he had expressed a hope in diplomatic intervention by the European powers to resolve the Croatian Question in Croatia's favor. But his abuse of the Radicals at this time doubtlessly went too far. During the celebration of Bastille Day (July 14), he went even further by connecting the Karadjordjevics with that day's significance and by insinuating that Belgrade had lost its last friend in Croatia. He used the same occasion to reiterate what he called the true aspirations of Croatia, that is, to insist on the full right to national self-determination. Another speech in the same vein convinced the government to seek his arrest.

When Radic got wind of his imminent arrest, he secretly crossed the Hungarian border (July 21). He continued his journey to Vienna under the name of Stjepan Fleisig. A few days after his arrival in Vienna he left for London with his wife, his son (Vladko) and his son-in-law (Kosutic)), hoping that he could enlist British public opinion for the Croatian cause. During his stay in London, he made no contact with any notable British official, but cultivated relations with the pacifist wing of the Labor Party which centered around Noel Buxton and the Lelland brothers who were publishers of the weekly paper, the *New Leader*. His experience in London was negative. His contacts assured him that there was no man in England who would endorse or support the idea of a separation between Serbia and Croatia.

After his failure in Great Britain, he returned to Vienna, cherishing hopes for the formation of a democratic alliance consisting of his Federalistic Bloc, Davidovic's faction of the Democrats and the Serbian Agrarians. Seeking Pasic's downfall, he worked to strengthen the opposition in Parliament through the participation of the Peasant Party. On March 7, the first group of members from the Peasant Party presented their credentials to the Parliament for verification. Their arrival in Belgrade immediately provoked a governmental crisis and a split in the Democratic Party. Pribicevic's faction left the Party and on March 26 formed the Independent Democratic Party which joined Pasic's government two days later. Unable to resist the pressure of the opposition majority, the government contrived a way to adjourn Parliament from May 27 to October 20, thus, at least for the time being, thwarting Radic's design for toppling the government.

Radic did not personally participate in these maneuvers. He stayed in Vienna and from there watched the development of the crisis. It was at this time that he finally accepted the repeated invitation of Chicherin, Commissar of Foreign Affairs of the USSR, and of the recently formed International Peasant Union in Moscow, to visit the Soviet Union. There were several plausible justifications for this step. At that time many people in Europe believed in the imminence of Russia's return to the fold of the European nations. Germany had recognized the Bolshevik regime on April 16, 1922, followed by Great Britain on February 1, 1924, Italy on February 7, and France on October 28. The introduction of the New Economic Policy (N.E.P.) was, outside of the Soviet Union, generally regarded as the first step toward reversion to a capitalistic economy. Moreover, temporary measures favorably affected the peasantry. Obviously, Radic was impressed by the new trend in the Soviet policy regarding the peasants.

At about the same time the Comintern discussion of the Balkan issue was in the news. In a resolution which was voted in July 1924, the Comintern Balkan Section recognized for Croatia, Slovenia and Macedonia the right to break from the Kingdom of the Serbs, Croats and Slovenes in order to form independent republics. Thus the Comintern's attitude regarding the Kingdom was more or less like Radic's own concept of a "neutral peasant republic of Croatia." Moreover, one should bear in mind that all his life Radic had had a weakness for Russia insofar as it appeared to him as a Slavic and Christian, pesant and democratic, symbol and protector. And this remained true for Radic whether Russia was ruled by the Romanovs, by Lvov and Kerenski, or by the Bolsheviks.

Before leaving Vienna, he went to see Johann Schober, Chief of the Austrian State Police and former Chancellor, and explained to him his reasons for going to Moscow. He insisted that under no circumstances would he accept the Bolshevik program of its methods.

He arrived in Moscow on June 2 accompanied by Kosutic. He immediately got in touch with the Commissariat of Foreign Affairs and the International Peasant Union. He enrolled his party as a member, but retained for it its own program and methods. He passed his time by lecturing and attending conferences. He was prevented from visiting Russia outside the limits of Moscow. On August 4 he was back in Vienna.

* * *

The presence of Radic's deputies in Parliament upset the balance of Pasic's government and compelled him to tender his resignation. On July 27, Davidovic formed a coalition government consisting of Spaho, Korosec and Nastas Petrovic. The latter was the King's trusted man and a Radical. Petrovic was appointed Minister of Interior. The Coalition relied on Radic's deputies for parliamentarian support.

After more than a year of wandering between Vienna, London and Moscow, the Croatian peasant leader was politically wiser, even though most of his experiences were disillusioning. London had turned a deaf ear to all his plans, and his visit to Moscow, in addition to proving to be a total failure, left him with the stigma of being an apparent Communist sympathizer. This unpleasant reputation was to cling to him and his party in the months ahead. With hopes for international intervention on behalf of Croatia shattered, he had no choice but to avail himself of the regular channels of parliamentarian struggle to coerce a revision of the *Vidovdanski Ustav*. Toward this end, he revived his Croatian Bloc, imposing his views regarding an understanding with Serbia on his partners. In a series of public speeches, he strongly emphasized anti-monarchism and antimilitarism, thus undermining the precarious position of the Davidovic government.

After Davidovic's fall, Pasic formed a coalition government with Pribicevic. This government decided immediately to apply to Radic and his party the *Obznana*, the extraordinary law for State security. This was done on the basis of the party's affiliation with the International Peasant Union in Moscow. On January 1, 1925, the entire leadership of the party was jailed. While Radic was in jail, the general elections took place. They gave the Pasic-Pribicevic faction of the National Bloc 1,040,492 votes and 142 mandates; while Radic took 532,972 votes and

67 mandates. Davidovic took 284,527 votes and 37 mandates; Korosec 121,369 votes and twenty mandates; Spaho 132,207 votes and fifteen mandates; the Agrarians 121,639 votes and five mandates; the Montenegro Federalists 8,651 votes and three mandates; and the Germans 45,010 votes and five mandates. After the elections, all of Radic's deputies, except Radic and those who were in jail, presented their credentials to the *Skupstina.*

Radic was completely isolated from his collaborators in prison. Pasic sent an examining judge to him to open preliminary pourparlers. Nikola Nikic, who was Radic's deputy, served as intermediary between the two men. The result of the talks was an agreement with Pasic permitting the transmittance of the text of a declaration drafted by Radic to his nephew, Pavle Radic, who was also a member of the *Skupstina.*

On March 27, 1925, Pavle Radic read his uncle's declaration to the Belgrade Parliament. It recognized the country's political setup which was established by the *Vidovdanski Ustav* and which included the Karadjordjevic Dynasty. Hopes were expressed for a revision of the Constitution that would satisfy all legitimate claims of the Croats and Slovenes on exercising self-determination. This declaration brought a complete chapter of Croatian politics to an abrupt end. The sudden about-face proved too violent and unexpected for Radic's political entourage to digest. Only a few months earlier he had rammed his intransigent program down the throats of the Croatian bourgeois politicians; and now, with no warning, he unveiled this contradictory surprise. Trumbic, Lorkovic and their friends could not swallow it. They defected from the party to form the new Croatian Federalist Peasant Party.

Radic never made public his reasons for so radical a change. He explained it to his followers as simply a natural political move. But the circumstances speak more plainly: (1) Radic's plan for a self-determined Croatia had definitely been defeated; (2) his exile and visits to London and Moscow seeking foreign intervention had failed; (3) Pasic proved an undeniable success in the general elections; (4) although legally an elected member of the Parliament, Radic remained in prison; (5) despite the Court decision that their arrests were illegal, the Executive Committee of the Party, composed of legally elected deputies, remained in custody; and finally (6) Radic expected his own assassination at any time.

In the meantime, the Party dropped its republicanism and became the Croatian Peasant Party, henceforth referred to as the HSS. On April 26 the Central Committee and elected deputies of the Party voted to grant full confidence to their leader and endorsed the new direction. As a consequence of this Pasic-Radic understanding, Pasic formed a new government of "national understanding". Radic's followers took the places of the followers of Pribicevic, receiving four minor ministries.

Upon Radic's capitulation, Pasic had, beyond all doubt, scored a major victory. But Radic succeeded in preserving, although in a somewhat diminished form, his popularity with the Croatian peasants.

On August 15, the Croats celebrated the thousand year anniversary of the establishment of the Kingdom of Croatia. (Tomislav had assumed his title in 925.) For the occasion, Zagreb became the festive center of a huge Croatian *Sokol* gathering. (The *Sokol*, or Faulcon, was a gymnastic society which enjoyed popularity among all Slavic peoples and was created according to the pattern of the German *Turnverein*.) Radic became involved in preparations for the visit of the Royal couple on this occasion. King Aleksandar and Queen Marija were enthusiastically received and hailed as "King and Queen of Croatia".

* * *

Although Radic had renounced his national program, he continued to work for a Constitutional reform that would permit the country's reorganization along federalistic lines. He had already obtained the Radical's support for the enactment of new laws dealing with the self-rule of the communes, the unified taxation system, Agrarian reform in Dalmatia, the use of natural resources, the drainage of swamps, the canalization and regulation of waterways, maritime trade, and the fisheries along the Adriatic Sea. He had also introduced such administrative measures as a civil service law, providing for its independence from politics and the reduction of government personnel, and a law providing amnesty for political and military offenses. Despite the thorough preparation of these bills by the ministers of the HSS, they never had a chance to be submitted to Parliament due to the dilatory tactics of the Radicals.

When Radic, himself, joined the government on November 17 as Minister of Public Instruction, he presented an elaborate plan for the reorganization of the national educational system. This plan took into account his own party's program as well as the most recent pedagogical methods. But it shared the fate of the other bills that had formerly been introduced: It met with constant rebuttal from the Radicals.

Instead of pursuing a genuinely constructive policy which would deal with the pressing problems of the country (at least as they were presented in the bills of the HSS), and instead of directing its energy toward a revision of the Constitution, the government became involved in another conflict. The latent corruption of Pasic and his entourage erupted into the open in a series of scandals surrounding his son, Rade. This gave King Aleksandar a welcome excuse for ridding himself of the old Premier's irksome tutelage. In a determined and merciless campaign against Pasic, the King enlisted Radic's help, since Radic's proclaimed principles had given him a reputation as an outspoken enemy of corruption.

A manysided attack from the press, unpleasant questions asked in the *Skupstina* and a crisis in the government provoked Pasic's resignation on April 4, 1926. The new government, a coalition of the Radicals and the HSS, was formed by Nikola Uzunovic. Thus, Pasic's fall became chiefly a personal victory for the King, and due to a complete reshuffling of the Cabinet, he became supreme arbiter. All the great political leaders, viz. Pasic, Davidovic, Radic and Pribicevic, were relegated to a more or less latent and frustrated opposition while the government carried out the policy of Aleksandar.

Although Aleksandar had not flinched at condemning Pasic's corruption, he availed himself of every legal loophole to build a huge family fortune. His efforts made Pasic's practices seem mere child's play. From complete bankruptcy in the years before the ascent to the Serbian throne (1903), the Karadjordjevic family became one of the wealthiest of the minor reigning European dynasties. Outwardly everything had a perfectly legal aspect, since the King, with Pasic's consent, passed ordinances to legalize certain forms of graft. In 1922 he made a decree which entitled him to convert the country's currency (the *Dinar*) into Swiss *Francs* at the rate of 2.08 *Dinars* to the *Franc*. Out of the 1,086,297,782 *Dinar* total on the Civil List, 612,527,753 had been transferred into Swiss banks while the Stock Exchange was averaging ten to fourteen *Dinars* per *Franc*.

The new government was caught in a permanent cycle of crisis. All remedial measures divised by the Croatian ministers were, on the instruction of their Serbian ministerial colleagues, immediately sabotaged by insubordinate officials. Thus, as an example, Pavle Radic, Minister of Agrarian Reform, was constantly overruled by mere district chiefs who acted on the surreptitious orders of the Minister of the Interior. In May, Radic attempted to force the issue by provoking a new governmental crisis, but he met resistance from his own deputies who were headed by Nikic and Superina.

On December 10, in the thick of a general political crisis which rocked the government and undermined the political parties, Pasic died. By this time, not only his internal but also his foreign policies, had failed. On November 27, contrary to the provisions of the Treaty of Rome (January 27, 1924), a Pact of Amity between Italy and Albania was signed in Tirana. Pasic's close friend, Nincic, Minister of Foreign Affairs and author of the Treaty of Rome, was forced to resign.

Another crisis induced by the malpractice of the Minister of the Interior, Boza Maksimovic, forced Uzunovic to resign. The new government was formed by Velja Vukicevic, a second-rater of the Radical Party, but a man who held the King's confidence. He based the government on a coalition with Korosec and Spaho, as well as with Vojislav Marinkovic's faction of the Democratic Party. The government did not present itself to the *Skupstina*, which was soon dissolved. Elections were called for September 11.

Prior to the elections, a Radical-Democrat agreement predetermined the distribution of all deputies from Macedonian and Albanian parts at a ratio of three for the Radicals to every two for the Democrats. A similar agreement took care of the German, Magyar and Rumanian electors of the electoral districts of Vojvodina. Thus the electing of some fifty members to the *Skupstina* was a farce.

General apathy characterized the elections. The results were: The Radicals 505,735 (93); the Radical-dissidents 195,039 (17); the Democrats 375,789 (61); the HSS 381,371 (61); Pribicevic 202,127 (23); the Agrarians 146,425 (9); Korosec 139,932 (20); Spaho 120,336 (18); the Socialists 23,474 (1); the Croatian Bloc 48,626 (2); etc.

The elections left both Radic and Pribicevic, formerly implacable antagonists, in similar positions with respect to the government. Radic lost no time preparing the ground for a "Parliamentarian union of democracy", cooperating toward that end with Davidovic, Pribicevic and the Agrarian, Joca Jovanovic. Davidovic, however, joined the government while Radic and Pribicevic formed the Peasant Democratic Coalition on November 10. That such formidable antagonists who had waged merciless war on one another for nearly two decades should open a new chapter in Croatian politics as allies, and this at the sunset of their public careers, created a sensation.

The primary purpose of the Coalition was to fight for a truly democratic regime within Constitutional limits. It sought to promote legislation which would permit local and provincial self-government, and it hoped to pave the way for a change in the Constitution which would allow the reorganization of the country on a federal basis. But the Coalition was greatly outnumbered. It faced a new government which had been formed by Vukicevic through a Coalition of Radicals, Democrats, as well as Korosec and Spaho, and which the opposition derisively labeled the *tvrdi grad* (stronghold).

As soon as the *Skupstina* convened, the opposition put forward one interpellation after the other. It became known that for the past years Croatia had paid 686 million *Dinars* more in taxes than Serbia, although Serbia nearly doubled Croatia in size and population. But besides the evident inequality in taxation, the question of the mismanagement of the National Bank, the National Mortgage Bank and the State Monopoly arose. All of these institutions had a national character, yet they were controlled by ten Serbs and two Russian emigrees, but not a single Croat. Pribicevic suggested that the extent of Serbian hegemony could be judged by the fact that eighty to one hundred percent of all important government positions were held by Serbs from Serbia. Similar conditions prevailed in the Army where all generals and ninety percent of the superior officers were Serbs, even though the Croat's military qualities were outstanding and had distinguished them in their service in the former Austro-Hungarian Army. The temperature in the *Skupstina* was going up daily.

The crisis reached its peak when the government negotiated a substantial loan in London. British financial circles wanted to be assured of a certain amount of stability in the country's domestic and, above all, foreign policy. London always had had a weak spot for Mussolini, thus it put pressure on Belgrade to ratify the Nettuno Conventions, a move that would strengthen Mussolini considerably. There were thirty-one conventions, all of which formed a corollary to the Treaty of Rome and granted special privileges to Italy and the Italian population in Dalmatia regarding the eastern shore of the Adriatic.

In the beginning of April, the Italian press violently attacked its Adriatic neighbor and incited the Venetian population to a series of demonstrations. The Coalition reacted with counter-demonstrations which were particularly violent in Zagreb and

Belgrade as well as in various towns in Dalmatia. The idea was to force the reluctant government to bring the issue of the loan before the *Skupstina*. The pro-government press, especially the *Samouprava*, the *Balkans* and, to some extent, the *Politika*, launched a systematic and violent attack on the Coalition, even going so far as to call for blood. The scenes in the *Skupstina* were equally as violent, reeking with accusations of blatant corruption in the government. During the June 20, 1928, session, three members of the government majority openly declared that they were ready to seek Radic's blood. Following a staged incident, Punisa Racic, a Radical deputy, killed Pavle Radic and Djuro Basaricek with a revolver and mortally wounded Stjepan Radic. He also wounded Ivan Pernar and Ivan Grandja. All of these victims were members of the HSS.

Following the shooting, Racic fled the *Skupstina* Hall, and passing through the governmental chamber he exclaimed to those present: "Long live Greater Serbia."

After an immediate reaction of consternation, the assassination in the *Skupstina* provoked searing hatred and violent demonstrations all over Croatia and especially in Zagreb. They were aimed as much at Serbia as they were at the government. Thus, the "Croatian Question" was dragged from the *Skupstina* into the streets and assumed the proportions of an open conflict.

When Radic was in the hospital in Belgrade, his second in command, Vladko Macek, paid him a visit. It was on this occasion that Radic outlined for him the new aspects of the Croatian Question: "After what happened in the Parliament we shall want to have little or nothing to do with them anymore. We might settle for common foreign affairs and defense, but maybe not even that much. It will depend on circumstances. . ."

King Aleksandar and Pribicevic were among Radic's other visitors. The King had made several attempts to separate Pribicevic from Radic and the Croats and once again advanced to him the idea of a separation from Croatia, but to no avail. Pribicevic remained as staunch a friend as he had once been a foe. Radic recovered sufficiently to return to Zagreb where he lingered between life and death. On August 8, 1928, he died.

Although the assassination conspiracy was organized by certain military and political circles closely connected with King Aleksandar, the Croats instinctively attributed the bloody deed to Aleksandar himself.

CHAPTER XXII

THE ROYAL DICTATORSHIP

Aleksandar Karadjordjevic — Crisis of parliamentarism — Royal dictatorship — Croatian reactions — Authoritarian constitutional regime — Zagreb Resolution — Yugoslav foreign policy — Aleksandar's assassination — Regency — Prince Paul — Jeftic's premiership — Stojadinovic's premiership.

Aleksandar Karadjordjevic (1888-1934) was born at the Montenegran capital of Cetinje. He was the youngest son of Prince Petar, a pretender to the Serbian throne, and Princess Zorka, daughter of the ruler of Montenegro, Prince Nikola. Born in exile, Aleksandar spent his youth and received his education in foreign countries, chiefly Russia. He was ultimately to die at the hands of an assassin on the foreign soil of Marseilles, France. Because of the protection he received from his two maternal aunts, who were married to Russian Grand Dukes, Milica and Anastazija, he was accepted into the Page Corps of the Imperial Corps in St. Petersburg. His sister, Jelena, was also destined to marry a Russian Grand Duke. His third aunt, Elena, married Victor Emanuel, King of Italy. His education was exclusively militaristic with a distinctive autocratic, imperialistic slant.

For centuries the Russian emperors had excelled in carrying out the special mission of liberating all Greco-Orthodox and Slavic populations from the Ottoman or Habsburg yokes. This idea found a devoted pupil in Aleksandar. According to his contemporaries, strict military discipline, martial bearing, personal courage, limited general culture, and limited intelligence were his most evident characteristics. He possessed natural personal charm when he wanted to employ it. He had instinctive cunning, unlimited personal ambition, and a stubborness and outright ruthlessness which made him lucrative as a possible partner and formidable as an antagonist.

After the ascension of his father to the royal throne in Serbia, brought about by the bloody events of 1903 which annihilated the rival Obrenovic Dynasty, Aleksandar's family returned to Serbia. He and his older brother, Crown Prince Djordje, became fervent members of the nationalistic Greater Serbian movement. The members of the secret military organization, the Black Hand, as well as the leaders of the ruling Radical Party, became their daily companions and in a certain sense their educators. Aleksandar was not slow in proving himself an outstanding student in the area of conspiracy. With Pasic's help, he masterminded a conspiracy to deprive his brother of his right to the succession to the throne. When Djordje was badgered into losing his temper and signing his resignation, Aleksandar moved ahead of him and, in 1909, became the Crown Prince. Employing the same methods and the same ally, in 1914 he pushed his father aside. He assumed royal prerogatives as the Prince Regent on the eve of the fatal events of that year. During the war, Aleksandar showed an equal ruthlessness when he staged the famous Salonika Trial to settle accounts with the Black Hand.

According to the general assessment of contemporaries who had to deal with him, Aleksandar could not tolerate any personality stronger than his in public life. This propensity had been reinforced by his autocratic education. Using position, charm, persuasion, bribe, corruption and brutal force, which did not exclude juristic murder and even political assassination, he systematically paved the way for his personal regime. Even at the initial formation of the Kingdom of the Serbs, Croats and Slovenes he was using Protic to undermine Pasic's position. Pasic was not entrusted with the formation of the government, but his second in command, Protic, was instead, and later even Vesnic. (Pasic was subsequently quite happy to repay Protic in the same coin.) Ultimately, Radic's attacks on corruption served Aleksandar in dealing the Patriarch of Serbian politics the final blow. (Davidovic, as another potential contender, was never able to establish his leadership in the Democratic Party because of the intrigues of either Pribicevic or Marinkovic, both of whom received their inspiration from the Court.)

It was a well established fact that although the Kingdom was a constitutionally based parliamentarian monarchy, no government was voted into or out of power according to parliamentarian procedures. The governments were formed or toppled at the whim of backstage maneuvers which were directly or indirectly manipulated by the King's entourage or by the King himself. Following Pasic's death, the Cabinet became the property of the King's stooges, e.g. Uzunovic and Vukicevic, and later Zivkovic, Srskic and Marinkovic. Even Pribicevic, after outliving his usefulness, was dismissed without proper procedures or even a pretense to them.

Radic's assassination freed Aleksandar of the last political leader who enjoyed popular support in the country. Thus the stage was set for the experiment of personal rule, either accompanied by the pretense to parliamentarianism or without it.

In general, the Croats believed that Aleksandar never made an attempt to become the King on an equal basis for the Serbs, Croats and Slovenes. Above all, he was a proponent of Serbian exclusivism; more a political force for the idea of a "Greater Serbia" than a monarch to all the peoples under his crown. And it was in this spirit of absolute Serbian domination that he approached the crisis created by Radic's assassination.

* * *

After the shooting of June 20, the members of the Peasant-Democratic Coalition decided to boycott the *Skupstina*. They left Belgrade and gathered at the old *Sabor* Hall in Zagreb on August 1. Under Pribicevic's chairmanship, they voted a resolution in which they enumerated their grievances and demands:

The rump National Assembly, called into session on August 1, 1928, has no right to vote any decisions affecting the entire country. All such decisions, particularly in financial matters, are forthwith declared null and void for all territories of former Austro-Hungary. These territories, of which Croatia is a special part, shall henceforth be represented by the Coalition.

The Coalition emphasizes that the Kingdom of Croatia, as well as that of Montenegro and all other historically defined entities in the National Council, in forming the common State of the Serbs, Croats and Slovenes with Serbia, did not intend to surrender their separate existence to any other country but did so only for the benefit of the common State. Because of the recent tragic events and because of the Act of December 1, 1918, and the Constitution of 1921, which have served to impose the hegemony of the former Kingdom of Serbia on all other lands joining the common State, we declare that the organization of the State, as it has existed up to now, must be considered null. Furthermore, with the utmost determination, we shall continue our struggle for a new and better organization of the State, seeking to secure complete equality for all lands. Other steps shall be taken when the president, Stjepan Radic, assumes his post again.

The Peasant-Democrat Coalition invites all political parties and groups of the former Austro-Hungarian territories to join it in the struggle for equality. We expect the peasants of Serbia to give us their support, which would be in their own interest, inasmuch as a victory in accordance with the principles previously outlined constitutes the only guarantee strong enough to save the common State.

At this meeting, Pribicevic reversed his stand from that of a convinced unitarist and centralist to that of an equally adamant federalist. With Macek, who acted in the name of the absent Radic and who would succeed him after his demise on August

8, he formulated the Coalition demand for the dismissal of the "rump" Parliament and the setting up of new elections aimed at constitutional changes which would help implement federalism. Aleksandar dismissed this demand, contending that the assassination was an unfortunate accident. Moreover, he insisted on the continuation of the government and the Parliament as though nothing had happened. The government and the Serbian political parties also flatly rejected the Coalition's demands. But shortly thereafter, Vukicevic tendered his resignation and Korosec assumed the Premiership of what remained basically the same government. (Korosec was a Slovene and the only non-Serb to ascend to this position.)

The tension between Belgrade and Zagreb was growing daily. Aleksandar continued to prepare for his personal regime. He secured French approval in advance. Paris was simply interested in being able to rely on its ally's military preparedness. It had no objections to the royal dictatorships in Rumania and Yugoslavia, both of which were formal French allies, even though it was the symbol of European democracy Nor did Bucarest, of course, have any objections; and such staunch "democrats" in Prague as Masaryk and Benes gave their wholehearted support to Aleksandar's policy. Thus securing foreign support, Aleksandar turned his attention to the internal arena.

After some maneuvering, he invited Macek and Pribicevic to the Royal Court on January 4, 1929, for consultation. It was on this occasion that Macek presented Aleksandar the Croattian plan for resolving the country's crisis. The gist of his proposal was the reorganization of the Kingdom on a federal basis with due respect to the existing historical units as they existed at the time of the formation of the common State in 1918, viz. (1) Slovenia, (2) Croatia, Slavonia and Dalmatia, (3) Bosnia and Hercegovina, (4) Montenegro, (5) Serbia, (6) Vojvodina, and (7) Macedonia. But the consultation appeared to be a mere formality since the list of members of the projected government had already been completed.

On January 6, 1929, Aleksandar published a manifesto addressed to the people of the Kingdom in which he announced his dictatorship. The General of the Royal Guard, Petar Zivkovic, became the new Premier and at the same time assumed the post of Minister of Interior. Zivkovic was a typical product of Obrenovic and Karadjordjevic Serbia. His first entry into the public stage was as the officer on guard at the Royal Court in 1903 who opened the gate to the conspiratorial band which had come to assassinate the last Obrenovic. Later he joined with Aleksandar and Pasic in forcing the split in the Black Hand which resulted in the formation of a new conspiratorial organization known as the White Hand. Although Serbia waged three wars during his military career (two Balkan wars and World War I), Zivkovic never distinguished himself in a military operation. Nevertheless, he was granted the most distinguished military honors and the highest promotion.

The new government was a spitting image of the previous government, consisting of the same Serbian political personalities who had dominated the parliamentarian governments and the Slovene and Moslem allies of these governments. However, the King also appointed two forgotten Croatian politicians of the National Council, Drinkovic and Alaupovic, and he added to these two representatives from the Croatian business community, Franges and Sverljuga.

By Aleksandar's manifesto, the name of the country was officially changed to "Yugoslavia" and obtained a single official flag. The use of the national names Serbia, Croatia and Slovenia was strictly forbidden and the hoisting of the respective national flags constituted a crime against the state. But this stipulation was cleverly by-passed by the Serbs. Since the Serbian Orthodox Church enjoyed semi-official status and since the Serbian Patriarch and the Serbian national flag were the symbols of the Church, the flag was proudly hoisted under religious pretexts on every public occasion. Yet, the use of the Croatian flag was criminal.

* * *

The Croats promptly reacted to the new regime. Two of the most outstanding of Macek's lieutenants, Krnjevic and Kosutic, secretly went into exile intending to inform public opinion and enlist it in favor of the Croatian cause. But an even more extrème reaction came from the *Frankovci*. Headed by Ante Pavelic, their only member in the Belgrade parliament, they formed a revolutionary and terroristic organization called the *Ustasa* (Insurgent). Pavelic and some of his closest friends emigrated to Hungary and finally to Italy, where they came to enjoy Mussolini's hospitality. They immediately launched a series of terroristic acts, including political assassinations, in full collaboration with the similar Macedonian organization headed by Vanca Mihajlov. They held the common goal of the complete destruction of Yugoslavia with the subsequent erection of an independent Croatia and an independent Macedonia on its ruins. Several attempts were made on Aleksandar's life. Thus the special law for the Protection of the State was invoked and directed at all agitators. It resulted in centuries of prison sentences and a substantial number of hangings.

The old administrative division of the country was exchanged for nine *banovinas* each named for the principal river flowing through its territory. Croatia was splintered into the Savska, Primorska, Vrbaska, Drinska and Zetska *Banovinas*.

Within two years of his announced personal rule, Aleksandar began to experiment with an authoritarian concept of constitutionalism. In 1931 he promulgated his constitution toward the end of perpetuating his personal rule on a strictly unitarian basis. A special electoral law was introduced which required the presentation of a national list derived from the country as a whole so that any resurgence of a nationalistic or local challenge to the government might be prevented. The new and only political formation was decreed from above with the pompous title, the Yugoslav Radical Peasant Democratic Party. General Zivkovic was its head. It announced the aim of its program as the preservation of the royal authoritarian regime. The elections were a one-horse-race which officially gave the government an overwhelming majority, although in Croatia only a small percentage of the electors bothered to cast their votes.

To aggravate the already existing tensions on the political level, the country was badly hit by the economic crisis of the thirties. The impact was particularly felt in the villages. But the government was too preoccupied with exclusively political issues to pay any attention to the plight of the peasants. The political issues in question seemed to be stringently limited to the persecution of the Croatian opposition as well as of the underground Communist organizations.

*   *   *

At their meeting in Zagreb on November 7, 1932, the leaders of the Peasant-Democratic Coalition reacted to Aleksandar's constitution. Meeting secretly under Macek's chairmanship, they voted the following resolution known to history as the Zagreb Punctation:

(1) Subscribing to the principles of democracy, we consider the sovereignty of the people the basis on which the entire system of the State must be built and we consider the people as the sole and unique source of all sovereignty and political power.

(2) The Peasantry as a unit is the depositary of the national culture and therefore the foundation of economic life and upholder of the social structure and national moral values. Thus it should be the cornerstone for the organization of our national life.

(3) We must point out that Serbian hegemony, imposed on Croatia and the other lands from the start, has acted destructively through an obvious incapacity to rule and through tyranny and other such immoral actions. Serbia has monopolized all the powers of the State and has destroyed our moral values, progressive institutions and traditions. It has not respected the material possessions of the people and

has robbed them of their spiritual peace. The misrule reached its peak with the introduction of the absolutist regime on January 6, 1929, which reinforced Serbian hegemony and resulted in fatal consequences and, worst of all, annihilated civil and political liberties.

(4) Considering these disastrous experiences, we have come to the inevitable conclusion that we must return to the starting-point of 1918 in order to respond to the pressing need to wage a decisive and organized struggle on the said hegemony and free our lands from it by depriving it of its power and influence through the elimination of its bearers.

(5) Only by carrying out the program previously outlined can be the new organization of the common State be undertaken. Without going into details at this time, the basic ideas underlying such an organization may be summarized as follows:

The commonwealth, as we conceive it, must be an association of interest arrived at with the free consent of each member with the domination of one or more over the others ruled out, thereby giving each the right to safeguard its particular interests on its own territory or to administer, in concert with the others, common affairs of mutual concern on the strength of general agreement. Thus progress shall be assured in respect to moral development, as well as in respect to the material conditions of the Serbs, Croats and Slovenes. Individual interests of minorities speaking foreign languages shall be specifically guaranteed.

Besides regular administrative and judicial prosecution, the government made extensive use of its undercover agents in dealing with recalcitrant Croats. The University Professor, Milan Suflay, was assaulted and killed at noon in the heart of the city. The murderer remained undiscovered. After spending three years in the penitentiary, Predavec, Macek's second in command, was murdered under similar circumstances. Due to his strong constitution, Mile Budak survived a similar attack and joined Pavelic in exile. It was not until years later that it was discovered that these assassinations were organized by the military command in Zagreb and executed by its secret agents.

Macek had his turn when he was brought to trial before the extraordinary Court for State Protection. He was sentenced to three years in prison for signing the said resolution and granting an interview to the visiting correspondent of the French paper, *Le Petit Parisien.*

* * *

The smoldering dissatisfaction in Croatia was more and more giving ground to the more explicit hatred for Aleksandar and Serbian domination. Endless political trials of Croats who were simply political offenders resulted in heavy penalties. Assassins, or would-be assassins were executed. And while this approach to the situation by the government steadily undermined the already precarious existence of Yugoslavia, the Belgrade regime was facing an equally dangerous situation on the European chessboard.

France, the chief protector and ally of Yugoslavia, was slipping into internal chaos and losing its dominant position in Europe. Aleksandar soon realized that the Belgrade alliance with Prague and Bucarest (known as the Little Entente) and directed against Hungarian revisionism was merely a wistful dream without French support. Nevertheless, he built a similar alliance with Rumania, Greece and Turkey (called the Balkan Entènte) to oppose Bulgarian revisionism.

Bulgaria still had an unsettled account with Serbia, i.e. Yugoslavia, on the issue of Macedonia. But for all practical purposes the newly formed Balkan Entente was as lifeless as the Little Entente. The longstanding Italian conspiracy against the very existence of Yugoslavia was not only permanently embodied in Mussolini's protection of the Croatian *Ustasa,* but also in his policy regarding Albania. And the omnipresent danger of Habsburg restoration in Austria made for another unpleasant speculation for Belgrade diplomacy. Aleksandar took a serious view of the prospect of the Habsburg return due to

316

Mussolini's machinations in Austria and therefore tried to harmonize his policies with those of the new master in Germany, Adolf Hitler, who had a similar distaste for the Habsburgs.

*　　*　　*

After five years of personal dictatorship and sham constitutionalism, Aleksandar was compelled to admit the complete failure of his policy. It is not known what prompted him to make his visit to France, but that it was to secure additional support from Paris for his new course would be a tempting speculation. Regardless, upon stepping onto French soil in Marseilles on October 9, 1934, he was killed by Croato-Macedonian assassins who were waiting for him. Louis Barthoux, the French Minister of Foreign Affairs, who was host for the reception, also was killed.

Before his departure for Paris, Aleksandar left a testament which provided for a Regency in the event of his death, since his son, Prince Petar, was in his minority. Prince Paul Karadjordjevic, Aleksandar's cousin, Radenko Stankovic and Ivo Perovic were named. But Prince Paul virtually assumed royal power in King Petar's name.

Prince Paul was a man of vast culture especially in the arts, but, due to Aleksandar's intolerant attitude, his training in politics was negligible. He was hesitant by nature and lacked his late cousin's daring approach to the pressing problems of the country he was so suddenly called to rule. From the beginning he was at odds with Prime Minister Uzunovic who claimed the right to appoint the members of the Regency. Thus Paul made recourse to the former dictator, General Zivkovic, who immediately put Uzunovic in his place.

But the days of the government were numbered. As soon as the late King was in the ground, Uzunovic was replaced as government head by his former Minister of Foreign Affairs, Jeftic. Jeftic had an insufficient political background and was, as a matter of fact, considered a personal attendant to Aleksandar. He accompanied Aleksandar on his fatal journey and invented the legend that the King's last words were "Preserve my Yugoslavia".

Jeftic was a career diplomat who, from his position of Minister at the Royal Court, was promoted to head of Yugoslav diplomacy. He was the last Yugoslav Minister of Foreign Affairs who had the reputation of staunchly supporting the French alliance. It was more than obvious that his government, a slight reconstruction of Uzunovic's Cabinet, was a mere transition. Nevertheless, the new government started its life by showing a certain amount of conciliation toward the imprisoned members of the opposition, granting them amnesty. The action also affected the Croatian leader, Macek.

Because the Parliament elected under Zivkovic's government ceased activity, Jeftic called for new elections. The opposition took up the challenge. It hoped to stir up the people despite the fact that it was deprived of all means of electoral campaigning due to a strict censorship of the press and the radio which were in government hands. Since the electoral laws required the presentation of a single national electoral list, the Serbian opposition parties, i.e. the Democrats and the Agrarians, joined with the Coalition and the Bosnian Moslems to draw up a common list that would satisfy the formality of the law. Macek accepted the proposition that he head the list. But the government did not spare any means at its disposal to intimidate and persecute its challengers. In an encounter with the gendarmes in the village of Sibinj, twenty-eight Croatian peasants were killed. But despite all the weapons of the state aparatus, the opposition officially received 1,076,346 votes to the 1,746,982 cast for Jeftic's government. In Croatian sectors, viz. Croatia, Slavonia, Dalmatia and Bosnia and Hercegovina, the government received 520,144 votes to the opposition's 797,197. Moreover, everyone was skeptical as to the accuracy of the government's mathematics.

Jeftic's government fell a month and a half after its electoral victory. A new political formation was created behind the scenes. The parliamentarian majority of Jeftic promptly shifted

318

its allegiance to the new formation. Prince Paul entrusted Milan Stojadinovic, his personal friend, and a member of the Radicals, with the formation of the new government in coalition with the Bosnian Moslem, Spaho, and the Slovenian Clerical, Korosec. Although the new government announced a degree of liberalization of the regime, it continued to carry out the same kind of policy as the previous governments.

But the spirit of resistance prevailing in Croatia could not easily be put down. Numerous clashes between the police and the people resulted in bloodshed at several places such as Senj, Sibenik (where the police had the upperhand) and Kerestinec (where six members of Stojadinovic's organization were killed by enraged peasants).

The government that came into power recognized the existence of the Croatian Question, but did nothing to remedy it. Prince Paul proved to be a consummate procrastinator. His excuse was that he had to preserve the basic institutions of the Kingdom as inherited from the late King in order to pass them unblemished to Petar when he came of age. He was willing to grant a few audiences to Macek, yielding on some purely administrative, but otherwise insignificant, points.

Prince Paul's attitude is still an enigma. The question of whether his policy toward Croatia was due to the vacillations of a spirit that lacked confidence, or due to the well-calculated dilatory tactics of an autocrat, will always remain open. But, whatever his schemes, his Premier, Stojadinovic, fit into them perfectly. A clever financier who had made himself rich as Minister of Finance in the various governments of Pasic, a University Professor and a representative of British interests in Yugoslavia, he possessed the necessary requirements to serve the Prince-Regent policy. He was willing to give minor political as well as substantial economic, concessions to his two partners, Korosec and Spaho, both of them proven opportunists. The temptation to imitate his predecessors proved irresistible to him: Zivkovic's political concoction, the Yugoslav Radical Peasant Democratic Party, had given way to Uzunovic's Yugoslav Nationalist Party, and Stojadinovic yielded to the inclination to add a similar formation to the series. With his acolytes, Korosec and Spaho, he formed the Yugoslav Radical Union and became its leader. It might go without saying that all of the former followers of Jeftic, with a few exceptions, soon joined the ranks of the new party.

In time the economic crisis abated. This was due less to any clever governmental policy than to the new conditions created by Germanic economic penetration into the Balkans which was proving itself beneficiary to Yugoslavia. The economic injection stimulated Stojadinovic's temptations to make personal financial and political gains. As France gradually lost its influence on European affairs, Stojadinovic turned more and more to Berlin and especially to Rome. In the latter instance, all he had to do was revive the ancient Serbian Radical policy of friendship with Italy. This new turn in Serbian policy diminished Mussolini's interest in the Croatian *Ustasa* movement and brought their terroristic activities to a standstill. What Prince Paul had attempted as a tactic in diplomatically cooling the country's friendship with France and reaching a better understanding with Hitler and Mussolini, Stojadinovic turned into a definite foreign policy.

Stojadinovic, a self-styled successor to Pasic and an avowed "Great Serb", was especially impressed with Mussolini's position in Italy. He regarded it as exemplary. But while he had the Prince-Regent's confidence he lacked popular support. Thus he used the Yugoslav Radical Union, the *ad hoc* youth organization (the "Blue Shirts"), and the labor union, (the *Jugoras* or Yugoslav Labor Union) to imitate Mussolini's success.

Because of his good standing in Berlin and Rome, and counting on the support of Prince Paul, he called for general elections on December 8, 1938. Macek emerged as the leader of the opposition's list once again. But although the elections officially went in favor of the government, they were far from a personal success for Stojadinovic. Korosec and Spaho received the usual support of their following, and Stojadinovic was able to claim victory chiefly due to the usual support from national minorities such as the Germans, Magyars, Albanians, Macedonians and Turks. But after bringing all the pressure of the government apparatus to bear on the population, his victory even in Serbia was not impressive. In Croatia it was nonexistent, and the returns hinted at near disaster. Officially Stojadinovic received 1,643,783 votes to Macek's 1,364,524. In the Croatian sectors the government got 429,332 votes to 943,964 for the opposition.

CHAPTER XXIII

THE POLICY OF COMPROMISE

Stojadinovic's dismissal — Cvetkovic's government — Cvet-
kovic-Macek negotiations — Compromise — Serbian op-
position to the Compromise — Banovina of Croatia —
World War II — Prince Paul's diplomatic gamble and
Yugoslavia's neutrality — Yugoslavia joins the Tripartite
Pact — Military coup d'etat, (March 27, 1941).

On February 5, 1939, Prince Paul dismissed Stojadinovic.
Formally his dismissal resulted from the resignation of four members of his Cabinet. When he applied to the Prince for permission to replace them he was turned down and thereby was
forced to resign. The motivation for the resignations of the
Cabinet members, viz. Cvetkovic, Kulenovic, Kulovec and Krek,
was based on the government's unwillingness to solve the Croatian Question.

Officially the Belgrade government refused at all times to admit even the existence of the Croatian Question. The attitude
was the same for all Serbian political parties in the government, as well as those in the opposition. However, after effecting an electoral coalition with the Croatian Peasant Party headed
by Macek, the Serbian parties in the opposition somewhat
modified their stand. Through a joint declaration, the Croatian
Peasant Party, the Independent Democrats, the Democrats, the
Agrarians and the Radicals, declared themselves in favor of the
revision of the existing electoral law and of an election of a

new Constituent Assembly. Settlement of the Croatian Question in one way or another was deferred until a new democratic constitution could be voted. The same Serbian participants, Davidovic, Jovanovic, Trifunovic and Kostic, went a step further on August 15, 1938. At that time they recognized for the first time, at least in theory, Croatian national individuality and the Croatian right to a distinct political territory.

Stojadinovic paid little attention to the Croatian problem, seeking first of all to secure his own position through close cooperation with Germany and Italy and then to handle the internal problems of Yugoslavia in his own way and at his own pleasure. It was notorious that Stojadinovic belonged to the "Greater Serbian" political school, which, in an ultimate showdown, was ready to settle the issue by "amputating" Croatia.

The question reached its peak when, in January of 1939, Count Galeazzo Ciano, Italian Minister of Foreign Affairs, came to Belgrade to return Stojadinovic's earlier visit to Italy. Shortly afterward, rumors circulated that Ciano and Stojadinovic had come to an understanding regarding Italian policy in Albania which would ultimately lead to annexation. But what appeared more disturbing was that in the case of a general European war, Italy would occupy the Croatian territories of Yugoslavia conceded to her by the famous secret Treaty of London in 1915. Indeed, Albania was duly occupied and annexed by Mussolini's Italy on April 7, 1939.

The Yugoslav General Staff, pretty much all Serbian, pursued its own policy in much the same manner. It engaged in secret exchanges with the Hungarian General Staff, expressing its willingness to cede Prekomurje and Baranja, as well as the northern parts of Backa, to Hungary. At the same time, Colonel Vladimir Vauhnik, Yugoslav Military Attache in Berlin, a Slovene, was charged by the Yugoslav General Staff and General Milan Nedic, Minister of National Defense, to sound out the German General Staff about a scheme for the dissolution of Yugoslavia: It was proposed that Italy annex Dalmatia in accordance with the Treaty of London; that Italy also annex Slovenia, except for the city of Maribor and 'adjacent territory which would go to Germany; that Hungary receive Prekomurje and the northern part of Vojvodina, i.e. Backa and Baranja; that an autonomous Croatia within the administrative boundaries of the Savska *Banovina* should remain under Serbian domination, or be put under Italian protection; and that the remainder of Yugoslavia be proclaimed "Greater Serbia".

*   *   *

The new government was formed by Dragisa Cvetkovic, leader of the anti-Stojadinovic conspiracy and confidant of Prince Paul. From the beginning, Cvetkovic officially announced that the solution of the Croatian Question was one of the most important of his tasks.

Meanwhile a general meeting of the Croatian national representatives who were elected in 1938 was held in Zagreb. A resolution was passed the gist of which was an energetic appeal to European and World public opinion. Responsible elements both in Europe and in Yugoslavia were addressed as well. Attendants of the meeting demanded the application of the right to self-determination to Croatia in the interest of peace in the Balkan sector of Europe and voted full powers and confidence to their leader, Macek, in implementing its demands.

Following the change of government in Belgrade, Italy once again became interested in Croatian affairs and Count Ciano tried to get in touch with the Croatian leader, Macek. Because Macek had learned about the Ciano-Stojadinovic secret dealings, he was willing to sound out Ciano regarding Italian plans for Croatia. These contacts did not, however, bring to the interested parties the hoped for and in some cases, expected, continuation.

The Czechoslovak tragedy, the Munich conference of September 29, 1938, and the ultimate extinction of an independent Czechoslovakia on March 16, 1939, had a sobering effect on both Belgrade and Zagreb. Moreover, Prince Paul received the friendly suggestion from both London and Paris to seek accommodation with the Croats. Macek, too, realized that an imminent compromise between Belgrade and Zagreb within the framework of Yugoslavia was more advantageous than the adventure of a more radical solution. Thus Prince Paul adopted a policy of compromise and imposed it on the government.

* * *

On April 3, 1939, Premier Cvetkovic appeared in Zagreb to open negotiations with Macek. After reaching an agreement in principle, Macek insisted on widening its significance by bringing in the Serbian opposition as well. But the Serbian politicians rejected his invitation. Cvetkovic and Macek agreed on the unification of the Savska and Primorska *Banovinas,* and that the city and district of Dubrovnik was Croatian territory. They also agreed that the remnants of eastern Croatia (Srijem and Bosnia and Hercegovina) were to decide by popular plebiscite between Serbia and Croatia.

But Prince Paul did not accept the agreement. He was obviously still playing for time and hoping against hope. The imminence of the war prompted both sides to go ahead anyway, giving the agreement at least a provisional character: Cvetkovic, acting in the name of Prince Paul, and Macek, solidified the agreement on the basis of Article 116 of the Constitution which pertained to extraordinary measures permitted during a national emergency such as war or general crisis. Thus the *Banovina* of Croatia was formed by the unification of the Savska and Primorska *Banovinas,* the city and district of Dubrovnik, and several districts of Bosnia and Hercegovina which had an uncontested Croatian majority. The definitive boundaries of Croatia would be determined for the remnants of Croatia, Srijem, Bosnia and Hercegovina, Dalmatia and Vojvodina later by popular plebiscite.

The *Banovina* of Croatia was to have its own Croatian *Sabor* or parliament and an autonomous government headed by a *Ban.* The *Ban* was appointed by the King and was solely responsible to the *Sabor*. The autonomous affairs of Croatia were comprised of Interior Administration, Justice, Public Education, Social Policy, Agriculture, Forestry, Mining, Commerce and Industry, Finance, Public Construction and Public Health. Foreign Affairs, including Foreign Commerce, National Defense, the Post, Telegraph and Telephone, and Transportation, remained under the control of the central government in Yugoslavia.

Prince Paul gave the arrangement his sanction on August 22. At the same time, the Ordinance for the formation of the Hrvatska *Banovina* was issued and immediately put into effect. Then Cvetkovic resigned from his post as Prime Minister and was entrusted with the task of forming the new government. Macek joined it as Vice-Premier and so did four members of his party. The agreement, known as the *Sporazum*, was subsequently (August 26) put into full effect. On the proposal of Macek, Ivan Subasic, a little known member of Macek's party, was named *Ban* of Croatia. This appointment was made at the special request of Prince Paul who considered Subasic a man devoted to the cause of the common State.

With the formation of the new government came a new political alignment. The agreement had been accepted only by those Serbian politicians who surrounded Cvetkovic and who were known as men under the control of the Court. But the Independent Democrats, as members of the Peasant-Democratic Coalition, and the Agrarians, at least officially, also accepted it. The Croatian Peasant Party of Macek was its principal supporter (and beneficiary). The Slovene Populists and the Bosnian Moslems gave their support too.

Croatian public opinion shared Macek's view that the agreement was simply a preliminary solution which should be followed by the State's gradual evolution from dictatorship to a parliamentarian system which would open the way to elections for a new Constituent Assembly. The new Constituent Assembly would provide the key not only to a definitive solution of the Croatian Question, but also to a reorganization of the State on a federal basis. However, the Croatian nationalist extremists, sympathetic to the *Ustasa* movement, declared the agreement unacceptable.

Except for Prince Paul and his mandatory, Prime Minister Cvetkovic and some of his personal friends in the Radical Party, and the small Peasant Party of Dragoljub Jovanovic, practically all Serbian political groups, including some members of the government, began to violently fight the agreement. The powerful Serbian Orthodox Church, with semi-official status in the State and immense influence in State affairs, joined ranks with the even more powerful Serbian military circles, famed for their longstanding tradition of conspiracy, toward the end of overthrowing the government and invalidating the Cvetkovic-Macek agreement. Furthermore, a new organization by the name of the Serbian Cultural Club was called into life under the presidency of Slobodan Jovanovic who was a Professor of Constitutional Law at the University of Belgrade. This organization openly declared its aim to be the establishment of a "Greater Serbia" and the effecting of an immediate nullification of the concessions made to the Croats.

The former electoral allies of Macek from the Serbian opposition — the Democrats, Radicals and some Agrarians — made a common front with such Serbian political groups as the Yugoslav National Party and the authoritarian formations called the *Zbor* and the *Borba*. These groups launched a merciless campaign against the government and against the very existence of the *Banovina* of Croatia. They were simply awaiting the propitious moment to destroy the Serbo-Croatian rapprochement that had been engendered by the agreement.

But even within the government two opposing views prevailed. While the Serbs saw the compromise as the maximum concession that could be made to the Croats and hoped for a later rectification of Serb losses, the Croats saw it as the beginning of their independence and the adumbration of the end of Serbian hegemony in the common State.

The new government had scarcely been formed when, on

September 1, Europe was plunged into war by German aggression in Poland. Great Britain and France declared war on Germany. Due to Mussolini's unpreparedness, Italy remained neutral for a time. The Yugoslav government followed Italy's example and declared its neutrality. But the previous German agreement with the Soviet Union and the rapid victory in Poland presented the Belgrade government with a new problem. Early in the Spring of 1940, Moscow and Belgrade had come to an understanding by granting diplomatic recognition to one another and by establishing diplomatic missions in the respective cities.

Prince Paul, who alone was responsible for his country's foreign policy, anticipated that Mussolini would maintain the neutrality upon which the maintainance of the *status quo* in the Balkans was chiefly reliant. But when Mussolini joined Hitler in the war on June 10 after the French collapse, Belgrade's maneuvers became highly restricted. Mussolini constantly dreamed of launching an attack on Yugoslavia with the aid of Croatian dissatisfaction, but he met with an equally constant veto from Berlin. Thus Belgrade was quick in realizing that its best protection against Mussolini's schemes was to be found in Berlin. Thus, in order to maintain neutrality and achieve security against Mussolini, Prince Paul had several talks with Hitler.

After the annexation of Austria in 1938, Germany had become Yugoslavia's immediate neighbor. Then came the extinction of Czechoslovakia and Rumania. The Soviet Union had presented its demand for cession of Bessarabia and the northern Bukovina on June 26. Rumania had no choice but to yield. On August 30, by Germano-Italian arbitration in Vienna, Rumania was compelled to cede northern Transylvania to Hungary. But Bulgaria was swift in demanding the return of Dobroudja on September 8.

The political picture of Central and Eastern Europe was changing radically. Crippled Rumania "invited" German troops to protect its integrity and independence. In just a few months,

Slovakia, Hungary, Rumania and Bulgaria became members of the Berlin-Rome-Tokyo "Tripartite Pact." Mussolini surprised Hitler with his aborted invasion of Greece on October 28. The Italian disasters in northern Africa, Abyssinia and Greece, as well as the German preparation for war on the Soviet Union, brought Hitler closer to the Balkans.

To help Mussolini out of his humiliating situation in Greece, on March 1, the German army entered Bulgaria. Thus, except for the boundary on the side of Greece and the Adriatic Sea, whose entrances were nevertheless controlled by Italy, Yugoslavia found itself surrounded by Axis forces. This was the general situation when Hitler formally presented Prince Paul with the demand that Yugoslavia join the Tripartite Pact.

After some hesitation and more negotiating, Belgrade gave in. But a considerable number of exceptions were made in the case of Yugoslavian membership. By superimposed declarations, Germany and Italy granted Yugoslavia the practical continuation of neutrality: Yugoslavia would not take part in the war; its territory would not be occupied; and there would be no military or war materials transported through its territory. Prime Minister Cvetkovic and Cincar-Markovic, Minister of Foreign Affairs, signed the document of adherence to the Tripartite Pact in Vienna on March 25.

The opposition to the Serbo-Croatian agreement chose the precise moment of the signing of the Tripartite Pact to carry out a military *coup-d'etat*. The intention was to deprive the Croats of the concessions made them by Prince Paul rather than to resist Hitler's demands. The *coup* was executed by the younger officers of the Belgrade garrison and had the political support of the Serbian political parties, the Serbian Orthodox Church and the Serbian Cultural Club. Thus they administered a fatal blow, not only to the first positive results of the Serbo-Croatian rapprochement but to the very existence of the State itself.

CHAPTER XXIV

LITERATURE AND ARTS

The beginning of literacy among Croats — Latin — Glagolitic — Cyrillic — Humanism — Renaissance — Marko Marulic — Dubrovnik Literature — Venetian Dalmatia — Northern Croatia — Protestantism — Catholic reformation — Jesuits and Paulists — Juraj Krizanic — Pavao Ritter Vitezovic — The Illyrian Movement — Modern and contemporary literature — Medieval arts on the Adriatic coast — Renaissance — Modern development — Ivan Mestrovic — Contemporary tendencies — Musical life.

After settling on the Adriatic shores the Croats came into permanent contact with the remnants of the Greco-Latin civilization. Some of them fixed their abodes amongst the ruins of Latin towns and colonies, mixing with the survivors of the Roman population from whom they gradually accepted Christianity and its cultural impact. As the Church in the former Dalmatia used the Latin language in religious services, Latin became familiar to those Croats converted to Christianity. Moreover, Latin was the language of everyday life and particularly the most important instrument for transmission of the Latin civilization. The Croats then either adopted or imitated the Latin example before they started to develop their own civilization with distinct Croatian characteristics. This trend manifested

331

itself first in religious matters. In order to bring Christianity closer to the large segments of the Croatian newcomers, the Latin gave way to the spoken Croatian language in certain religious ceremonies. Subsequently, during the ninth century the Croatian clergy developed its own liturgical services using the old Croatian, or Slavonic, language in which the holy books were written. An original Glagolitic alphabet was used in written Croatian texts. The Glagolitic alphabet was of unknown origin, obviously oriental, although the later romantic Croatian historians attributed its invention to the "Slavonic apostles" Cyril and Methodus, who had invented and introduced the Cyrillic alphabet in their missionary work among Moravian Slavs while spreading Christianity. The Cyrillic alphabet appeared on the Croatian territory only a century later with the event of the Pataren heresy, both alphabets then were adopted, the Glagolitic chiefly by the Benedictine monks along the Adriatic shores, and the Cyrillic by the members of the Franciscan Order some time later in the Croatian interior and Bosnia.

* * *

With the emergence of the Croatian political power, the coastal towns were gradually losing their distinct Latin character. Through marriages and general mixings their population was croatized and the Croatian language replaced Latin in use. The Latin alphabet, however, remained in use in writings. Thus, all three alphabets, Latin, Glagolitic and Cyrillic, were used among early Croats in their literary endeavors.

The oldest preserved inscription in the Croatian language written in the Glagolitic characters is the *Bascanska ploca* (the Baska Plate), made on the stone in about 1100, commemorating King Zvonimir's donation to the church at the village of Baska on the Island of Krk. Copies of the *Chronicles of the Priest of Dioclea* were written in Latin but also in the Croatian languages in either Latin or Glagolitic alphabets dating from the same period. The Glagolitic characters were also used in writing of the *Codex of Vinodol* (1288). The Glagolitic alphabet was chiefly in use for writing and copying of liturgical books, especially the missals. The best preserved example of this copying art is the *Glagolitic Missal,* an illuminated copy, executed for Novak, Croatian nobleman and courtier of King Ljudevit I of Anjou (1368). The oldest known document written in the Cyrillic characters was a treaty between *Ban* Kulin of Bosnia and the Republic of Dubrovnik (1189). Hrvoje Vukcic Hrvatinic, *Ban* of Croatia and Duke of Split, a militant Pataren himself, ordered the copying of several religious books, of which the illuminated *Missal* is of a special distinction, executed in 1404.

The regular ties the Croatian lands maintained with western Europe by the intermediary of Italy brought to the country western literary contributions, chiefly in the field of religion, which were then duly translated and adapted for use in the Croatian language. The Latin language, however, was predominant not only in the religious life but also in the public and educational life as well. Of special interest for scholars in history are two manuscripts: the *Codex of Korcula,* originating in the twelfth century, and the *Historia Salonitana,* written by Toma, Archpriest of Split (1200-1268).

With the introduction of the printing press, the painstaking process of hand-copying gave way to the new art of book production. The first book printed in the Croatian language, the *Glagolitic Missal* (1483), followed by the *Breviarius* (1493), were done in Venice, which was then a center of the printing art. The first established printing press in Croatia was set up at Kosinj in 1483. From there it was moved to Senj the next year.

* * *

The educational facilities of the country were at a modest level thus prompting the more ambitious students to complete it in Italy. This was already a generally accepted practice for the members of the clergy. The Croatian scholars attending Italian universities became thus the beneficiaries of both Humanism and Renaissance. The principal contacts with Italy were maintained chiefly through Venice since the Republic held in its hands major parts of the Croatian coastline and Adriatic islands. The famous Venetian *Riva degli Schiavoni* (the Slavonic coast) was named after a multitude of the Croats who landed there. The Venetians, officially as well as privately, called all Croats *Slavi* or *Schiavoni*. Among the most famous Croatian humanists, Janus Pannonius, by his Croatian name, Ivan Cesmicki, Vespasian's Archbishop of Strigonia, his nephew, Ivan Cesmicki, junior, Marko Marulic and Matija Vlacic, Flacius Illyricus, deserve special mention.

* * *

Croats developed and preserved their own popular poetry, sagas and proverbs, which were then adapted for use in religious celebrations and theatrical performances as became a general practice at these times. These elements of folklore also found their way into works of Croatian writers when they appeared on the national scene.

* * *

The beginning of Croatian literature properly speaking is related to the name of Marko Marulic, writer and humanist (1450-1524). He was born in the well-to-do family in Split, where he also received his education. After becoming a member of the clergy, he left for Italy where, at the University of Padua, he continued the advanced studies in the fields of theology and philosophy. While in Italy he fell under the spell of the contemporary Humanism. His first literary products were written in Latin, chiefly dealing with the Catholic renewal. These works were generally well received and his books were printed in Venice, Florence, Rome, Basel, Cologne, Antwerpen and Paris for the church use. Some of them were translated into Italian, German, French, Portuguese and Czech. Besides these scholarly contributions in religious matters, he also wrote poetry in his native Croatian. In order to fullfil the wishes of his sister, a nun, who did not possess sufficient knowledge of Latin, he wrote in the Croatian language a historico-religious epic, *Judita* (Judith) in 1501. The epic was in a way an allegoric comment on the plight of his native land exposed to the Ottoman onslaughts. The *Judita* was first printed in a book form in Venice in 1525. Its publishing, therefore, could be considered the beginning of Croatian literature.

In the meantime, the Republic of Dubrovnik, already enjoying a great amount of political independence, had achieved a remarkable material prosperity, which, combined with the political and civil liberties, created a favorable atmosphere for the cultural efforts. In order to elevate the general standard of its children's education, Dubrovnik had brought in some enlightened educators from Italy to take care of the city's schools who brought with them the spirit of humanism and renaissance prevailing then in Italy. Furthermore, the most promising, or well-to-do, students were sent to Italy to complete their studies. Following the example set up by different Italian city-republics, Dubrovnik on its own became a center of a flourishing literature written in Croatian. In addition to the literature of the spiritual revival, the wordly literature was highly cultivated. The early poets of Dubrovnik, Andrija Cubranovic, Sisko Mencetic, and Djore Drzic, fell under Petrarch's influence. The most prolific poet of the sixteenth century, Mavro Vetranovic, a Benedictine monk, wrote spiritual-religious poetry with a strong satirical tendency. He was also the first to introduce on the Dubrovnik stage the pastoral dramas based on popular saga and customs.

Croatian territory under Venetian domination witnessed also considerable literary activities. Hanibal Lucic, a nobleman from Hvar, excelled in love poetry but was also preoccupied with epics in which he lamented the tragic destiny of Croatia after the fatal battle of Krbava in 1493. Petar Hektorovic wrote a realistic description of the lives of the fishermen in *Ribanje i ribarsko prigovaranje,* while Petar Zoranic, native of Zadar, wrote the first Croatian novel in prose, *Planine* (the Mountains).

Marin Drzic (1508-1576), a playwright from Dubrovnik,

wrote well-constructed pastoral dramas and comedies of which *Novela od Stanca* (A Story of Stanac), *Pomet,* and *Dundo Maroje* are still produced not only on the Croatian stages but on different European stages as well. Brno Karnarutic, a captain of the Venetian cavalry, wrote the epic *Vazetje Sigeta grada* (The Fall of the City of Szigeth) on the theme of the heroic deed of *Ban* Nikola Zrinjski. For their contributions in the poetry of this period Dinko Ranjina, and two ladies from Dubrovnik, Julija Bunic nad Cvijeta Zuzoric, should be mentioned.

Due to the Turkish conquests and Venetian acquisitions the center of the country's public life shifted to its northwestern corner to the territory situated between towns of Zagreb and Varazdin. The population of these parts was speaking the "Kajkavski" dialect of the Croatian language which ultimately led to the beginning of a literature written in this dialect. The first noteworthy literary attempt in this field was a translation of Stephen Verboeczy's *Decretum Tripartitum* by Ivan Pergosic published at Nedelisce in 1574. Anton Vramec, a priest and humanist, educated in Croatia and Italy, under suspicion for his lenient catholicism, published *Kronika* (the Chronicle) in Ljubljana in 1578. The book is of a kind of the general historical survey but most valuable in the description of the Croatian past and especially of the contemporary events. The literary activities in the northern part of Croatia were chiefly in the practical field dealing with the religion, law and other public affairs. It could not be otherwise. The country was but a mere permanent armed camp exposed to the daily Turkish onslaughts, hardly suitable for inspiration of higher artistic life.

Although the attempts of the Protestant Reformation in Croatia were short-lived they produced considerable activities in the field of literary productivity. Some members of the Croatian clergy took an active part in the general Protestant movement in Germany which then reverberated to the country itself. Croatian territory of Istria were anyway part of the Holy Roman Empire and became thus immediately involved in its religious convulsion. The Lutheran Protestant Reformation was one of the most important. The center of the Protestant activities for Croatia and Slovenian lands as well as in Wuertemberg whose Duke Christopher became their principal sponsor and protector. Primoz Trubar, Canon of the Ljubljana Cathedral, started there publication of the Protestant books in the Slovenian language in 1550. Petar Pavao Vergerije, former Bishop of Kopar in Istria, who became one of the most influential advisors of the Duke, published a pamphlet in Croatian, *Razgovaranja meju papisku e jednim luteranom* (the Discussion between a Papist and Lutheran), printed in Tuebingen in 1555. Due to his influence, the Duke, with the support of the German Protestant nobility, established the Croatian press and publishing house at Urach which remained active from 1561 to 1568. Finally, Christopher Ungnand, former *Ban* of Croatia, a chief sponsor of the Protestant cause in Croatia, when he left the country to settle himself in Wuertemberg took over the care of the Protestant Croatian press. During this period several translations and adaptations of Protestant writings, as well as the text of the Old and New Testament, were published in the Croatian language using either Latin, Glagolitic or Cyrillic alphabets. The editors and chief translators of those texts were two eminent Croatian "Glagolitic" priests, Stjepan Konzul Istranin and Antun Dalmatin who in the preface to *Postile* (the Epistles) stated their motivation: ". . . to learn the God's truth and to spread it in the Croatian language. . ."

Far the most important Croatian Protestant was Matija Vlacic (Mathias Flacius Illyrians), a humanist whose activities spread over Saxony and the Habsburg lands of Austria. His violent radicalism alienated him from Melanchton and thus from the official German Lutheran Protestantism. After losing support of the Protestant nobility of Saxony, he tried to establish independent Protestant academies first at Regensburg and then at Klagenfurth, at the doorsteps of his native land, without achieving his aims.

* * *

The tide of the Turkish conquests was stopped first by the

Croatian victory at the battle of Sisak (1593) and ultimately with the signing of the Peace Treaty of Zitva-Toeroek (1606). Following the signing of the said treaty Croatia found itself split in four parts: the largest area fell to the Turks under whose domination practically all signs of national and cultural life were brought to general stagnation; the territory under Venetian rule after promising cultural beginnings in such Croatian centers as Split, Hvar, Sibenik and Zadar, witnessed soon after a general stagnation and lethargy except for such limited literary activities chiefly dealing with the spiritual religious life; Zagreb emerged as a principal cultural and political center of the remnnats of the country under the Habsburg rule; only the independent Republic of Dubrovnik, with its political freedom and economic prosperity, deserved from its contemporaries the honor title of the "Croatian Athens."

The new intellectual life of the country, especially in the field of literature, was greatly if not exclusively dominated by the spirit of the Catholic revival following the Council of Trent. Although the Catholic reformation was already undertaken by the existing orders of the Benedictines, Franciscans and Paulists, it became soon the exclusive domain of the Society of Jesus. The Jesuits put to it their own stamp especially by taking over education. They established a Classic Gymnasium in Zagreb in 1607 to be soon followed with the establishment of similar institutions at Varazdin, Rijeka, Pozega and Osijek. The Paulists manifested similar zeal. The Jesuit Gymnasium of Zagreb and the Paulist School of Lepoglava received charters from Emperor Leopold for their elevation to the rank of academies with the right to establish doctoral programs in 1669. The establishment of the Jesuit Academy of Zagreb marked the beginning of the future University of Zagreb.

The Jesuits used the Latin language as their means of instruction but soon they followed the Protestant example of using the Croatian in order to reach the common people. Since the people of Croatia are using different local dialects the Jesuits were facing the problem of establishing a common literary language. The study of grammar became the number one problem. For this purpose the Illyrian Academy in Rome commissioned Croatian Jesuit, Bartol Kasic, to prepare the *Institutiones linguae illiricae*, the oldest Croatian grammar, published in Rome in 1604. Another Jesuit, Jakov Mikalja, prepared the *Blago jezika slovinskoga* (the Treasury of the Slavonic Language), a Croatian, Latin and Italian dictionary, published at Lorèto in 1649. Juraj Habdelic published his *Dikcioner* in 1670, the same year Ivan Belostenec published in Graz the most outstanding book of this time, *Recnik* (the Dictionary).

There was not then a common denomination of the national language. The contemporary writers, chroniclers and linguists followed the foreign example sometimes called it Croatian, Slavonian, Slavonic, Illyrian, or even in some cases Gothic, or even Schythian (!), which created for the future generation fatal, sometimes ridiculous, confusion.

Latin would remain the official language of the country until 1845. The historians, until this time, would, therefore, use Latin, or Italian dialect spoken in Dalmatia, to write their works. Mavro Orbini, a Benedictine monk from Dubrovnik, published his history *Il regno Slavi* in Pesaro in 1601 in the Italian language. The first critical history of Croatia written on the basis of the documents of Ivan Lucic, *De regno Dalmatiae et Croatiae* (On the Kingdom of Dalmatia and Croatia), was published in Amsterdam in 1666.

The misery of their native land prompted many of her sons to seek Croatia greatness in the domain of fantasy. Under constant pressure of Turks, Germans, Italians and Magyars, Croatia and Croats were supposed to compensate her weakness by stressing out an idealistic union of all Slavic peoples. While the majority of such writers left their dreams within the limits of poetry, or farfetched treatises, such as Orbini, one among them decided to add more substance to his imagination. He was Juraj Krizanic, a member of the small Croatian nobility, a Dominican monk, educated in Zagreb, Graz, Bologna and Rome. He was sent by his superiors to Poland whose government was experimenting with an attempt to bring about the unification of Roman Catholicism and Greco Orthodoxy in the Greco Catholic Church, also known as Uniatism. At this time the King of Poland and the Polish nobility were deeply involvèd in Russian affairs trying to submit the Orthodox Russia to the sway of the Catholic Poland. Following his dreams and carrying out his superiors's orders, Krizanic journeyed from Vilna to Moscow where he approached the Russian ruler with the idea to put himself at the head of a huge federation of all Slavic peoples. His proposal, however, was not taken seriously and for his efforts he found himself exiled to Tobolsk, then on the limit of the Russian Siberia. The Romanov Tsar, Alexei, had different ideas of the Croatian monk. During his long years of Siberian exile Krizanic invented his own special Slavic language, a mixture of Croatian, Russian and the old Slavonic, in which he wrote a treatise *Politika* in which he expounded his aformentioned ideas. The exiled Croatian Dominican monk became thus a forerunner of the later Panslavism. Ultimately he was expelled from Russia just in time to join the Polish army of King Jan Sobiesky, on its way to bring help to the city of Vienna then besieged by the Turks. During this campaign Krizanic lost his life.

*   *   *

Although under Turkish rule the normal cultural life of the country was brought to a standstill, the members of the Roman Catholic clergy were tolerated to carry out their spiritual mission to some extent. The spiritual life of the Catholic population of Bosnia Pashalik was entrusted to the care of members of the Franciscan Order. Members of this order, Franjo Glavinic, Rafael Levakovic and Matija Divkovic prepared liturgical texts, written in a special kind of the Cyrillic alphabet known as "bosancica" for their spiritual needs and catechism. The population which had accepted the Islamic faith followed the general pattern of spiritual and cultural life as it was generally established in the Ottoman Empire, using either Arabic or Turkish language. Two native writers and poets, Hasan Kaini and Zorin Oglu, achieved some reputation by their contributions in Turkish and Arabic languages but in the Croatian as well.

* * *

The most important center of the cultural life and literary activities still remained Dubrovnik. Ivan Franjin Gundulic (1589-1638) deserved a special distinction. He belonged to the patrician family and took an active part in the public life of his native Republic. He was member of the the Senate and served for a time as the Republic Duke. Gundulic tried his hand in literature at an early age. His field of predilection was above all the theater. In the numerous plays, he had written, he followed the contemporary general trend of the didactico-religious genre. But soon he opted for a new trend when he wrote an heroic epic, *Osman,* on the theme of the struggle between the Cross and the Crescent. His lasting reputation was achieved by the pastoral drama *Dubravka* in which he glorified his native city by the added ode to liberty. In the shadow of Gundulic his contemporary epigons, Junije Palmotic, Dzore Palmotic and Vladislav Mencetic enriched the literary life of Dubrovnik.

* * *

In northern Croatia Juraj Ratkaj published his *Memoria* (Vienna, 1652) in which he covered Croatia's history and gave a vivid description of the contemporary Croatian society and general conditions of the country.

Pavao Ritter Vitezovic (1652-1713) achieved an early reputation in poetry written in the Latin or Croatian of which the most significant was the epic *Odiljenje sigetsko* (Linz, 1684). However, his historico-political treatises, *Croatia rediviva* (Zagreb, 1703), and *Bosnia captiva* (Trnava, 1712), as well as his writings dealing with the Croatian grammar and orthography, would make his lasting reputation.

After the exuberance of the seventeenth, the eighteenth century witnessed a steady decline of literary activities. Baltazar

Krcelic in his *Annuae* (Zagreb, 1776) gave a description on education in Croatia at the occasion of the elevation of the Jesuit Academy to the Royal Academy of Zagreb. Filip Grabovac, a vicar of the Croatian troops in the Venetian army, wrote *Cvit razgovora* (the Flower of the Words), published in Venice (1747). Andrija Kacic Miosic, a Franciscan monk, who extensively traveled in the Slavic territory of the Ottoman Empire, imitated the popular poetry in his epics *Razgovor ugodni* (Friendly Story), first published in Venice in 1756, and *Korabljica*, with a complete disregard for the historical facts which he manipulated. Matija Reljkovic under the influence of the Enlightenment wrote *Satir* (Dresden, 1762) in which he criticised popular backwardness and superstitions. Tito Brezovacki, a Latin poet, wrote also Croatian comedies in the "kajkavski" dialect, *Diogenes,* and *Matijas Grabacijas diak,* which are still occasionally performed.

During the French occupation of southern Croatia and the existence of the Illyrian Provinces, Sime Starcevic prepared a Croatian grammar, *Nova ricislovnica* (Trieste, 1812) to be used in the Croatian schools formed under the French regime. At the same time Maksimilijan Vrhovac, Bishop of Zagreb, called on his diocesan priests to cultivate the national language and to collect popular poetry and sagas. Antun Mihanovic, in Austrian diplomatic service, addressed a pamphlet to the Croatian public, *Rec domovini* (the Word to the Homeland) published in Vienna in 1815, advocating the cultivation of the national language, thus paving the way for the renewal of the national literature.

* * *

The development of modern Croatian literature could be attributed to Ljudevit Gaj and his proposal introducing linguistic reforms. In the pamphlet *Kratka osnova* (the Essential Basis) appearing in 1830 he proposed a common simplified orthography based on the phonetical principles, using a single letter for every sound. Ivan Derkos joinèd him with his pamph-

342

let, *Genus patriae* (1832), advocating the use of the "stokavski" Slavonia, Dalmatia, Bosnia and Hercegovina, and in Serbia as well. The birth and ascendancy of the common literary language marked the Illyrian Movement period with such significant authors as Ivan Mazuranic, Stanko Vraz, Petar Preradovic and Mirko Bogovic.

The Illyrian literary period prepared the way for Croatian romanticism which was, nevertheless, characterized with strong elements of realism. August Senoa (1838-1881), a poet, novelist, playwright, literary and theater critic, and journalist, left his undeniable mark on this period. While his novels, *Prijan Lovro, Barun Ivica, Mladi gospodin* and some of his short stories, were written with strong notes of realism, in his historical novels, *Cuvaj se senjske ruke, Turopoljski top, Zlatarevo Zlato, Saljacka buna, Diogenes* and *Kletva,* Victor Hugo's influence could be discerned. Franjo Markovic, an aesthetic poet, playwright and literary critic, and Josip Eugen Tomic, a novelist, were Senoa's most outstanding epigons.

Realism made its definite mark in Croatian literature with Ante Kovacic (1854-1889), author of novels, *Barunicina ljubav, Fiskal* and *U registraturi.* Eugen Kumicic, author of novels, *Preko mora, Gospodja Sabina, Zacudjeni svatovi, Kraljica Lepa* and *Urota Zrinjsko-Frankopanska,* was under the influence of Zola and Flaubert. Josip Kozarac (1858-1906) introduced the rustic subjects in his novels, *Prince djeda Nike, Biser Kata* and *Mrtvi kapitali,* Vienceslav Novak (1859-1905) dealt with the social problems in his novels, *Pavao Segota, Posjednji Stipancici, Dva svijeta, Zapreke* and *Tito Dorcic.* Ksaver Sandor Gjalski (1854-1935), a nobleman, a witness of the disappearance of the ancient social order, who followed Balzac, Flaubert, Turgenev, Goethe and Schopenhauer, and "explored the inner deepness of the Croatian soul" in his novels, *Pod starim krovovima, Iz varmedjijskih dana, Diljem doma, Na rodnoj grudi, Osvit, Za maternsku rijec,* etc. Silvije Strahimir Kranjcevic (1865-1908) was a poet of extreme sensibility and mysticism.

343

At the change of the century the new literary generation announced its breaking off with the tendency of the old literary school of "romanticism, realism and naturalism, firmly determined to put itself in the service of the nation in order to find out the true position for Croatia in the contemporary world" which became known as the "Croatian modern literature." Antun Gustav Matos (1873-1914), a versatile writer and merciless critic, followed the pattern established by his French idols, Saint-Beuve and Lemaitre. Milan Begovic (1876-1948), a poet, novelist and playwright, wrote the novels, *Dunja u kovcegu* and *Giga Bariceva*. Vladimir Nazor, Vladimir Vidric, Dragutin Domnjanic, Milutin Cihlar-Nehajèv, Dnko Simunovic and Viktor Car Emin deserved mention. Ivo Vojnovic (1857-1929), "the last aristocrat" of Dubrovnik, described the last days of the Republic in the drama *Dubrovacka trilogija*. Milan Ogrizovic, Ivana Brlic Mazuranic, Julije Benesic, Janko Polic Kamov, Fran Galovic left their marks on this period.

The basic characteristic of the Croatian literature on the eve of World War I was its negativism towards the traditional literary values, or the conflict of generations. Doubts were cast over former artistic, human and national concepts. The modern trend in its turn became greatly influenced by the polarization of the Croatian public life: Croatism versus Yugoslavism, dominated by personal antagonism. The resulting feud certainly enlivened the literary production although it contributed title to its creative artism. The formalism has replaced the artistic values.

* * *

The postwar period of the Croatian literature was dominated by contemporary trends of European public and artistic life, thus all imaginable "isms" found their way in the country's literary activities. The contemporary social and political problems resulting from the war and stimulated by the Russian Revolution, gave birth to the social-realism or literary expression of the Marxian school tending to reduce literature to a role of an ideological propaganda. The general anxiety in all human, national and social concepts became manifest. New literary magazines appeared and disappeared at fantastic rates, each one announcing a new era, however, without tomorrow. The most outstanding representative of the period, Miroslav Krleza 1893-) excelled in all fields of literary activities. Anarchist in achievement, Marxist by philosophy, decadent in aesthetical value, perpetual antagonist and pitiless polemist, he put his indeniable personal stamp on the contemporary Croatian literature. Fighting constantly with himself he was never able to settle the primary question of literature, i.e. of the literary language. He started his literary career using the Croatian literary language, then turning to the Serbian, back to the historical Croatian "kajkavski" dialect, to finally settle with what he had started, the Croatian literary language. Krleza is obviously the most typical example not only of the Croatian literary but also national anxiety. His opus is quite impressive: *Pjesme, Balade Petrice Kerempuha, Gospoda Glembajevi, U agonji, Vucjak, Leda, Hrvatski bog Mars, Povratak Filipa Latinocza, Banket u Blitvi, Na rubu pameti, Zastave* and other numerous novels, poetry and essays. August Cesarec (1893-1941) started his literary career as an expressionist to become the most outspoken Marxian interpreter of the Holy Scripture, wrote novels of inequal value: *Careva kraljevina, Zlatni mladic, Izraelov povratak,* etc. Augustin Ujevic, a bohemian in his life, an independent poet, living on the margin of society and its norms, with a tremendous creative drive seeking expression in perfection wrote poetry, *Lelek srebra, Kolajna, Auto na korzu* and *Zedan kamen na studencu.* Slavko Kolar, a humorist and satirist, left a singular picture of his country and its people, opposing the comic to tragic, in his novels, *Ili jesmo ili nismo, I mi smo za pravicu.* Djuro Vilovic, author of *Hrvatski sjever i jug,* and Djuro Sudeta, a religious mystic, should be added.

Between the two wars many literary personalities emerged, a few of whom are still active. Generally speaking they followed the then prevailing trends in European literature, ranging from the mystic religious tendency to the propagandistic social-realism of the Marxist school. Let us name some of them: Dragutin

345

Tadijanovic, Frano Alfirevic, Ante Bonifacic, Mile Budak, Miroslav Feldman, Luka Perkovic, Vladimir Kovacic, Slavko Batusic, Novak Simic, Sida Kosutic, Mate Balota, Drago Gervais, Nikola Pavic, Hasan Kikic, Ivan Doncevic, Olinko Delorko, Drago Ivanisevic, Ivo Kozarcanin, Mihovil Pavlek Miskina, Ivan Goran Kovacic, Josip Kulundzic, Tito Strozzi, Kalman Mesaric, Geno Senecic, Stanko Simic, Antun Branko Simic, Slavko Jezic, Zvonko Miljkovic, as well as some noteworthy literary historians critics, Ljubomir Marakovic, Ivo Hergesic, Josip Bogner, Mihovil Kombol, Antun Barac, etc.

As the consequence of World War II, Germano-Italian occupation and the then ensuing Civil War followed by the Communist victory, the literary activities underwent some drastic changes. During the bloody period of five years many writers fell victims of foreign occupation or domestic political revenge such as Cesarec, Kikic, Goran Kovacic, Pavlek Miskina, Budak and some lesser personalities. The resulting exodus prompted some to exile like Bonifacic, Nikolic, Nizeteo, Kestercanek, Vida etc. The literary life in the country was reduced to the strict ideological control by the Communist Party imposing as an exclusive topic the glorification of the Communist Partisan's deeds during the Civil War or to tackle all problems of life within the rigid lines of the social-realism. Briefly, it fell victim to the strict supervision of the Communist propaganda. Lately, however, the artistic tendency and the revolt against the rigid conformity could be felt. The noteworthy names of the contemporary Croatian literature are Petar Segedin, Ranko Marinkovic, Marin Franicevic, Vjekoslav Kaleb, Sime Vucetic, Josip Barkovic, Grgur Vitez, Zivko Jelicic, Vlatko Pavletic, etc. Some of them proved to posses undeniable artistic and literary qualities while some still have to prove their right to be included on the list of the Croatian literature.

* * *

After they settled in their new environment amid the ruins of the Dalmatian towns the Croats established contact with the

346

Latin artistic remnants and such activities as they were preserved and joined to participate in them. In their original primitive status the Croats were limited to build their huts and houses as necessary for protection against the inclemency of the nature, or to erect some kind of fortifications for the protection against the enemy. The only artistic contribution of that time could be considered the carving of a few decorative figures on spindles or gourds, some embroidery on their garments, and other similar samples of the primitive arts.

After accepting Christianity in their new country they were bound to imitate their Latin neighbors in building the places of worship, churches, monasteries and ultimately houses and palaces. The remnants of a few churches provide examples of their accomplishment. To the then prevailing romanesque style in architecture the Croats added some concepts and decorative characteristics of their own. The Basilica of the Holy Cross, the see of the first Bishop of Croatia, is the oldest preserved monument of this art. The same architectural elements could be observed in the church of St. Donat in Zadar dating from the eleventh century. The numerous excavations of the old churches confirm the above mentioned example of the architectural concepts. The subsequent prevailing style along the Adriatic coastline fell under influence of the Gothic style as it was then developed in Venice. Northern Croatia was exposed to the similar Gothic influence coming from Germany. As medieval art was generally anonymous, no names of architects or builders were preserved. With individualization of arts during the time of the Renaissance, master builders proudly carved their names on the stones of portals of churches they built. Juraj Dalmatinac (Georgius Dalmaticus), native of Sibenik, built the beautiful cathedral of his native town as well as many churches in Venetian Dalmatia and Italy. The Renaissance Italy attracted two gifted brothers, Luka and Franjo Vranjanin (Luciano and Francesco de Laurana) who became famous in their craft in Italy, of which the most outstanding example is the Ducal Palace of Urbino.

Renaissance art was under the influence of the Catholic Reformation gradually replaced by the Baroque style which left a considerable number of churches and palaces built in this style both in the north and the south of Croatia of which the Cathedral of St. Blaise in Dubrovnik is of a special distinction.

Sculpture was for a long time considered a part of architecture. This fact which was strongly emphasized during the period of the Rènaissance. The early Croatian artists, both architects and sculptors, fell under the influence of the remnants of the famous Diocletian Palace in Split, on which ground the town was built. Andrija Buvina (1214) decorated with several sculptures Cathedral of St. Dujam in Split, while Master Radovan (1240) excelled in his art decorating the portal of the Cathedral of Trogir. The already mentioned Juraj Dalmatinac and brothers Vranjanin were equal to themselves in both architecture and sculpture. Ivan Duknovic (1440-1509) decorated many churches in Dalmatia before he became the official artist at the Court of King Mathias Corvinus, a famous Renaissance patron.

The early painting in the churches along the Adriatic shores was definitely under Byzantine influence. The Byzantine style was, however, soon replaced by the Italian influence which became exclusive especially at the time of the Renaissance. Some of the promising Croatian painters emigrated to the more promising atmosphere of Italy where Julije Klovic (Julius Clovius) and Andrija Medulic (Andreas Schiavonne) left lasting traces especially in Rome, Naples and Venice.

The religious painting and church decorations in northern Croatia fell under the influence of the Baroque as it was practiced then in Austria. Members of the St. Paul Order, Ivan Ranger, Frederik Benkovic and Franjo Bobic decorated many churches during the seventeenth and eighteenth centuries of which those of Lepoglava and Belec are of particular beauty.

Medieval Bosnia, during the country's short lived independence, developed its particular style the samples of which are preserved in numerous tombstones, known as "stecak" which were decorated with symbolical figures honoring departed. After the Turkish conquest the oriental arts were introduced of which the most outstanding examples are such buildings as the Gazi Husref Beg Mosque in Sarajevo and the bridges at Mostar and Visegrad.

The national re-awakening at the beginning of the nineteenth century brought about a revival of the arts side by side with the literature. Bartol Felbinger in the architecture and Vjekoslav Karas and Ferdo Quiquerez in painting set up the pace. Later, under the influence of Bishop Strossmayer, the neo-renaissance style was introduced to the country with construction of the Cathedral of Djakovo and the Palace of the Academy of Arts and Sciences in Zagreb. The old romanesque Cathedral of Zagreb after the earthquake, was reconstructed in the neo-gothic style which then dominated European architecture.

Definitive organization of the artistic life of the country started only with Isidor Krsnjavi, an able and energetic Head of Department of Public Instruction of the Croatian government. Some young Croatian painters received their artistic education either in Paris or Munchen, such as Miroslav Kraljevic, Ivo Racic and Vlaho Bukovac. Due to their influence the artistic life of the country concentrated in Zagreb developed extensively and qualitatively. For the first half of the twentieth century in the field of painting such important artists as Vjekoslav Crncic, Ferdo Kovacevic, Branko Senoa, Vladimir Becic, Joza Kljakovic, Ljuba Babic, Jerolim Mise and the artistic group "Zemlja," headed by Krsto Hegedusic, emerged. The school of the primitive-peasant painters should be also mentioned.

Sculpture also made remarkable progress with Josic Rendulic and Robert Franges Mihanovic but above all with Ivan Mestrovic (1883-1962) the most important artistic personality of the Croatian origin. Mestrovic excelled in carving, sculpturing and architectural construction of the topics taken from the national epics and folklore or the later period on the themes taken from the Holy Scripture. Among his disciples and successors special mention is deserved by Tomo Rosandic, Frane Krsinic and Antun Augustincic.

* * *

The Croatian musical folklore is rich in its variety. Definitely Slavic in origin as in its tonalities and melodies, the rhythmic constructions carry on different influences such as German in the north and west, especially in the mixed territories such as Burgenland in Austria where Joseph Haydn originated, Hungarian or Gypsy in the north, oriental in Bosnia and Hercegovina and Italian along the Adriatic coast. Artistic music came to the Croats with the advent of Christianity and followed then the musical trends of development of Italy. Few of the Croatian musicians of the Renaissance and Baroque periods achieved some reputation in Italy and western Europe such as Rota Kolonic and Ivan Jarnevic.

There is also a strong indication that Joseph Haydn, a peasant-coachman's son, is of Croatian origin, being born in Burgenland, populated by Croats, where the original name is still in use as well as in general in northern Croatia, Hajdin.

The true artistic musical life of the country was closely related to the national awakening. Vastroslav Lisinski wrote the first Croatian operas, *Porin* and *Ljubav i zloba*. However, the definite organized musical life started only with Ivan Zajc (1832-1914) and the establishment under his direction of the Croatian National Opera and the Croatian Musical Institute. Always still popular is his opera *Nikola Subic Zrinjski*. The most noteworthy of his pupils and successors were Franjo Kuhac, Blagoje Bersa, Antun Dobronic, Josip Slavenski, Bozidar Sirola, Josip Zganec, Krsto Odak, Kresimir Baranovic, Lujo Safranek Kavic, Boris Popandopulo, Jakov Gotovac, followed by scores of contemporary musicians, composers and performers.

CHAPTER XXV

YESTERDAY AND TODAY

The twelve days war — Occupation — The Independent State of Croatia — The Yugoslav government in exile — The Civil War: 1941-1945: Ustasa — Cetnici — Partisans — The Communist victory — The Federal People's Republic of Yugoslavia — The old problems in today's realities.

The fact that Yugoslavia was formally still a member of the Tripartite Pact was reaffirmed by the new government of General Simovic. The Croatian members of the ousted Cvetkovic's government including Macek, as well as their Slovene and Moslem colleagues had joined without enthusiasm the putschist regime. Germany, therefore, without breaking off diplomatic relations, or, for that matter, presenting an ultimatum or a formal declaration of war, attacked her ally on April 6, 1941. In fact, the German official announcement was made when the first German bombs were already falling on Belgrade. Simovic's government fled Belgrade in the general direction of Sarajevo without even trying to organize any kind of military resistance. After an aimless criss-crossing of the Bosnian mountains, the government decided upon an unconditional military capitulation, which was duly signed on April 17. Three days before the signing of capitulation, the government and King Petar II left the country, going first to Greece, then Jerusalem, and then, by the way of Cairo, to London, where it joined similar governments in exile.

On April 10, German armor appeared in Zagreb as a consequence of military operations on the northern Yugoslav front on the River Drava where the resistance of the Yugoslavia units was broken. Croatian nationalists, who were organized into the *Ustasa* Movement, took advantage of this opportunity through Slavko Kvaternik, former Austro-Hungarian Lt. Colonel, who, in collusion with the Germans, proclaimed the Independent State of Croatia that same day.

* * *

After capitulation, Yugoslavia was split into several territorial units. Germany annexed the former Austrian province of Styria which made part of northern Slovenia; while Italy annexed the southern part of Slovenia, which was originally the Austrian province of Carniola. Italy also annexed the larger part of Dalmatia, including the city of Split, as well as the northern part of the Croatian Littoral. Hungary annexed Backa, Baranja, Medjumurje and Prekomurje. Bulgaria took possession of Macedonia, and Italy, in the name of Albania, annexed Kosovo and Metohija. Montenegro was proclaimed an independent State under Italian protectorate. Banat was put under a special German Donau *Gau*. Serbia fell under German military occupation under which General Milan Nedic, former Yugoslav Minister of the Army and Navy, formed a government. Thus, while the principle of legitimacy was maintained by exiled King Peter II and his government in London, Yugoslavia disappeared from the map of Europe.

* * *

The Independent State of Croatia, proclaimed on April 10, was accepted with genuine enthusiasm by the Croaitan nationalists organized in the *Ustasa* Movement, soon faced the bitter reality of the European New Order. Italian annexation of Dalmatia and the Croatian Littoral was particularly resented. With an equal disappointment was viewed the Hungarian annexation of Medjumurje. Furthermore, neither Germany nor Italy made any effort to respect the independence and integrity of the newly proclaimed State. In fact, even prior to military operations against Yugoslavia, they had agreed to split the Croatian territory into two zones of occupation, viz. German and Italian, reducing the Zagreb *Ustasa* government to mere puppet status. Ante Pavelic, head of the *Ustasa* Movement, who had spent twelve years of exile in Italy as a protege of Mussolini's, returned to Croatia to introduce a personal dictatorship which aped his Italian sponsor. Through the Germany-Italian occupation, under the name of the Independent State of Croatia, the personality of Pavelic cast a deep shadow on the life of the country.

Pavelic's political experiences were rather modest. He was elected a member of the Belgrade *Narodna Skupstina* in 1927. His principal political education and contribution could be reduced to the fact that he had been a chief of a secret terroristic organization of the *Ustasa* which carried out a system of political assassinations on Yugoslav territory with the secret support of Italian and Hungarian authorities. The crown of these activities was the assassination of King Aleksandar of Yugoslavia in Marseille on October 9, 1934.

Pavelic not only accepted complete subservience to his sponsors, Hitler and Mussolini, but on his own initiative introduced political terrorism as a system of government. In this endeavor he enjoyed the most complete support of the masters of the European New Order. Playing on the long-standing Croato-Serbian antagonism, using some legitimate, as well as invented or exaggerated, Croatian grievances against Serbian domination in Yugoslavia, he launched at once into a bloody persecution of the Serbian minority. He did not spare his Croatian opponents, and, in fact, sent many of them to established concentration camps or even outrightly to death. Macek was one of his most notable victims. He spent the entire life of the Independent

353

State of Croatia either in a concentration camp or under house interment. When Hitler invaded the Soviet Union on June 22, 1941, and transformed anticommunism into a new gospel, Pavelic subscribed to it whole-heartedly. Aping Hitler's anti-semitism, although his own wife was of Jewish origin, he began a persecution of the Jews. Besides his wife, the mothers and wives of some of his lieutenants were of Jewish origin.

* * *

The capitulation of the Yugoslav Army did not reconcile the population to the new order. At first conflicts broke out between Italian forces and Croatian population in occupied Dalmatia. Then, in more or less organized form in Serbia, where the *Cetnici* groups, allegedly under command of Draza Mihajlovic, Colonel in the Yugoslav Army, became active. The *Cetnici* were a semi-official, paramilitary organization recruited from the Serbian population to support the Belgrade government. They did so in two ways. First of all they exercised terror over recalcitrant Croats and the non-Serbian population, especially Macedonian and Albanian; and, secondly, in the case of war, they were to act as irregular units behind the front lines. The *Cetnici* units were particularly well organized in what was, properly speaking, Serbia, as well as in Bosnia and Hercegovina. Due to their activities during the war, they became, at the same time, an excuse for, and retort to, the *Ustasa* terror over the Serbian population. The clashes between the *Ustasa* and the *Cetnici* soon assumed all the proportions of a pitiless civil war in which both sides excelled in the extermination of an innocent population.

* * *

When the Communists, following Hitler's aggression against the Soviet Union, joined in the fray, the country was, for all practical purposes, exposed to complete lawlessness. Indeed, the only authority was that of the different, conflicting armed groups, one of which would gain the upper hand from time to time

354

and become master of the day in the disputed territory. Thus the Germans, Italians, *Ustasa, Cetnici,* Partisans, or *Domobrans* (the regular Croatian Army) very often succeeded each other in the same localities within a couple of days, bringing in not only a new order, but new masters as well, accompanied with revenge on suspects and innocents.

With the German attack on the Soviet Union, the Bolshevik government called all the Communists of the world to arms. Under the slogan "Death to Fascism, Freedom to the People," the Communist Party of Yugoslavia was the first to answer the call to enter the relentless and bitter struggle against the Germans and their allies. Although they had only a limited membership (no more than five thousand), the Yugoslav Communists were highly disciplined and well prepared for the underground work which was imposed on them due to the fact that the Party has been outlawed in the country since 1921. Furthermore, the Yugoslav Communist leaders played a prominent role in the Spanish Civil War, thus giving to many of them the necessary training for the guerrilla warfare which they now inaugurated.

As disciplined Stalinists, prior to the war, the Yugoslav Communists had adopted Stalin's official policy of friendship with Nazi Germany. In fact, they prepared, throughout the country, sporadic demostrations against the government and carried out a constant subtle propaganda against the Cvetkovic-Macek government, accusing it of war-preparation on the side of the western plutocracies, and against the proletarian and half-socialist regime in Germany. However, they easily adjusted themselves to the changed circumstances. Under the leadership of the somehow mysterious, new General Secretary of the Party, Josip Broz Tito — a man, a professional revolutionary, who was highly trained in conspiracy and military arts at home and abroad — they actively joined the insurrection against the German and Italian forces of occupation and their domestic collaborators, in July 1941.

Josip Broz Tito, a Croatian born locksmith, received his political training as a young socialist first in Croatia, and then in Austria and Bohemia. As a non-commissioned officer in the Austro-Hungarian Army he took part in the World War I on the Russian front, where he was made a prisoner of war. In this quality he witnessed the beginning of the Russian Revolution, and took an active part in it when the Bolsheviks took over, on which occasion he joined the Communist Party.

Due to the harsh reprisals exercised by the Germans against the forces of resistance, the mass executions of hostages, Colonel Mihajlovic, commander of the *Cetnici* units, desisted from further activities. Indeed, especially in Croatia and Bosnia as well as in Montenegro, some of his local commanders established mutual toleration and practical collaboration with German, and, above all, Italian units in occupation. Both, Germans and Italians, openly advocated a policy of Serbo-Croatian extermination in order to depopulate the country for their own designs, supporting, toward that end, both the *Ustasa* and *Cetnici* extremists. On the other hand, the exiled Yugoslav government in London gave to Mihajlovic its wholehearted support by making him the General and Minister of the Army and the Navy, thus the chief commander of the resistance and official representative in the country.

The Communists, for their part, took their campaign more seriously and utterly disregarded all possible compromise. Eventually, they transformed the alleged struggle against the occupants into a civil war which had the ultimate aim of elimination of all possible political opposition to their cause. The Partisans — as the Communists styled themselves — had an easy time of it recruiting new followers from among the Serbian population in Croatia persecuted by the *Ustasa;* or, on the same account, from among the Croatian population persecuted by the *Cetnici* or Italians.

As the fortunes of war changed over to the side of the Partisans, they boldly asserted their political program at two Anti-Fascist Congresses held at Bihac (1942) and Jajce (1943), where, according to the preconceived plan of the Comintern of 1926, they advocated transformation of Yugoslavia into a free federation of six republics, i.e., Slovenia, Croatia, Bosnia and Hercegovina, Serbia, Montenegro and Macedonia.

The official war policy of the British government worked in their favor as well. Churchill's sole purpose to fight the Germans at any time at any place with all available means, took the Partisans of Yugoslavia seriously into account. Disgusted with the constant bickering and fighting of the motley crowd which represented the Yugoslav exiled government in London, he decided to "give to every bandit a rifle to kill Germans." In doing so he undercut the power and any authority the Yugoslav government could claim. Moreover, subsequent to the Teheran conference of the "Big Three," Churchill turned his back on the exiled government, supporting outrightly the Partisans by sending them his official representative. This support proved to be decisive after capitulation of Italy in 1943, since the Italian units in Croatia, Montenegro and Slovenia were instructed to surrender to the Partisans. The Partisans were thereby furnished with undisputable possession of territory hitherto under Italian occupation, as well as with a huge amount of military equipment, arms and ammunition. Thus, the Partisans were enabled, in the space of a day, to come from the position of an embattled guerrilla to that of an internationally recognized belligerent. They were not late to announce transformation of their guerrilla bands into the National Liberation Army of Yugoslavia and elevated their leader Tito to the title of Marshal. Furthermore, Churchill put additional pressure on the weak and frivolous King Petar and his new Prime Minister, Ivan Subasic, former *Ban* of Croatia, to come to terms with Tito.

The Red Army, after making itself master of both Rumania and Bulgaria, tendered its support to the Partisans, on whose account it liberated Belgrade, thereby installing Tito in the capital of Yugoslavia by the end of October 1944.

With the retreating German army, the different regimes established on the Yugoslav territory during the occupation also disappeared. The Partisans, therefore, aided by the Red Army and the Bulgarian army (Bulgaria, after capitulation to the Soviet Union, joined in the war against Germany), were able to establish their undisputed authority over the liberated territory. Pursuing their defeated Serbian, Croatian, or for that matter, Slovenian foes, they relentlessly carried out bloody purges of all perspective enemies in order to consolidate their seizure of power.

* * *

When the war in Europe was over, the second stage of the Civil War in Yugoslavia was its logical sequel. The coalition government, formed under Churchill's sponsorship, with Tito as a Premier and Subasic as Minister of Foreign Affairs, including members of the Communist Party as well as some token representatives of the democratic parties, was soon done with. The general elections set up for November 1945, with a single list of candidates carefully selected, produced the so-called "popular democracy" — a euphemism for the dictatorship of the proletariat. Enjoying official diplomatic recognition of the Allied Powers, and above all, the benefit of the UNRRA economic aid, the regime was able to establish itself firmly in power within a few months.

The National Constituent Assembly, in record time and without a single vote of dissent, voted in the new constitution of the country. It was, more or less, ratification of decisions made at congresses of Bihac and Jajce. However, unable to draw a satisfactory boundary between Serbia and Croatia, the Central Committee of the Communist Party opted for a compromise solution by granting equal status to Bosnia and Hercegovina within the federation. By this constitution, Yugoslavia officially became the Federal People's Republic of Yugoslavia, consisting of six federal republics: Serbia, Croatia, Slovenia, Bosnia and Hercegovina, Macedonia and Montenegro; two autonomous provinces of Vojvodina and Kosmet were added to Serbia. By the Peace Treaty of Paris (1946), Italy ceded to Yugoslavia former Austrian provinces of Istria, Rijeka, Zadar, Gorizia and part of Carniola. Istria, Rijeka, Zadar and islands of Lastovo, Cres and Losinj were incorporated to their mother land Croatia. Croatia thus consisted of former Croatia, Slavonia (minus her eastern part, Srijem, which was added to the autonomous province of Vojvodina, which was part of Serbia), Baranja, Dalmatia (minus the Boka Kotorska, given to Montėnegro), and the territory liberated from Italy.

*　*　*

The retreating Germans were followed by the *Ustasa* government and its military units, as well as by the regular Croatian army, and score of people compromised by their collaboration with the *Ustasa* government, or for that matter, with the occupants, and by those who were simply afraid of their destiny under new masters. Thus started a general exodus.

Some of the leading personalities of the *Ustasa* government surrendered to the British forces in Austria, but were promptly delivered into the hands of the Communist authorities. The Communists made short work of them. Even more tragic was the destiny of the Croatian regular army, the *Ustasa* military units, the Serbian *Cetnici* of General Mihajlovic, and similar military organizations of Serbian and Slovenian collaborators. Delivered by the British authorities to their victorious Communist allies, they were summarily executed; and only a limited number survived the "death march" from the Austrian to the Rumanian border.

A multitude of refugees who escaped Partisan capture becamė, at first, "the displaced persons" *par excellence*, populating refugee camps in Austria, Germany and Italy. From these camps they were dispersed over "five continents," forming the so-called "Croatia beyond frontiers." The ranks of this "new Croatia" were inflated by additional refugees who, since 1945, have escaped Yugoslavia for political or personal reasons. Moreover, the number continued to swell following the collapse of the communist economy by 1960, due to the fact that it was an officially permitted, if not officially organized, "economic emigration" into Western Europe, especially to Germany, Austria, France, Switzerland, Sweden, etc., from where many of them found their way across oceans to the American countries or Australia. According to the official estimation of the Communist authorities of Croatia, at present every fourth Croat is living abroad.

For the first ten years of its existence, the new regime calling itself the popular democracy, a euphemism for the dictatorship of the proletariat, or the Communist Party, applied its principles in the best Stalinist tradition, that is, with full rigidity. However, with the break between Stalin and Tito in 1948, some dissatisfaction became manifest. This dissatisfaction had many aspects: the Marxist concept of industrialization proved to be costly and ineffective; the agricultural collectivization created a general chaos and a penury in production of the foodstuff. Finally, the highly centralized Communist bureaucracy fell into the hands of the Serbs who, asserting their dominant position, brought the crisis between themselves and the Croats to the climax in 1967 when it erupted in all magnitude on the language question, the Croats insisting on nullification of the "Serbo-Croatian" common language and on official recognition of the Croatian language pure and simple.

Thus, in consideration of the latest happenings, and despite the slogans and the relentless affirmation that Communism has discovered the golden key to the solution of all national controversies, the Croats, even those who are Communists, cannot shrug off historical realities. Indeed, they are bound now, more than ever before, to assert their specific national entity.

CHRONOLOGICAL OUTLINE

Paleolithic period: the Krapina cave man
Neolithic period: many findings in Bosnia and Slavonia
IVth century B.C.: The Thracian, Celtic and Illyrian settlements
    and the beginning of the Greek colonization
228 B.C.: Roman Consul Gneus Centimalis defeated the Illyrians
57 and 56 B.C.: Caesar invaded Illyricum
10 A.D.: Tiberius completed conquest of Pannonia and Dalmatia
289 and 294: Diocletian brought in the first Sarmatians (Slavs?)
VIth century: the Avaro-Slavic invasion
614: fall and destruction of Salona
670: Pope Agathon came to an understanding with Croats
800: Duke Viseslav, first Christian ruler of Croats
819-21: Ljudevit's wars against the Franks
852 Trpimir, Duke of Croatia
879-92 Branimir, first independent Duke of Croatia
925 Tomislav became the King of Croats
1058-74 Petar Kresimir IV, the strongest ruler of Croatia
1075-89 Zvonimir supported Gregory VII in the Struggle for
    Investiture
1097 Members of the First Crusade crossed Croatia; Death of
    Petar, last king of the national origin
1102 *Pacta conventa*
    Koloman of Hungary became King of Croatia
1202 The Fourth Crusade conquered Zadar for Venice
1222 Andrija II signed the *Bulla aurea*
1242 The Tartar invasion
1390 Stjepan Tvrdko of Bosnia assumed the title of the King
    of Croatia

1409 Ladislav of Naples sold Dalmatia to Venice

1463 Turkish conquest of Bosnia

1493 Turks defeated Croats at Udbina

1501 *Judita*, the first book written in the Croatian language

1526 Battle of Mohacs

1527 Archduke Ferdinand Habsburg elected the King of Croatia

1573 The peasant revolt of Matija Gubec

1671 Zrinjski-Frankopan conspiracy

1690 Serbian refugees from the Ottoman Empire settled in eastern Croatia

1712 The Croatian *Pragmatical Sanction*

1809-13: French rule in Croatia — Illyrian Provinces

1830 Beginning of the national awakening

1848 War with Hungary

1868 The *Nagodba*

1914-18: World War I

1918 Croatia severed relations with Austria and Hungary; Formation of the Kingdom of the Serbs, Croats and Slovenes

1928 Assassination of Stjepan Radic

1929 Introduction of the Royal Dictatorship

1939 The Serbo-Croatian agreement
Formation of the *Banovina* of Croatia

1941 The Belgrade military *coup-d'etat*
The war: occupation
Proclamation of the Independent State of Croatia
The Civil War

1945 The Communist victory
Formation of the People's Federal Republic of Yugoslavia

Siscia

Murala

Cibalae

Sirmium

Stridonium

Jadera

Salona

Epidaurum

ROMAN PROVINCES

PANNONIA

AND

DALMATIA

CROATIA

XTH CENTURY'S

CROATIA

PERMANENT BOUNDARY ▬▬

LARGEST EXTENSION ▬▬▬

RESTRICTED ••••••

MIVth CENTURY'S
CROATIA
BOSNIA
AND
DUBROVNIK

MDCTH CENTURY'S
CROATIA
BOSNIA
DUBROVNIK
VENETIAN DALMATIA

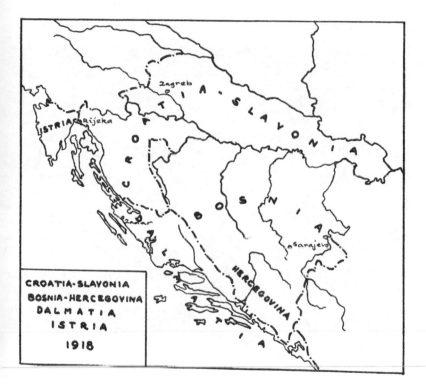

ISTRIA Rijeka
Zagreb
C R O A T I A - S L A V O N I A
Zadar
B O S N I A
Sarajevo
D A L M A T I A
HERCEGOVINA

CROATIA-SLAVONIA
BOSNIA-HERCEGOVINA
DALMATIA
ISTRIA
1918

o Zagreb

BANOVINA
OF
CROATIA
1939